Beasts
FROM THE
East

First published in October 2005

A catalogue record for this book is available
from the British Library

ISBN 1 84425 222 1

Library of Congress catalog card no. 2005926085

Published by Haynes Publishing,
Sparkford, Yeovil, Somerset, BA22 7JJ, UK

Tel: 01963 442030 Fax: 01963 440001
Int. tel: +44 1963 442030
Int. fax: +44 1963 440001
E-mail: sales@haynes.co.uk
Web site: www.haynes.co.uk

Haynes North America, Inc.,
861 Lawrence Drive, Newbury Park,
California 91320, USA

Jurisdictions which have strict emission control
laws may consider any modifications to a vehicle
to be an infringement of those laws. You are
advised to check with the appropriate body or
authority whether your proposed modification
complies fully with the law. The author and
publishers accept no liability in this regard.

While every effort is taken to ensure the
accuracy of the information given in this book,
no liability can be accepted by the author
or publishers for any loss, damage or injury
caused by errors in, or omissions from the
information given.

Designed by Richard Parsons

Printed and bound in England
by J. H. Haynes & Co. Ltd, Sparkford

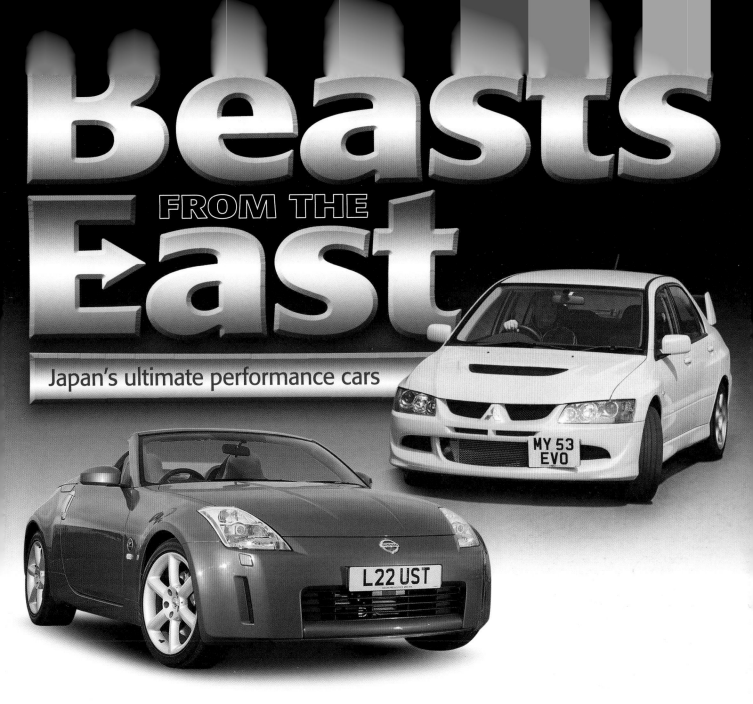

Beasts
FROM THE
East

Japan's ultimate performance cars

PAUL GUINNESS

Haynes Publishing

CONTENTS

CONTENTS

INTRODUCTION

The Japanese car scene has changed immeasurably since the 1970s, when the odd machine that was actually exciting or interesting was soon outnumbered by mass-selling models carrying such daft names as Sunny, Violet, Cherry and Gloria. These days, a big proportion of the models from Japan are very fine cars indeed, and many of them are seriously desirable by any standards.

Whatever your particular Japanese car penchant, you'll probably be able to think of a few models that ideally should have been included in this book. But with a finite number of pages available, we had to stick resolutely to 40 different models – and that meant a long time spent agonising over the final list.

Here it is then. Forty of the top Japanese fun, sports and performance cars. They're not all blisteringly quick or amazingly expensive, and neither are they all from one particular era. In fact, we've managed to cover every decade from the 1960s through to the early years of the 21st century, so we're pretty sure there's something for everyone.

Over the next 40 chapters, you'll find 240Zs, CRXs, GTI-Rs, VR-4s, GTIs, NSXs, GTs, Type Rs and lots more brought together as a tribute to all that's great about Japanese sports and performance cars. And that makes this book essential reading matter for anybody who loves Japanese cars, owns a Japanese car or is thinking of venturing into the Japanese car scene for the first time.

Some fantastic cars for drivers have emanated from Japan over the years, and it's these that this book is here to celebrate. Each one has a fascinating story to tell. Each one is a bit of a beast.

ACKNOWLEDGEMENTS

Researching a book that involves no fewer than 40 different models of Japanese sports and performance cars is no mean feat, so I am grateful to everybody who has offered advice, help and encouragement along the way.

Among the many names I could mention, I'd particularly like to thank Rod Jones for always being there, Howard and Sarah Darber for their unstinting support, and Frank Westworth for so much authorial inspiration over the years.

I am also indebted to Haynes Publishing's Mark Hughes and Steve Rendle for their professional help and personal encouragement through this and all other projects. I'm equally grateful to Tim Wright and Kathy Ager at LAT for helping to source some terrific photography.

Finally, to all the hard-working people in the various UK press offices that represent Japanese motor manufacturers, a heartfelt thank you.

I hope fellow Japanese car fanatics enjoy what follows…

Paul Guinness
July 2005

DAIHATSU
CHARADE GTti

turbo terror

Up until 1987, anybody in the market for a minuscule hot hatch was faced with the usual predictability of a Fiesta XR2, Nova GTE or – horror of horrors – an MG Metro Turbo. Ah yes, the joys of consumer choice. Then along came the all-new Daihatsu Charade GTti to give the market the shake-up it so desperately needed; and how.

The new Charade line-up of 1987 was, generally speaking, nothing to write home about. It comprised a range of perfectly competent five-door runabouts, perfect for keeping the pensioners of Bournemouth happy on their weekly shopping trips. But the GTti was something else entirely.

This exciting new three-door version used the same basic 993cc three-cylinder engine as the rest of the range. In this form, though, it was a DOHC design with a 12-valve cylinder head, fuel injection, turbocharger and intercooler. The result was a spectacular-for-the-time power output of

99bhp at 6500rpm, far more than any other sub-1000cc production engine of the late 1980s.

Just as useful was the fact that the lightweight Charade tipped the scales at a mere 1808lb, which gave it a class-beating power to weight ratio of

WHAT WE LIKE...

Arguably the ultimate pocket rocket of the 1980s, the GTti combined the thrill of a turbo with the fastest acceleration in its class – and all at a bargain price.

...WHAT WE DON'T

Compared with mainstream rivals such as the Fiesta XR2, the GTti was a technically complicated little beast. But it was also a far better driver's car.

more than 117bhp per tonne. No other similarly priced hot hatch could hope to come even close.

Not unexpectedly, the Charade GTti proved a formidable newcomer out on the road, with a top speed of 114mph and the all-important 0–60mph dash in under 8.0 seconds. Remember, these were figures for a cut-price go-faster 'supermini' rather than a grown-up Golf GTi rival; no wonder the GTti was arousing the interest of petrolheads everywhere.

It wasn't just the Daihatsu's on-paper performance that mattered. In fact, this turbocharged terror was the most fun thing on four wheels that the hot hatch market had seen in a very long time. Its free-revving 12-valve engine provided unlimited joy for your right foot, while the sudden kick-in-your-back boost provided by prodigious turbo lag made the whole thing even more exciting.

Once the front wheelspin was under control, the GTti would race forward at a rate unprecedented at this price level, while its super-sharp steering provided all the feedback even the most critical of drivers could wish for. As for the handling, the old 'kart-like' cliché so favoured by motoring hacks was rarely so appropriate.

In one fell swoop, the GTti managed to make oh-so-staid rivals such as the Fiesta XR2 seem dull and unappealing, and yet – in the UK at least – it remained very much a niche product. This was partly due to import restrictions on Japanese cars at the time, combined with the buying public's distrust of what it saw as a complex and highly technical piece of equipment.

But over its six-year run the GTti built up a loyal following among enthusiasts who appreciated something a bit different from the norm. As the years went by, it managed to prove itself a dependable machine, too. Daihatsu's reputation for reliability remained undiminished, despite the relative complications of the GTti's technical make-up.

These days, the Charade GTti continues to offer spectacular value for money as a second-hand buy, though only an excellent example with a guaranteed mileage and a full service history should be considered by anyone looking for daily transport.

Yet find a good one and you'll soon be wearing a grin bigger than you ever thought possible. The Daihatsu Charade GTti: such fun to drive, it should be available on prescription as a viable alternative to Prozac. ∎

SPEC

ENGINE: 993cc DOHC fuel-injected 12-valve turbocharged three-cylinder

POWER: 99bhp @ 6500rpm

TORQUE: 96lb ft @ 3500rpm

PERFORMANCE: Top speed 114mph, 0–60mph 7.9 secs

TRANSMISSION: Five-speed manual

CHASSIS: Rack-and-pinion steering; independent coil-spring suspension all round; servo-assisted disc brakes all round

▼ GTti drivers could expect a well-equipped interior and a terrific driving position. And with 117bhp per tonne on tap, it was an exciting place to be. (*Daihatsu*)

TIMELINE

1987	Latest-generation Charade introduced, including new GTti hot hatch
1993	Production of GTti ceased
1993	New 1.3/1.5 Charade range launched, but GTti not replaced

DAIHATSU CUORE AVANZATO TR-XX

mad but fun

If you were the manufacturer of a tiny hatchback and you wanted to make a go-faster version, you'd probably consider fitting a bigger engine. Well, not if your name was Daihatsu. So when the idea occurred to them that a 'high performance' version of their tiny Cuore might be a good idea, they ripped out its 850cc engine and replaced it with a 659cc unit instead.

Confused? You needn't be, because this was no ordinary 659cc engine. It was a 16-valve fuel-injected four-cylinder twin-cam lump with turbocharger and intercooler strapped on for good measure. While its resultant output of 64bhp may not sound that exciting, it was enough to give the Cuore Avanzato TR-XX a very fine turn of speed.

The key to the Avanzato's decent performance was its extremely light weight, tipping the scales at less than a tonne. For a four-wheel-drive machine, that's not a lot. And did I forget to mention that this diminutive Daihatsu also offered

all-wheel traction? Yes, you can add that to the list of features fitted as standard to this technology-crammed mini-marvel.

WHAT WE LIKE...

One of the most enjoyable forms of transport ever to come out of Japan, the Avanzato provides more grins per mile than just about anything else on the road.

...WHAT WE DON'T

Minuscule proportions mean limited accommodation and a tiny boot. Furthermore, it's not the kind of car we'd choose to have a serious accident in...

In 1997, when the Cuore Avanzato TR-XX went on limited sale in the UK, it was sold at a price that represented something of a bargain for a hi-tech machine limited to British imports of just 150 examples. Even so, could anything this small really be any good where it mattered most: out on the open road?

Oh yes; piloting the Avanzato was an exhilarating experience, its tiny stature and eager performance combining to give it the feel of a roller skate on steroids. With its four-wheel drive permanently split 50/50 front and rear, this pocket rocket would pull away from the line with zero wheelspin and an eagerness rivalled only by a whippet. Top speed wasn't great at 102mph (well, what do you expect from just 659cc?), but hitting 60mph in 8.5 seconds was pretty impressive. The fact that it felt much, much quicker than that was even better.

Although it rolled a bit when pushed really hard into a corner, the Cuore Avanzato simply refused to let go. Grip was exceptional for a machine with city-car proportions, while its sharp rack-and-pinion steering helped make the most of such 'chuckability'.

No car this small can ever be perfect, of course. The Cuore Avanzato was noisy, unrefined, uncomfortable on long journeys and just too tiny for most owners to use as an only car. But so what? This machine was all about maximising thrills and fun behind the wheel, and in that sense it was a huge success.

It's just a shame the Avanzato had such a limited shelf life in the UK, all 150 examples selling out quickly, snapped up by budget-conscious buyers with a sense of fun and a love of the unusual. As an antidote to the dreariness offered by many manufacturers in the late 1990s, the Avanzato was a revelation.

So promising was the Cuore Avanzato, it was even offered in rally spec at extra cost, enabling buyers to take part in the specially created Daihatsu Rally Challenge, a seven-stage series aimed at novice enthusiasts looking for a little excitement.

The Avanzato wasn't the fastest car on the street in 1997, but it was one of the most fun cars around, and from a company more renowned for its superminis and 4x4s, that was an amazing achievement. Its passing was mourned by a small but enthusiastic crowd. ■

SPEC

ENGINE: 659cc twin-cam 16-valve fuel-injected four-cylinder with turbocharger and intercooler

POWER: 64bhp @ 7500rpm

TORQUE: 74lb ft @ 4000rpm

PERFORMANCE: Top speed 102mph, 0–60mph 8.5 secs

TRANSMISSION: Five-speed manual

CHASSIS: Power-assisted rack-and-pinion steering; MacPherson front struts with anti-roll bar; semi-trailing arms and coil-sprung rear suspension; front disc and rear drum brakes

▼ The minuscule twin-cam powerplant came complete with a 16-valve cylinder head, turbocharger and intercooler for maximum performance. No wonder it was so much fun to pilot. (Daihatsu)

TIMELINE

| 1997 | Cuore Avanzato TR-XX goes on sale in UK |
| 1998 | All 150 examples sell out early in the New Year |

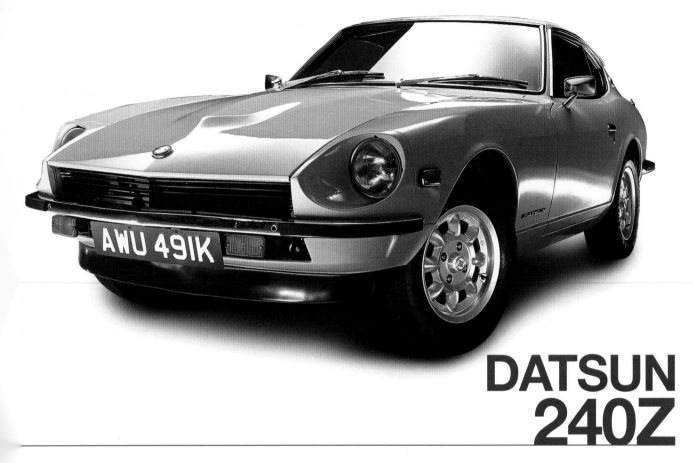

DATSUN 240Z

the mould-breaker

▲ The pure lines of the 240Z hid a sportster that was both exciting and exhilarating by the standards of 1969. (*Nissan*)

Until the announcement of the Datsun 240Z in 1969, Japanese sports cars had generally been seen as quirky, oddball and rather eccentric. They did well in their homeland, but their export potential was rarely exploited as fully as it could have been. They were the sports cars for people who dared to be different – and in Britain in those days, such people were in short supply.

But then along came the 240Z, unveiled to an eager press in 1969 and on sale throughout much of the world by the following year. And what an amazing machine this was.

All right, so the 240Z wasn't entirely new. It used an engine borrowed from elsewhere in the Datsun line-up, in the shape of a 2393cc overhead-cam six-cylinder unit that had already given good service in various Datsun saloons. So how would it cope with life inside what was meant to be an impressive new sports car? Time would tell.

Indeed, much of the 240Z's mechanical make-up had been seen in other parts of the Datsun range before now, so from a purely technical point of view the newcomer wasn't light years ahead of its time. Where the 240Z really scored was in its styling and in its uncanny timing. The world market – and particularly the USA – was waiting for a car like the 240Z, and Datsun was only too happy to oblige.

In fact, the 240Z can lay claim to being the first Japanese car ever created with American success as its prime target. American buyers still loved sports cars, but the MGB was woefully unexciting and the six-cylinder Austin-Healey 3000 had been killed off in 1968 as a direct result of new American safety and anti-pollution legislation.

What Britain needed to do was replace the Healey and even the Triumph TR6 with a brand new sports car that would comply with every new American regulation, and one which would

SPEC

ENGINE: 2393cc OHC straight-six with alloy head and twin Hitachi carbs

POWER: 151bhp @ 5600rpm

TORQUE: 146lb ft @ 4400rpm

PERFORMANCE: Top speed 125mph, 0–60mph 7.9 secs

TRANSMISSION: Five-speed manual

CHASSIS: Quick-ratio rack-and-pinion steering; independent coil-spring suspension all round with MacPherson front struts; front disc and rear drum brakes

capture the imagination of a younger audience. Britain failed to deliver, but Japan filled the gap brilliantly.

The result was the Datsun 240Z and, as even the briefest of driving experiences would confirm, it was a machine with the finest sporting credentials of its time. It may have been a mechanical amalgam of parts already in existence at Datsun HQ, but that didn't stop the 240Z from being a real sports car, and a rather impressive performance machine despite its affordable price tag.

With its lightweight alloy cylinder head and twin Hitachi carburettors, the 240Z's version of the Datsun six-cylinder engine was a lusty and potent affair by the standards of 1969. It pumped out an impressive 151bhp at 5600rpm, enough to propel it to a top speed of 125mph, passing 60mph along the way in a scenery-blurring 7.9 seconds. Remember, we're going back to the end of the 1960s. Bear that in mind when reading those performance figures again and you can't fail to be impressed. ▷

▲ The 240Z's 2.4-litre straight-six powerplant sounded impressive – and went even better! (*Nissan*)

▼ The addition of a tailgate gave this all-time classic coupé surprising practicality for such a sporting machine. (*Nissan*)

But the 240Z wasn't just about straight-line performance. Datsun's engineers had to be congratulated on putting together totally standard components in such a way that the 240Z was so accomplished out on the open road. The all-independent suspension with MacPherson struts up front provided the Datsun with predictable but delightful handling without sacrificing ride quality. And the 240Z's close-ratio transmission provided some of the slickest, quickest gear changes the world of affordable sports cars had ever seen. When it came to stopping in a hurry, the fact that the Z came with front disc brakes as standard was seen as an essential safety feature.

More important than any of this was that the 240Z simply felt right. It was a communicative machine, its sharp rack-and-pinion steering allowing any keen driver to make the most of its precise handling, its impressive spread of power and its all-round fun factor. With that masculine-sounding straight six throbbing away under the 240Z's lengthy bonnet, this masterpiece could make any driver feel good, not to mention excited. This was all emphasised by the Datsun's two-seater layout, with its low-down seating position, its modern but sporting interior and sheer eagerness when right foot met right-hand pedal.

Anybody who grew up in the 1970s knew about the 240Z. So popular was this car the world over, it featured heavily in teenage thoughts everywhere and quickly became a performance icon, which when you think about it, was a remarkable thing to happen.

FAIRLADY FEVER

What's in a name? Well, for its home market, the 240Z wore the different badge of Fairlady Z, a continuation of the earlier Fairlady semi-sporting machines offered in Japan. Datsun decided, with infinite wisdom, that the Fairlady badge just wouldn't go down well in the USA or Europe, and so adopted the 240Z moniker instead. A sensible move from a company that has also used such bizarre model names as Cedric and Bluebird over the years...

▼ The ultra-long bonnet and short cabin area were almost reminiscent of a Jaguar E-Type, reckoned some admirers. This was a very sexy machine by any standards. (*Nissan*)

WHAT WE LIKE...

Superbly styled coupé that broke the mould for Japanese sports cars, going on to become bestseller in its class throughout the world. You just can't argue with that kind of success.

...WHAT WE DON'T

Interior wasn't the highest quality in the world, but that didn't deter many buyers. This was still the best-value sporting car of the early 1970s.

You see, prior to 1969, Japanese cars in both the USA and Britain were still minority products, each country boasting a generally loyal and patriotic car-buying public. When it came to sports cars, though, the Americans just couldn't get enough of British products, with sales of MGs being particularly buoyant. So surely something like a sporting Datsun would have a tough fight on its hands against such established buying patterns?

Not a bit of it. In every country where the 240Z was launched, it became an immediate hit. Indeed, in the USA, twelve months after the model's debut, second-hand versions were selling for more money than brand-new examples, such was the Z's popularity and its shortage of supply. Datsun increased production in an attempt to keep up with demand, but it was a difficult task. The 240Z was fast becoming the world's best-selling sports car of its day.

Despite its keen pricing, the 240Z was seen as an aspirational product. Perhaps it had something to do with that seemingly never-ending bonnet, slightly reminiscent of a Jaguar E-Type's. Or maybe it was the allure of a powerful, throaty and strong-performing six-cylinder powerplant. Either way, it was a car that people lusted after, despite being one that a great many could easily afford.

Popular though the 240Z may have been, Datsun wasn't going to rest on its laurels, and ▶

▲ The 240Z's super-sharp rack-and-pinion steering helped ensure this was one of the finest driver's cars of its era – even compared with far more expensive 'rivals'. (*Nissan*)

by 1971 a few minor changes were under way. Nothing dramatic, but the relocated air vents, redesigned seat belts, new-look steering wheel and restyled speedometer and oil pressure gauge were all seen as improvements. The following year also saw a redesigned centre console, new-style flip-forward seats for easier access to the in-car storage area, and new hubcaps and wider rims being introduced. But really that was about it for the duration of the 240Z's four-year production run. It just shows that if a design is right from the start, it doesn't need changing just for the sake of it.

Mind you, that didn't stop Datsun creating a rather intriguing version of the 240Z early on, as a direct result of heavy taxes for vehicles over 2000cc in Japan. Very early examples of the 240Z were released in its homeland with a twin-cam six-cylinder engine that came in just under the all-important 2-litre bracket. This vehicle was known as the Fairlady Z 432, the '432' part of the name referring to its mechanical configuration.

It employed four valves per cylinder, triple Solex carburettors and twin overhead camshafts – and you couldn't get much more of a contrast with a regular 240Z than that. In fact, with such a high level of engineering, this new engine was a technically fascinating piece of kit, producing almost 160bhp at 7000rpm. Acceleration was seriously impressive, but that didn't stop the 'normal' 240Z from grabbing almost all the limelight.

Fewer than 500 examples of the Z 432 were produced, with some even put to use by the Japanese police. A lightweight Fairlady Z 432-R was also made available for racing purposes, though this was a real rarity.

As for the regular 240Z … well, things took a turn for the worse in 1973 with the arrival of the 260Z, a bigger-engined version of the 240Z, created to combat ever more stringent American legislation. New emissions rules and anti-pollution specifications meant that, despite its larger 2.6-litre engine, the 260Z was substantially less powerful than its predecessor, offering a mere 126bhp in American spec. To make matters worse, Datsun decided to introduce a 2+2 version of the 260Z, featuring a stretched wheelbase and space for a couple of small children in the rear. This latter move ruined the whole balanced look and perfect proportions of the design, and the 260Z was soon seen as a poor imitation of an original masterpiece.

Consequently, these days it's still the 240Z that's considered the finest of the early Z-car scene. In fact, until the launch of the turbocharged 300ZX model of 1989, the Z-series seemed to be in terminal decline with each new generation, going from raw and exciting sports coupé to overweight and soft-handling boulevard cruiser within just a few years.

What we're left with now then, is a near-fanatical following for the original Datsun 240Z in every country where classic performance cars are revered and respected, and that can only be a good thing. Any car that virtually takes over a whole sector of the market and is so undeniably impressive in every way deserves to be put on a pedestal.

Anybody given a chance these days to pilot a classic 240Z should do so without hesitation, for this is still a joyful experience. The engine of a well-sorted 240Z still sounds fantastic and its performance is enough to put a wide grin on your face within a few seconds. Acceleration remains impressive, and the gear changes are incredibly slick and fast for such an aged design. When you get a well-maintained 240Z on your favourite B-road, you realise that for enjoyable handling, tenacious grip and pure entertainment value it's still got what it takes.

The biggest enemy of the 240Z, as with so many of its rivals from the early 1970s, is rust. Japanese cars were no better or no worse than their American or European peers in this respect, although popular opinion has suggested otherwise over the years. Get yourself an all-original or superbly restored 240Z now, though, and you'll discover one of the most delightful ownership experiences of your life; and unlike most British sports cars from the same era, at least a Datsun is going to be reliable.

Such reliability enabled the 240Z to create a name for itself in competition over the years, and in its heyday was very successful on the track. From 1970 onwards it was winning its class in the Sports Car Club of America's annual series, as well as enjoying considerable success internationally as a rally and long-distance enduro car. It wasn't long, too, before a whole aftermarket accessories and performance scene developed for those enthusiastic 240Z

owners who wanted to make the most of the potential of their beloved new hero.

No wonder the 240Z became known as 'The First American Sports Car Built In Japan', a tag that would accompany it for many years. It was exactly the kind of sporting performance machine that America – and much of the rest of the world – had been waiting for. That it was designed and built in Japan came as a major blow to every rival car company and a major surprise to enthusiasts everywhere. ▨

TIMELINE

1969	240Z two-seater coupé announced
1970	Right-hand-drive 240Z is launched in UK
1971	Changes include new air vents, restyled steering wheel and new speedo
1972	Minor mods include flip-forward seats and new hubcaps
1973	American-spec 240Z fitted with power-sapping emissions equipment
1973	240Z replaced by 260Z

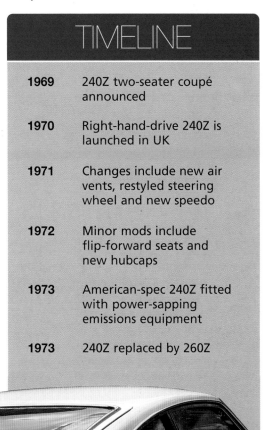

▼ America couldn't get enough of the 240Z. No wonder it became known as The First American Sports Car Built In Japan. (*Nissan*)

HONDA S800

the early power

▲ As one of the world's most compact sporting models of its time, the S800 was most popular in hard-top coupé guise. But it's what lay under the bonnet that was soon generating headlines worldwide. (*LAT*)

Back in the 1960s, Britain ruled the world of affordable sports cars. Models such as the MGB and Triumph Spitfire were selling in big numbers worldwide, despite being propelled by basic and unexciting engines. But then Honda created the amazing little S800 in 1965 – and the world sat up and took notice.

Enthusiasts weren't snapping it up in vast numbers, but at least they realised there was real talent in Japan as a result of its existence. This was the most technically advanced small sportster ever to be launched, and it made its British 'rivals' seem dull and ancient by comparison.

The new S800 of 1965 was actually a development of the previous S600, launched a year earlier. Where the latter had been powered by a 606cc engine, the S800's capacity had been increased to a heady 791cc. But this was no ordinary little powerplant. On the contrary, it was a very grown-up double overhead-cam four-cylinder unit with a hemi-head and no fewer than

four carburettors, and despite its limited size, it managed to pump out a mightily impressive 70bhp at a whopping 8000rpm.

WHAT WE LIKE...

The first ever genuinely exciting Honda is still one of the most desirable on the classic car circuit. Fantastic high-revving little powerplant made British sports cars of the 1960s seem archaic by comparison.

...WHAT WE DON'T

There's not much to dislike about the oh-so-gorgeous S800, apart from the fact it tended to rust a lot in Britain. But then, so did most cars of its era.

Now, I know what you're thinking: a mere 70bhp isn't that much, is it? But don't forget, we're going back to the mid-1960s, a time when double overhead camshafts and multiple carburettors were new territory in the affordable sports car market. Compared with the MG Midget, the 100mph S800 was a technical masterpiece and was light years ahead of its time.

Available in both coupé and convertible guises, the S800 was a joy to drive, its incredibly rev-happy and eager engine being complemented by the slickest four-speed gearchange the sports car scene had ever experienced. Handling and roadholding were best described as fun, thanks to the initial chain-drive set-up and independent rear suspension; this was altered two years later, when a live rear axle became a standard fitment. Around the same time, the original all-drum braking was altered to incorporate front discs, a move much appreciated by the S800's enthusiastic owners.

That the S800 was so technically advanced and such a thrill to drive was even more remarkable when you bear in mind its arrival was only three years after the first ever Honda production car. Up until 1962, this most innovative of Japanese companies had concentrated solely on motorbikes – and with great success. But the arrival of the S800 (among others) meant that by the end of the decade, Honda would be a 'proper' car manufacturer and was even about to enter the grand prix scene.

The S800 was always a niche product, particularly in the UK, with a total of just 11,536 examples rolling off the line by the time production ceased in 1970, but it will always be remembered as one of the most significant cars ever created by Honda.

Whatever type of sporting Honda you drive now, it owes a great deal to the S800; and as one of the world's most innovative producers of petrol engines, Honda learned much from its most exciting offering of the 1960s. The automotive world would be a much poorer place if the stunning little S800 had never existed.

Only a fool would underestimate the importance of the S800, one of the most characterful – and advanced – machines of its era. Those who experienced it for themselves in the late 1960s were given a unique insight into just how technologically clever the good folk at Honda were. No wonder the future for the company looked so exciting; the S800 was truly paving the way for even more greatness. ∎

SPEC

ENGINE: 791cc DOHC quad-carb roller-bearing four-cylinder with hemi head

POWER: 70bhp @ 8000rpm

TORQUE: 49lb ft @ 6000rpm

PERFORMANCE: Top speed 100mph, 0–60mph 13.4 secs

TRANSMISSION: Four-speed manual

CHASSIS: Rack-and-pinion steering; chain-driven rear-wheel drive and independent rear suspension to 1967 (then live rear axle with radius rods); drum brakes all round (front discs from 1967)

TIMELINE

1965	S800 launched to replace similarly styled S600
1966	First production examples of S800 go on sale in Japan
1967	Spec update includes live rear axle and front disc brakes
1967	S800 launched in the UK to critical acclaim
1968	S800M announced, aimed at American buyers
1970	Production of the S800 ceases in May

◄ How's that for the ultimate in classic wind-in-the-hair motoring? The soft-top S800 was a hilarious and rewarding drive. (*LAT*)

HONDA CRX

the fun and funky civic

▲ The second-generation CRX was smoother and faster than its predecessor, with up to 150bhp available in its most powerful guise. (*LAT*)

Cast your mind back to 1983. In the UK and throughout much of Europe, the Honda Civic was selling well but usually bought by older drivers looking for something that was reliable, comfortable and good value for money, which is why the Honda Civic was the vehicle of choice in Bournemouth and Eastbourne at that time. But as an enthusiast's machine, it held about as much appeal as a food mixer.

Then, in Japan, Honda unveiled the new Civic CRX coupé. And, even better, they confirmed it would be coming to the UK and to most other export markets by the spring of 1984. Finally, at long last, the Civic range had something interesting to show.

Not just interesting but pretty stylish, too. Despite being based on the platform of a basic three-door Civic, the new CRX was a fairly low-slung fastback coupé that looked cool from any angle. It was sharp, it was angular and it was the most handsome affordable sportster out on the street back in the mid-1980s.

It wasn't merely good looking, either, because despite its humble origins the front-wheel-drive CRX was also an amazingly competent driver's car. Its coil-sprung suspension had been beefed up and stiffened, which made for a hard ride by Honda standards; fortunately, this resulted in a car with impressively flat handling characteristics, loads of grip and a real wow factor on the open road.

The CRX's 100bhp 1.5-litre 12-valve engine was both eager and free-revving, while the knife-through-butter gearchange helped exploit every last drop of power. The rack-and-pinion steering was sharp and precise, giving plenty of feedback at speed. The combination of all this excellence resulted in a 2+2 with all the fun and feel of a grown-up go-kart.

With good looks and so much driver appeal in its favour, the CRX was soon being hailed as a more interesting alternative to a conventional hot hatch, and this was a market that Honda was happy to explore. But as hot hatches became increasingly sophisticated through the 1980s, so the CRX had to develop in a similar direction.

It was no surprise then, that a new CRX – generally known as the Series II – was launched in 1986, combining softer, more curvaceous styling with very much more power. In fact, once the VTEC-engined version of the new CRX came along, this little firecracker of a coupé was boasting up to 150bhp – enough for a top speed just this side of 130mph, and the 0–60mph sprint in under 8.0 seconds. The CRX was growing up fast.

The newcomer may have been quicker and more highly developed than the original (as the twin-cam VTEC's variable valve timing and 16-valve head happily proved), but the CRX had lost none of its directness, its poise or its sheer fun. It was still one of the most entertaining four-wheeled devices this side of a roller skate, and its combination of ultra-sharp steering and near-faultless handling ensured continued appeal to hot hatch converts everywhere.

What Honda did with the second-generation CRX was really very clever, because although ▶

SPEC

CRX 1.5 SERIES I

ENGINE: 1488cc fuel-injected 12-valve four-cylinder

POWER: 100bhp @ 5750rpm

TORQUE: 96lb ft @ 4500rpm

PERFORMANCE: Top speed 115mph, 0–60mph 8.5 secs

TRANSMISSION: Five-speed manual

CHASSIS: Rack-and-pinion steering; independent coil-spring suspension all round with front MacPherson struts and anti-roll bar; front disc and rear drum brakes

CRX 1.6 VTEC SERIES II

ENGINE: 1595cc 16-valve fuel-injected DOHC four-cylinder VTEC

POWER: 150bhp @ 7500rpm

TORQUE: 108lb ft @ 6500rpm

PERFORMANCE: Top speed 129mph, 0–60mph 7.9 secs

TRANSMISSION: Five-speed manual

CHASSIS: Rack-and-pinion steering; independent coil-spring suspension all round with front MacPherson struts and anti-roll bar; disc brakes all round

CRX 1.6 VTEC SERIES III

ENGINE: 1595cc 16-valve fuel-injected DOHC four-cylinder VTEC

POWER: 158bhp @ 7600rpm

TORQUE: 111lb ft @ 7000rpm

PERFORMANCE: Top speed 132mph, 0–60mph 7.5 secs

TRANSMISSION: Five-speed manual

CHASSIS: Power-assisted rack-and-pinion steering; independent coil-spring suspension all round with front MacPherson struts and anti-roll bar; disc brakes all round

▲ The CRX was always a top-handling machine, with levels of grip and roadholding that made it serious fun to drive. It was a refreshing alternative to some fairly mundane hot-hatch opposition. (*LAT*)

WHAT WE LIKE...

Whichever generation of CRX takes your fancy, you'll find it a swift, nimble and highly entertaining choice. It offers real driver feedback and is now very, very affordable on the used market. It's a little gem

...WHAT WE DON'T

The Series I's fairly angular styling may be dated, but there's very little to dislike about any CRX. It was the most fun thing to happen to the Civic in the 1980s

this was a far more attractive and up-to-date design than its predecessor, it was still immediately recognisable at a glance as a CRX.

Honda's designers had taken the original, rounded off its edges and made it near perfect in the process.

Sold in the UK and most European markets as a 2+2, the CRX was marketed in the States as a strict two-seater. Whether that makes a statement about the size of the average American driver and passenger, we're not sure. Either way, the CRX was about as spacious as anybody could reasonably expect a compact coupé to be, particularly up front. But its boot space was usefully large compared with other coupés, and this helped to ensure its appeal to buyers who demanded practicality as much as style.

The major appeal of the most expensive CRX derivative was, naturally, its VTEC engine. This 1.6-litre lump was – and still is – an absolute star, combining a seriously high-revving nature with all the flexibility and performance we've come to expect from the VTEC family. It was enough to make rival engine manufacturers feel like heading back to the drawing board.

In spite of its excellence, the Series II CRX wasn't to be allowed to live much longer than the latest Civic range on which it was based. As the more humble Civic offerings bit the dust in 1991 to make way for an all-new line-up, so the CRX followed suit.

So ... would Honda continue its own trend of replacing the CRX with a replacement still instantly recognisable as a CRX? This time, there was no way. By the time the very latest CRX was unveiled in 1992, it was immediately obvious it was a drastic departure from what had gone before.

It's true that the best engine of all – the 1595cc twin-cam VTEC – remained available on the most expensive version, this time pumping out 158bhp and endowing the new CRX with a 132mph top speed, but in terms of the car's style and image, just about everything else had changed.

The Series III CRX had evolved into what some people described as a Fiat X1/9 for the 1990s. It wasn't mid-engined or rear-wheel drive. But it did 'borrow' the Fiat's original idea of a removable metal roof (in this case made of aluminium) which could then be stowed in the car's boot when the sun appeared. But the really novel feature was that, on the most expensive version, this roof was electrically operated.

Nowadays, of course, convertibles with steel roofs are all the rage, with numerous versions offered by various manufacturers. But in 1992, it was a brave step on such an affordable car, and Honda had to be congratulated for devising this unique selling point. As that year's motor shows throughout the world proved, it was a novelty that drew crowds and fascinated potential buyers alike.

But in the UK, the third-generation CRX failed to capture the imagination of enthusiasts in quite the same way as its predecessors. It was less practical, as being a two-seater with a tiny boot, it had to be. But was that enough to deter the fanatics? Some people suggested it had become too much of a hairdresser's car … and maybe, despite its performance potential, there's a grain of truth in that.

As for us, we'd take an immaculate, low-mileage, second-generation CRX VTEC over any of the others. It's a cut-price second-hand super-coupé … and it's still one of the most rewarding drives you'll find for sensible cash. ■

TIMELINE

1983   Series I CRX unveiled in Japan

1984   CRX goes on sale in most export markets, including UK

1986   Restyled CRX (Series II) launched with softer styling and more power

1987   New 130bhp twin-cam version of CRX introduced

1989   160bhp VTEC model becomes available

1991   New Civic range means the end of the CRX Series II

1992   Series III CRX launched – removable roof panel is its unique selling point

1993   Third-generation CRX goes on sale in the UK in the spring

1996   Fastest VTEC model dropped from UK line-up

1997   CRX American and UK sales discontinued

1998   CRX production ceases

▼ The final incarnation of the CRX saw it fitted with a targa-style roof, electrically operated on the most expensive versions. This was revolutionary stuff back in 1993. (Honda)

HONDA
CIVIC VTi 1991–2000
the gti-beater

▲ Over the years, the VTi was available in a bewildering array of guises, including thee- and five-door hatches, four-door saloon, two-door coupe and five-door estate. Still, at least it meant there was a Civic VTi to suit most tastes. (*Honda*)

A confusing array of cars comes under the banner of Honda Civic VTi, such is Honda's expertise when it comes to creating niche-filling performance machines. And even by restricting this chapter to two generations of Civic sold between 1991 and 2000 (with a complete change for the 1995 model year), there's still a wide range of VTi versions to mention.

It's to Honda's credit that they managed to transform an ordinary machine with real pensioner appeal into a top-performing hot hatch capable of eating a Golf GTi for breakfast. Enthusiasts everywhere always knew the Civic had great potential, such was the excellence of its chassis design, its high levels of grip and its all-round responsiveness. But it wasn't until the all-new fifth-generation Civic came along in 1991 that the concept of a go-faster Civic really took off.

It was at this time that Honda's VTEC engine development had been hitting the headlines; its combination of variable valve timing and ultra-

high-revving capabilities proving its potential for future performance machines. That the concept ended up being used in so many Honda models throughout the 1990s and beyond says a lot about Honda's technological wizardry and the sheer practicality of its engineering.

The new-generation three-door Civic of 1991 was a likeable machine in many ways, with clean uncluttered styling and an easy-going nature. Its ride wasn't the finest, but its neat handling and adequate grip made up for this. Then Honda decided to launch a high-performance version.

It was probably inevitable, given the success of (mainly European) hot hatches throughout the 1980s and into the1990s, but not everyone was prepared for just how good – and how powerful – the Civic VTi would be.

This hot new Civic was going to take on the GTi version of the new MkIII Golf that Volkswagen were about to launch, and both models ended up costing roughly the same in the

UK. But whereas the 2.0-litre Golf managed only a miserly 115bhp, the 1.6-litre all-conquering Civic VTi developed a very healthy 158bhp at an impressively high 7500rpm. It was enough for a claimed top speed of 134mph, with 60mph from rest in only 7.5 seconds.

Even better news was that the Civic was an even greater car to drive than its impressive figures suggested. The incredibly responsive powerplant just loved to be worked hard, sounding ever more glorious the higher you revved it. Front wheel spin was a minor problem, but with that under control the VTi would just keep on accelerating right through the 8000rpm red line. The gear change was fantastically slick too, which helped aid rapid progress, while the independent all-coil suspension was suitably stiffened and lowered to enable remarkably flat cornering without reducing the Civic's ride quality any further. ▶

SPEC

CIVIC VTI THREE-DOOR, 1991–1994

ENGINE: 1595cc DOHC 16-valve fuel-injected VTEC four-cylinder

POWER: 158bhp @ 7500rpm

TORQUE: 111lb ft @ 7000rpm

PERFORMANCE: Top speed 134mph, 0–60mph 7.5 secs

TRANSMISSION: Five-speed manual

CHASSIS: Power-assisted rack-and-pinion steering; independent coil-spring suspension all round with front anti-roll bar; front disc (ventilated) and rear drum brakes

▲ Whichever VTi you choose, you'll find a thrilling and high-revving VTEC powerplant under the bonnet. And that's a very desirable piece of kit by any standards. (Honda)

CIVIC VTI THREE-DOOR, 1995–2000

ENGINE: 1595cc DOHC 16-valve fuel-injected VTEC four-cylinder

POWER: 158bhp @ 7600rpm

TORQUE: 113lb ft @ 7000rpm

PERFORMANCE: Top speed 129mph, 0–60mph 7.4 secs

TRANSMISSION: Five-speed manual

CHASSIS: Power-assisted rack-and-pinion steering; independent coil-spring suspension all round with front anti-roll bar; disc brakes all round (ventilated fronts) with ABS

CIVIC VTI FIVE-DOOR, 1995–2000

ENGINE: 1797cc DOHC 16-valve fuel-injected VTEC four-cylinder

POWER: 167bhp @ 7600rpm

TORQUE: 122lb ft @ 6300rpm

PERFORMANCE: Top speed 134mph, 0–60mph 8.0 secs

TRANSMISSION: Five-speed manual

CHASSIS: Power-assisted rack-and-pinion steering; independent coil-spring suspension all round with front MacPherson struts and anti-roll bar; disc brakes all round (ventilated fronts) with ABS

▲ The VTi managed to transform the otherwise fairly ordinary Civic into a GTi-beating high-performance beast, with up to 158bhp on tap in this guise. (*Honda*)

WHAT WE LIKE...

Great performance, incredibly responsive engines and nimble handling help to make the VTi an exciting alternative to lots of less interesting hot hatches. Exceptional reliability is the icing on the high-performance cake.

...WHAT WE DON'T

The five-door versions of 1995-onwards share essentially the same bodyshell as the Rover 400 hatchback range – and that's nothing to be proud of. If you don't need five-door versatility, the smaller-engined VTi three-door is a far more tempting choice.

▶ In some markets, the Civic VTi was available in four-door saloon guise, too – boosting the number of body styles to no less than five in total. (*Honda*)

Lowlier versions of the new Civic were competent but fairly unexciting creations. But the VTi was something else, and the world's motoring press just couldn't get enough of its massive fun appeal and its exciting driving style.

Honda never leaves a Civic range untouched for too long, which is why the sixth-generation model to wear that famous badge was announced towards the end of 1994 for the 1995 model year. With the success of the previous VTi still getting talked about, it wasn't long before a similarly quick version of the new model was introduced.

This, however, is where the Civic range became just a little complicated. Logically enough, the new three-door Civic replaced the previous three-door model of the same name. However, a five-door Civic would also join the range, replacing the unexciting old Concerto and sharing its bodyshell and underpinnings with the new-for-1995 Rover 400 series – which left almost nothing in common with the three-door Civics. An American-built (and, again, very different) Civic Coupé would also become available, as would an estate car based on the five-door Civic. What's more, each model of the new Civic line-up would eventually have its very own VTi version.

It was, perhaps, a sensible move, meaning that Honda could offer a high-performance Civic to suit all tastes, irrespective of whether buyers needed a three- or five-door hatchback, a coupé or an estate. However, the five-door Civic's closeness to the rather dull Rover 400 range meant this would never be a top-selling version of the VTi, not helped by its rather staid styling and (thanks to Rover) old-fashioned image.

This was a shame, because the five-door Civic VTi was fitted with a 1.8-litre, 167bhp VTEC lump that certainly held a lot of performance potential. However, no doubt thanks to the extra weight of the five-door's bodyshell, performance was little better than that of the 1.6-litre three-door version. In fact, with a 0–60mph time of eight seconds dead, the new five-door VTi was slower accelerating, despite its extra cubic centimetres.

For enthusiasts everywhere, the ultimate Civic VTi was still the three-door hatchback, using the latest version of the 1595cc DOHC unit found in its predecessor. In this application, it offered the same 158bhp output (at marginally higher revs), together with a slight increase in torque, giving it a top speed just this side of 130mph, with 60mph from standstill in 7.4 seconds – strong enough figures to make a Golf GTi head back to Germany in shame.

As before, the driving experience was an exciting and joyous affair, the high-revving nature of the VTi's superb engine proving better at putting a smile on drivers' faces than any amount of anti-depressant pills. Into a corner, with the power held high and the double-wishbone suspension doing the business, this latest VTi would hang on in there with the best of them. When it came to standing-start acceleration and being first away from the lights, the VTi simply trounced the opposition.

The Civic VTi had achieved so much by the time production ceased towards the end of 2000 that fans of the model were understandably saddened by its passing. But, of course, they had little to fear. Honda's new-for-2001 Civic line-up would surely include a scorching VTi version … wouldn't it? Well, no. But, even better, the incredible new Civic Type R was waiting in the wings instead. The high-performance Civic was here to stay. ■

TIMELINE

1991	New-generation Civic range announced; UK sales start in November
1992	VTi version launched, with 158bhp from 1.6 litres
1994	New sixth-generation Civic three-door models unveiled
1995	Rover-based five-door versions join the range
1995	VTi derivatives of both three- and five-door models go on sale
1996	New five-door 1.8 VTi Estate announced
2000	Production of current Civic range ceases by year's end
2001	All-new Civic goes on sale, with Type R replacing previous VTi

▼ You need high performance combined with family-style practicality? A four- or five-door VTi will provide one of the ultimate solutions to your dilemma. (*LAT*)

HONDA
CIVIC TYPE R
hotter than ever

▲ The idea of a hot Civic really came to fruition with the debut of the Type R, offering the kind of power and performance never before seen in such an affordable performance machine. (*Honda*)

The high-performance Honda Civic concept really came of age in 2001 when the all-new Type R model was displayed at that most exciting of European motor show venues: Geneva. It wasn't unexpected that Honda would unveil a sporting Civic for the new millennium; what did come as a shock was just how powerful the production version would be.

The new-generation Civic was already winning praise for its combination of refinement, build quality, value for money and easy driving style. But such attributes are usually far from the minds of those who prefer spending their hard-earned cash on brand new hot hatches. In any case, the latest three-door Civic range was – like so many of its rivals – bigger and taller than any of its predecessors, so would a high-performance version really fit the bill?

It would and it did. By the time the new British-built Civic Type R went on sale in the UK and several European export markets in October

2001, it was already being hailed as the fastest-accelerating front-wheel-drive hot hatch on the planet, thanks to its fantastic 2.0-litre twin-cam i-VTEC powerplant, a normally-aspirated engine with an incredibly rev-happy nature and the ability to produce 197bhp at 7400rpm.

Just think about that. It represents almost 100bhp per litre – and all from a non-turbo engine. Honda's experience of developing high-revving, high-performance engines with variable valve timing placed it at the forefront of petrol engine technology. Indeed, few other manufacturers could hope to have matched such an output from a normally-aspirated powerplant. It gave Honda a huge advantage in terms of headline-grabbing publicity.

That the fastest-accelerating car in its class was also one of the best value was equally typical of Honda. By the time the 197bhp Civic Type R went on sale in the UK in 2001, it cost about the same as a 115bhp VW Golf 2.0 GTi, a 134bhp Vauxhall

ENGINE: 1998cc fuel-injected
16-valve DOHC i-VTEC four-cylinder

POWER: 197bhp @ 7400rpm

TORQUE: 196Nm @ 5900rpm

PERFORMANCE: Top speed 146mph,
0–60mph 6.6 secs (2004 model)

TRANSMISSION: Six-speed manual

CHASSIS: Electric power-assisted
rack-and-pinion steering; independent
coil-spring suspension all round;
servo-assisted disc brakes all round
with ABS and EBD

Astra 2.0 SRi or a 140bhp BMW 318ti Compact. With a whopping 82bhp difference between the Civic and the Golf, there was simply no comparison in terms of power, performance or real driver appeal.

The big question was whether an output of very nearly 200bhp could be successfully pushed through the front wheels of a hot hatch. Many pundits suggested such power needed rear drive or all-wheel drive in order to be successfully used. But Honda disagreed; and so did the thousands of enthusiasts (not least the British fanatics) who swiftly became Type R converts. Honda found itself with an instant hit on its corporate hands.

The Civic Type R certainly needed to be treated with respect. It wasn't one of those high-powered cars anybody could jump into and drive at full throttle with virtually no skill or experience. In other words, this was no Impreza Turbo. What it offered instead was a driving style that demanded concentration, respect and a certain amount of mechanical and technological sympathy in order to extract the most performance; and the most pleasure.

Sliding yourself into a Civic Type R's body-hugging driver's seat for the first time is when you begin to fall for the model's charms. The interior is fantastically well laid out and the dashboard is both practical and sporting in style. But it's when you fire up the lusty 2.0-litre DOHC powerplant, blip the throttle and start unleashing all 197 horses that you get a taste of what's to come.

The Type R's close-ratio six-speed ▶

▲ Almost 200bhp from the Type R's 2.0-litre engine was a phenomenal achievement by the standards of 2001. (*Honda*)

◀ Body-hugging seats are a must in any hot hatch with this kind of performance potential. (*Honda*)

◀ Dashboard-mounted gearstick looked odd in a high-performance car, but the super-slick six-speed gearchange more than made up for it! (*Honda*)

WHAT WE LIKE...

The fastest accelerating front-wheel-drive hot hatch in the land is just like one of the 'old school' – but much, much better. Drive it with respect and you'll be going faster than you ever thought possible in a Honda Civic.

▶ The handling of the fastest front-drive Civic brought new standards to the hot-hatch class. (*Honda*)

▼ The demise of the Type R in 2005 was a sad occasion for so many enthusiasts of the model. (*Honda*)

...WHAT WE DON'T

Wheelspin can be a problem, especially on damp or smooth surfaces, which makes it a hot hatch for the enthusiast rather than the novice – and that's something to be celebrated.

transmission is a joy to use, which means the minuscule movement to select first gear ready for your inaugural Type R experience is delightfully quick, but even if you're convinced the clutch is being released at a steady rate, nothing quite prepares you for what's about to happen. On anything but a perfect road surface in perfect weather conditions, the Civic Type R spins its wheels like a potter on speed. Even when conditions are as near perfect as it's possible to be, it's still a handful – in the wrong hands, that is.

But this is just what makes us adore the Type R. This is no blandmobile that goes fast but gives its driver little in the way of reward or feedback. This is a machine that demands to be driven hard, but equally demands to be respected; and in many ways, it makes you a better driver.

Think about it; there's nothing more humiliating than sitting at a set of traffic lights that have just turned to green, your engine revving and front wheels spinning, desperate to make rapid progress but in reality being beaten away from the standing-start by a sales rep in a diesel. Instead, you pull away fairly gently (or as gently as any Type R allows you to) and, once you're under way, you then start to accelerate. Hard. In no time at all the scenery is a blur and everything else on the road is fast disappearing in your rear view mirror.

Once you're under way, things still aren't totally straightforward. This awesome i-VTEC engine of Honda's is so eager throughout its extensive rev range that it's still possible to be spinning the front wheels as you're changing up from second to third and giving the accelerator a bit of a seeing to. But you adjust your driving style to suit. You soon get used to making the most of that ultra-slick six-speed transmission to cut short any wheelspin time, and you soon learn to use the

Civic's go-faster pedal in such a way that you're bringing in the power in a steady but steep curve rather than adopting an all-at-once policy. You soon learn; and the sooner you do, the more you warm to the whole Civic Type R driving experience.

But the Type R isn't just about outright performance or ultimate power. It's also one of the most rewarding hot hatches you'll ever come across, with tenacious grip and impressively roll-free handling even at the limit. The electric power steering gives the driver plenty of 'feel' and feedback at all speeds, while the braking system (with ABS and EBD as standard, of course) is one of the most competent at the price.

Because this isn't an over-complicated four-wheel-drive machine, it feels almost like an old-school hot hatch with all that this means for driver enjoyment, skill and involvement. It's a Japanese performance car with character, and that fact alone needs shouting about until every Golf driver in the land sits up and takes notice.

What's more, things got even better at the beginning of 2004 when a round of very minor styling updates was accompanied by a lighter flywheel, enabling the engine to spin even more freely. Suddenly the vital 0–60mph time dropped from 6.8 to 6.6 seconds, making the Type R even more desirable among performance fanatics. The Type R was once again the hottest of all affordable hatches. ∎

TIMELINE

2001	High-performance Civic Type R unveiled at Geneva show in February
2001	Production version goes on sale in UK in October
2001	British-built versions of Type R exported to Japan in December
2004	Revised model announced with styling updates and faster acceleration
2005	All-new Civic unveiled; final Type R is produced

▲ Wheelspin from standstill can be a problem in the Type R, although your driving style soon adjusts as a result. (Honda)

▼ This is a Japanese performance machine with real character. Who needs all-wheel-drive and over-complication when a high-performance car is this good? (Honda)

HONDA
PRELUDE
the coupé with class

▲ While the earliest Preludes were based on the rather dull first-generation Accord saloon, later models boasted the power and driving experience they truly deserved. (*Honda*)

If ever there was a Beast From The East whose image held it back, this was it. Not because the poor old Honda Prelude wasn't a sales success; it clearly was. But it was the kind of people who were snapping up brand-new Preludes that deterred many other potential buyers. Just like so many Hondas throughout the 1980s and 1990s, the Prelude wasn't seen as a car for the young.

Perhaps that had something to do with the fact that it always tended to be based on the platform of the rather dull Accord, or maybe it was because so many people ended up having a mid-life crisis, trading-in their sensible Civic for a more stylish Prelude in the process. Either way, Honda's svelte coupé was not a new car for the average 18–25 year old.

The story of the Prelude goes back to 1978, when a two-door coupé based on the dreary but reliable Accord saloon of the time suddenly appeared. It was badged the Prelude, offered a 1.6-litre four-pot and was distinctly unexciting.

An all-new Prelude appeared five years later, though it wasn't until 1986 that Honda's coupé offering finally started getting interesting. The styling was tidied up that year, even if it still looked a bit bland. More importantly, a new 2.0-litre twin-cam engine was introduced, as well as the revolutionary idea of four-wheel steering on top-of-the-range models. The latter transformed the front-wheel-drive Prelude's handling characteristics, as well as its driver appeal. I remember covering many miles in a four-wheel-steer Prelude back in 1989 – and, rather unexpectedly, I loved it.

Nothing stays still forever, and a brand new Prelude range was unveiled in 1992. Things were looking up yet again, thanks to big, more masculine styling, a dose of attitude and a new range of engines. It was a surprisingly good driver's car, even if most of its drivers were still in the 50-plus age bracket.

Even that new-look Prelude had disappeared by the end of 1996, its successor being squarer,

ENGINE: 2157cc fuel-injected 16-valve DOHC four-cylinder VTEC

POWER: 183bhp @ 6500rpm

TORQUE: 156lb ft @ 4500rpm

PERFORMANCE: Top speed 139mph, 0–60mph 7.5 secs

TRANSMISSION: Five-speed manual

CHASSIS: Rack-and-pinion power-assisted steering; double-wishbone independent coil-spring suspension all round; servo-assisted disc brakes all round

TIMELINE

1978   Original Prelude launched, based on Accord floorpan but with two-door body

1983   Bigger, sharper Prelude introduced with more power and more space

1986   Latest Prelude looks less cluttered. Twin-cam engine introduced

1987   Rear-wheel steering becomes available on top-of-the-range model

1992   Latest restyle gives new Prelude a meaner, moodier image … at last

1996   Yet another new look for the Prelude, cleaner but with less attitude

2001   Prelude discontinued as Honda focuses on hot versions of other models

simpler looking and more in tune with mid-1990s tastes. Even so, the appeal of the Prelude remained depressingly narrow in terms of market penetration.

That was a real shame, because some very fine Preludes have been built over the years. In 1996, the most expensive Prelude VTEC was pumping out 183bhp, giving it a top speed just this side of 140mph and a 7.5-second dash to 60mph. Even better than such figures was the grin-cracking behaviour of the engine. Like the rest of the Honda VTEC range, the 2.2-litre Prelude offered one of the most free-revving powerplants this side of a superbike, encouraging the driver to really work the car hard and make the most of its agile handling and eager nature. For a machine with a relatively aged customer base, this particular Prelude really knew how to party.

Fast versions of later Civics and Accords, and the arrival of the S2000 sports car at the start of the 20th century, meant Honda's interest in replacing the Prelude – particularly for export markets – was non-existent. And so it was that the Prelude name disappeared from most countries' price lists, becoming history by the end of 2001. A car with real ability – and up to 200bhp in its final days – had bitten the dust. ▪

WHAT WE LIKE…

Hugely underrated Japanese coupé that offers great value on the used market. With decent performance from various VTEC models in particular, it's a bit of a Q-car on the side.

…WHAT WE DON'T

Thousands of pensioners bought brand new Preludes when they were still in production, which means its image isn't exactly youthful. On the other hand, you're guaranteed a service history and plenty of wax on the paintwork…

▼ By 1986, top-of-the-range Preludes were boasting 2.0-litre twin cam power and the revolutionary idea of four-wheel steering. It was an advanced specification for the time. (*Author*)

HONDA BEAT

the sports car is back

With Mazda bringing attention back to the open-top sports car market with the MX-5 in 1989, it was only a matter of time before other Japanese makers started cashing in on the same sector. And, as ever, Honda was anxious not to be left out.

In typically innovative style, Honda ignored the temptation to create a direct rival to the MX-5, preferring instead to come further downmarket in size, power and price. The result was the cute-looking Honda Beat, launched in 1991 and an immediate hit in its homeland.

Not only was the Beat smaller, lighter and less expensive than the MX-5, it also boasted a mid-engined layout, a major contribution to its excellent handling, terrific rear-end grip and sheer fun appeal. In fact, so accomplished was the Beat's chassis, it could easily have handled far more power than the unexceptional 64bhp offered as standard.

Such an output wasn't bad, considering this tiniest of sporting Hondas found itself with just a 656cc 12-valve three-cylinder lump for propulsion, but at least it was a high-revving little unit, its maximum output being achieved at a buzzy 8100rpm. This was another of those tiny

WHAT WE LIKE...

Cute looks, lively engine and terrific handling resulted in a real fun car for fans of open-top motoring. Honda had reinvented the truly affordable sports car.

...WHAT WE DON'T

Not the quickest machine around, although it felt much faster than its figures suggested.

Japanese engines that just seemed to thrive on hard work and massive revs.

Which was just as well, since most Beat owners found themselves exploiting the upper part of the Beat's extensive rev range most of the time, in an effort to make the most of that fantastic mid-engined layout and grippy handling. The fact that the car's top speed was artificially limited to just 87mph was frustrating (though removable); but getting there was great fun. For anybody who wanted an urban runabout with style, charisma and the facility to top up their tan, the Beat was just perfect.

For some odd reason, the Beat was never officially sold in the UK, though a number of 'grey' imports have appeared over the years. Perhaps its non-appearance had something to do with the fact that Japanese buyers just couldn't get enough of the little Honda in its first couple of years, which made export less of a priority.

By the time Beat production ceased in 1996, around 33,600 examples had found buyers. Its popularity was in decline by then, however, and its novelty value was a thing of the past. Nowadays, the model has a strong and loyal following among enthusiasts who appreciate the charms of this delightful Honda. And, of course, the sheer value for money it offers on the used market.

Get hold of a 'grey' import Beat now and you'll find it fun to drive, cheap to keep and a great summer plaything. You'll also find it surprisingly well equipped, every Beat coming as standard with electric windows and air conditioning. Very thoughtful…

At just 3295mm in overall length, this is a diminutive sports car; in fact, it's 693cm shorter than the original MX-5, which gives a good idea of just how tiny this little buzzbox is. But as is so often the case, smaller really does mean more fun. So what if the Beat doesn't boast neck-snapping acceleration? Who cares if its top speed is almost on a par with the average milk float? The emphasis here is on fun, feedback and funkiness. In all three categories, the Honda Beat still reigns supreme if an eager little soft-top is what floats your boat.

What a shame Honda never got round to replacing the Beat in the 21st century. It could well have given the Smart Roadster a run for its money; well, you never know. ∎

SPEC

ENGINE: 656cc fuel-injected 12-valve OHC three-cylinder

POWER: 64bhp @ 8100rpm

TORQUE: 44lb ft @ 7000rpm

PERFORMANCE: Top speed 87mph, 0–60mph 10 secs

TRANSMISSION: Five-speed manual

CHASSIS: Rack-and-pinion steering; MacPherson struts front and rear; servo-assisted disc brakes all round

▼ The Beat's low-down driving position and seriously compact dimensions meant it was a fun and entertaining experience for any young-at-heart buyer. (*LAT*)

TIMELINE

1991	Production of the Beat gets under way in May
1992	First year's production runs at 20,000-plus cars
1992	Full range comprises two versions with different trim and options
1996	Beat production ceases in February

HONDA
INTEGRA TYPE R
racing pedigree

The Integra model name wasn't particularly well known in the UK prior to 1997. Honda did try selling a rather tedious five-door hatchback going by the name of Integra in the late 1980s, but its British sales levels were about as uninspiring as the car itself. In fact, a good many Integras – mainly aimed at the Japanese market – that have come and gone over the years could be described as terminally dull.

The range took a turn for the better when a new-generation Integra arrived in 1997, a line-up that comprised decent-enough four-door saloons and two-door coupés with a range of perfectly competent engines available between them. But by the end of the year Honda would do the almost unthinkable, metamorphosing the Integra coupé into the now legendary Integra Type R. It was a move that transformed the Integra range's image overnight, as well as providing Honda with another high-performance offering for power-loving petrolheads.

The significance of the Integra Type R shouldn't be underestimated, for this was the real start of the Type R revolution that was to come, with seriously upgraded and similarly-badged versions of the Accord and new-for-2001 Civic set to follow in the footsteps of the hottest new Integra the world had ever seen.

The best news of all was that Honda seemed keen to spread the Type R message abroad, which meant a good proportion of export sales for the awesome new Integra. That included the UK, where from the end of 1997 the Integra Type R became part of the official Honda line-up.

No other model from the 1997–2001 Integra range would be offered in the UK, so why did Honda decide to import limited numbers of the Type R? Primarily because the British market had always enjoyed healthy sales of affordable, high-performance machines, so there was a ready market for Honda's most exciting offering, and also because it introduced the British car-buying public to the Type R moniker, which would mean essential new models like the forthcoming Civic Type R having a real image advantage from the outset.

Enthusiasts and motoring journalists around the world were soon bowled over by the power and performance that came as standard with the Integra Type R. By applying their previous experience as F1 engine manufacturers, combined with the latest developments in VTEC engineering, the boffins at Honda managed to extract a mighty 187bhp from just 1997cc of normally-aspirated twin-cam engine. Even better news for enthusiasts everywhere was that such power was created at an incredible 7900rpm.

Think about those figures for a moment. Without the aid of superchargers, turbochargers or intercoolers, Honda had managed an immense output equating to 106bhp per litre. This was astonishing by production car standards of the time, and it marked the Integra Type R out as something very special indeed.

Like every other VTEC engine before and since, the Integra's four-cylinder unit thrived on very high revs, which is when Honda's variable valve technology really comes into its own. Pottering round town with the revs kept low and a using a cautious right foot, you had little clue as to the Type R's true potential. But with the Integra's extensive rev band being exploited to the full and the VTEC unit doing what it does best, there was

◀ Clean and uncluttered dashboard wasn't the most exciting design around; but it didn't need to be. (*Honda*)

no other affordable coupé capable of keeping pace with a Type R.

You could take the revs right round to 8500 and beyond before the artificial limiter would take over and demand a cutback. And yet, this marvel of an engine never protested; in fact, the more it was used and abused, the better it sounded. At anything above 6000rpm, the Type R developed an F1-like howl that quickly turned into a roar, in time with the blurring of the scenery.

Britain's *EVO* magazine, reporting on the Integra Type R in its May 2000 issue, said it '…makes the best noise of any four-pot in production.' That was impressive praise from a title renowned for getting the most out of any performance machine. Just as crucially, *EVO* reported: 'You would never believe a front-drive car could possess as much poise and adjustability as the Integra Type R.'

So, despite its front-drive set-up, the ▶

▼ In its day, no other four-cylinder engine sounded quite as good or quite as exhilarating as the Integra's awesome powerplant. (*Honda*)

SPEC

ENGINE: 1997cc DOHC fuel-injected VTEC four-cylinder

POWER: 187bhp @ 7900rpm

TORQUE: 178Nm @ 7300rpm

PERFORMANCE: Top speed 145mph, 0–60mph 6.2 secs

TRANSMISSION: Five-speed manual

CHASSIS: Power-assisted rack-and-pinion steering; independent coil-spring double-wishbone suspension all round with limited-slip differential; ventilated discs all round

▲ American-spec versions of the Type R were sold under the Acura brand name, a curious move given the success of Honda in the States. (*Honda*)

▶ Distinctive looks provided only the smallest clue as to the Type R's amazing performance potential. (*Honda*)

WHAT WE LIKE...

Fantastic performance from an F1-sound-alike engine makes any Integra Type R a terrifically entertaining machine. It's serious stuff, so don't underestimate this awesome car's potential. It marked the start of a whole new generation of Type R Hondas – and for that we must be grateful.

...WHAT WE DON'T

Fairly limited British imports, so an Integra Type R in perfect condition may take a bit of tracking down. But do persevere – your patience will get you one of the most dynamic driver's cars of the late 1990s.

Integra managed to keep all 187 horses under remarkable control. Front-wheel spin could be generated, of course, but the Honda's highly-developed double-wishbone independent suspension (suitably sharpened and honed in this guise, of course), limited-slip diff and ventilated discs all round helped ensure going round corners and stopping in a hurry were both achieved without too much drama.

Unlike four-wheel-drive super-saloons such as the Mitsubishi Evo and Subaru Impreza, the Integra was a machine that demanded respect. Should you drive foolishly, it was possible to get into very serious trouble in a Type R – but somehow that was all part of the fun. This was a performance beast with real enthusiast appeal, a car that demanded to be driven well rather than simply driven fast. It was raw, thrilling and exhilarating by any standards, and it was the most exciting thing to wear a Honda badge in a very long time.

When it arrived for the 1998 model year, the 187bhp British-spec Integra Type R also managed to offer spectacular value for money, undercutting far lesser coupé rivals such as the 150bhp Alfa Romeo 2.0 GTV, 170bhp BMW 323i Coupé, 140bhp Fiat Coupé 20V and 173bhp Toyota Celica 2.0 GT. Nothing else came close in terms of its performance-meets-value compromise, and even the most fanatical BMW enthusiasts were running out of excuses not to try an Integra Type R for themselves.

Unlike some of its 'softer' coupé competitors, the Integra was a pretty raw piece of kit; its lack of refinement at motorway speeds, its racing interior, hard ride and all-out high-revving power

◀ Fantastically body-gripping seats were essential in a car that offered such fast cornering abilities. (*Honda*)

◀ So much power from just a 2.0-litre normally-aspirated engine was unique to Honda, and a great sales pitch for the Type R. (*Honda*)

source proving less 'relaxing' than many people demanded. But that was fine, because UK supplies of the Integra Type R would be fairly limited, so that there were just about enough to go round among the hardcore performance car buyers.

Britain's motoring press always raved about the Integra Type R, still mourning its passing long after the final examples were sold in 2001. *Auto Express* enthused that it was '…pure, simple but blindingly quick, the finest front-wheel-drive car we've ever tested.' And during an exciting time at the wheel, *Car* magazine claimed the Integra Type R was a '…road-rocket bargain.'

A new-generation Integra arrived in 2001, with the Type R now propelled at an even more impressive rate by a 2.0-litre i-VTEC unit driven through a six-speed gearbox. But with the Civic Type R already attracting so much interest, Honda decided the Integra was no longer needed in the UK, and the latest version remained officially unavailable.

Still, at least that leaves the 1997–2001 Integra Type R as a fantastically tempting and very affordable used buy now. It's one of the finest ways of spending the price of a basic new 'supermini' on something that's guaranteed to thrill every time you get behind the wheel. It was yet another all-time gem from Honda, and it's as exciting now as it ever was. ■

TIMELINE

1997	Latest Integra range unveiled in Japan; homeland sales get under way
1997	Type R version announced by the end of the year
1998	Integra Type R goes on sale in UK to rave reviews
2001	Final UK imports of Integra Type R arrive
2001	New-look, bigger-engined replacement announced for 2002 model year

▼ As the old-style Type R faded away, there was a newcomer waiting in the wings to carry forward the name – though not in every export country. (*Honda*)

HONDA
S2000

soft-top heaven

▲ In typical Honda fashion, the all-new S2000 was soon hailed as the world's most powerful normally-aspirated production car – quite an achievement in the convertible class. (*Honda*)

Anybody who has yet to drive a Honda S2000 for themselves may well be under the illusion that this is either an upmarket hairdresser's special or an affordable alternative for people whose finances can't quite stretch to a new Porsche Boxster. Let's face it; the world is full of pseudo-performance two-seater convertibles that place head-turning glamour higher up their list of priorities than real performance and driver appeal. So perhaps the S2000 is just another one to add to that list?

Wrong! The S2000 is as much of a Beast From The East as anything else you're likely to find in this book: it's a world-beating driver's car with top performance, tenacious handling and sheer excitement all thrown in. In fact, upon its launch back in 1999, the S2000 was hailed as the most powerful normally-aspirated 2.0-litre production car available at any price. The fact that it managed to be notably cheaper than most of the opposition was the icing on the cake.

Let's deal with the value-for-money aspect of this stunning roadster first. By 2000, twelve months on from its introduction in most export markets, a brand-new Honda S2000 in the UK managed to undercut the purchase price of both the Porsche Boxster and the BMW Z3M, while matching that of the less powerful Audi Quattro 1.8T. Against such obvious opposition, the Honda seemed a remarkably good buy. And once word got round that the S2000's residuals were among the very best in the business, there suddenly seemed very little sense in not opting for the Honda.

SPEC

ENGINE: 1997cc DOHC 16-valve four-cylinder VTEC

POWER: 237bhp @ 8300rpm

TORQUE: 208Nm @ 7500rpm

PERFORMANCE: Top speed 150mph, 0–60mph 6.2 secs

TRANSMISSION: Six-speed manual

CHASSIS: Rack-and-pinion electric power-assisted steering; double-wishbone independent coil-spring suspension with anti-roll bar; servo-assisted disc brakes (vented fronts) all round with ABS and EBD

Plenty of people did, although not all of them chose the S2000 for its stunning driving style, which is why upmarket seaside towns and trendy inner cities soon became natural habitats for S2000s driven by immaculately dressed middle-aged ladies whose main purpose in life was to 'do lunch', which didn't do all that much for the S2000's image, it has to be said.

But if you let that bother you, you were missing out on an amazing experience. In fact, the S2000 was – and is – such a driver's car that many of its image-conscious earlier buyers soon found themselves annoyed by the way it had to be worked so hard. This is a machine that ▶

▲ Honda's VTEC engineering reached a new peak of excellence with the S2000's amazing powerplant. (*Honda*)

▼ The S2000 could be bought as much for its head-turning good looks as for its hugely impressive performance. (*Honda*)

▲ Manufactured at the same specialist factory as the legendary NSX, the S2000 has always been a top-quality product in every sense of the term. (*Honda*)

needs to be thrashed in order to make the most of its capabilities. That's because its maximum power of 237bhp isn't developed until a motorbike-like 8300rpm, although the engine will spin freely right up to 9000rpm before the rev limiter brings things back under control, so compared with some of the more user-friendly, boulevard-cruising convertibles out there, the awesome Honda is a bit of a monster.

Not only does it have a powerful engine, but also one that sounds fantastic. The VTEC four-pot screams like a banshee when it's near the limit, giving the S2000 driver the kind of aural thrills that would delight any airline pilot. With this amazing engine linked to a super-slick, extremely fast, six-speed gear change, you're able to make rapid progress indeed.

Not just in a straight line, either. Honda invested a great deal of time, energy and hard cash into ensuring the new S2000 was an

impressive handler – and it all paid off. Britain's *Auto Express* magazine praised the Honda for its '...perfect weight distribution and sharp, precise handling', going on to describe cornering as '...predictable and fun.' *Autocar* was also impressed, though suggested the S2000 was really only suitable for those who liked '...edgy handling and performance you have to work for.' Well, that's what enthusiasts' cars are all about, surely?

The fact that the S2000 boasted a rear-drive chassis gave it the feel of a 'proper' sports car, but Honda weren't about to leave it at that. The S2000 boasted an extremely low centre of gravity, 50/50 weight distribution and an engine mounted well behind the front axle. These three crucial factors were complemented by the S2000's immensely rigid bodyshell, so that the age-old convertible problem of scuttle shake was now a thing of the past.

▶ The S2000's clean and simple detailing adds to the styling's timeless appeal. (*Honda*)

Electric power steering with plenty of all-important 'feel' at speed was developed for the S2000, enabling any keen driver to really exploit the Honda's impressive suspension arrangement – an independent coil-sprung double-wishbone set-up with all-important anti-roll bar. The result was impressively flat handling and lots of grip when the car was treated with respect. But go a bit wild at the wheel and you'd soon find the S2000's rear end popping out of line, easily brought back under control with a bit of opposite lock and a broad smile on your face.

Going fast is all well and good, as long as a car's anchors are up to the job – and again, this is an area where the S2000 excels. You'll find discs all round (vented up front), plus the usual arrangement of ABS and electronic brakeforce distribution. So even when you're making the most of the Honda's performance potential, you know you'll be in safe hands when you need to stop in a hurry.

It's just as well, too, because this really is a quick car by the standards of most two-seater convertibles from mainstream manufacturers. Flat out, the S2000 will hit 150mph with ease, its almost absurdly free-revving engine almost instinctively offering more, no matter how hard you push it. On the way, you'll pass the 60mph mark in a mere 6.2 seconds, an experience that feels even quicker thanks to the Honda's low-down seating position and its terrific driver feedback.

It was the driving style of the S2000 that raised so many eyebrows when the model first took a bow. It had been an open secret for a long time that Honda was developing an all-new two-seater rag-top for worldwide markets, and most onlookers assumed it would be a fairly predictable piece of kit – the kind of machine to rival the Mazda MX-5s and Toyota MR2s of this world. When it became obvious that Honda was aiming more upmarket than that, the same industry prophets assumed it would be with a fairly 'soft' sports car aimed particularly at American buyers who tend to drive in straight lines at 55mph and who demand big, comfortable seats. How wrong they were.

Yes, the Honda S2000 was a relatively upmarket sportster from a mainstream manufacturer. But soft it most definitely was not. In fact, the way this non-turbocharged beast had to be driven in order to extract the most from ▶

WHAT WE LIKE...

Clean styling hides an engine that revs to almost crazy heights and a level of performance that surprises most drivers of other two-seater convertibles. Don't confuse the S2000 with any ordinary sports car; this is a beast through and through. It also just happens to be the most powerful non-turbo 2.0-litre motor you can buy.

...WHAT WE DON'T

Not everyone appreciates just how powerful and quick this drop-top really is, which elicits the occasional taunt about its being a hairdresser's special. Just get them behind the wheel and they soon shut their mouths.

◀ With a low centre of gravity and near-perfect weight distribution, it's little wonder the S2000 was soon being praised for its superlative handling characteristics. (Honda)

▶ Fantastic driving position adds to the S2000's enthusiast appeal. (*Honda*)

▶ Cleverly designed dashboard is an ergonomic masterpiece. (*Honda*)

▼ Even with the hood in the raised position, this rag-top Honda is still a cool looking machine – from any angle. (*Honda*)

its awesome performance potential was a huge shock all round.

It would have been so easy for Honda to have included a turbocharger in the S2000's specification in order to transform it into a tarmac-burning performance machine. But remember, this is one of the world's most admired companies when it comes to engine design and manufacture. It wanted to do things differently, and that required taking the basic VTEC concept a stage further – by developing an engine that would run at far higher than normal revs.

How does VTEC (an acronym of variable valve timing and lift electronic control) actually work? Basically by maximising the amount of air-fuel charge entering and the exhaust gas leaving the cylinders over the complete range of engine speed. Ideally the valves should remain open for a longer duration and with greater overlap at high engine speeds to give the gases sufficient time to overcome their inertia and to enter and depart

from the cylinder. For each pair of inlet valves and each pair of exhaust valves, there are three rocker arms and three corresponding lobes on the camshaft.

From idle to around 5850rpm, the valves are operated by the two outboard cam lobes, their short duration and low lift ensuring good cylinder filling. Above 5850rpm, pins in the rocker arms lock the two outboard rockers to the centre one which is operated by a high-lift, long duration cam lobe. Valve opening now matches the timing required for good output at high engine speeds. So now you know.

Honda has always had a reputation for producing high-revving powerplants, but according to the company's then chief engineer Shigeru Uehara, moving past an 8000rpm maximum brought a new set of problems: "New noise and vibration patterns were discovered. This was an untried zone for us."

His response to this technical challenge was not only to concentrate on advanced detail engineering, including lightweight high-precision valve gear, but also painstakingly to reduce weight and operating friction whilst ensuring good breathing efficiency. By

◄ No other sports car in the S2000's class boasts such a high-revving engine and such a rewarding driving experience. (*Honda*)

combining advanced design and materials, as well as key racing-inspired technologies, the Honda team achieved exceptional engine efficiency for the S2000.

Virtually every engine component was designed and refined to aid the quest for high revs, from the straight port intakes, which sharpen engine response, to the low back-pressure exhaust and the light race-influenced valve springs. Particular attention was paid to ensuring efficient combustion through advanced combustion chamber design, making full use of the knowledge gained from the company's racing activities.

The key features in realising a 9000rpm maximum are a relatively short-stroke design (short-stroke engines have the ability to rev higher, while connecting rod length is kept to a minimum), low friction valve gear and a very efficient oil pump. Certain components also feature a low-friction plating technique on bearing surfaces, a technology adapted directly from Honda's Formula 1 experience.

The result of all this technology was one of the most impressive normally-aspirated four-cylinder engines ever created, and one that would do the S2000 proud. No other four-pot of similar size offers as much power and performance, or as broad a rev band as the S2000's amazing unit.

The subsequent sales success of the S2000 throughout the world probably came as no surprise, despite just 12,000 examples being built

each year at the same Takanezawa plant as the legendary NSX. Relatively limited supply has helped to ensure an eager queue of buyers anxious to join the S2000 experience, as well as aiding those industry-leading residuals mentioned earlier.

Development of the S2000 since its launch has been relatively limited, restricted mainly to suspension changes, rigidity upgrades for the bodyshell, a few new colours and some interior enhancements. But then, when a car is this good and is still as popular with punters as the day it was first launched, why meddle? ■

TIMELINE

2001	S2000 unveiled and goes on sale later in the year
2002	Modifications include colour-coding, new sound system and retuned suspension
2002	GT version launched with detachable hardtop
2004	Stiffened bodyshell and uprated suspension head list of latest mods

HONDA
NSX

the japanese ferrari

When news broke in the late 1980s that Honda were busy developing an upmarket performance machine, many assumed it would be to rival the finest coupés and sports cars offered by the likes of Nissan and Toyota. But no, Honda were going more upmarket than that; much more upmarket, in fact. They were aiming fairly and squarely at Ferrari and Porsche.

Many thought the idea was pure madness. What did a company whose previous performance successes consisted mainly of go-faster Civics really know about the supercar sector of the market? Surely, the likes of Ferrari had absolutely nothing to worry about? Fans of Europe's traditional supercar marques couldn't resist gently mocking the concept.

The sniggering was to stop, though, in early 1989, when the wraps finally came off the long-awaited Ferrari-beating Honda project – and the NSX officially took a bow. It was at the Geneva Motor Show, world-renowned venue for some of

the world's most exciting new cars over the years, where Honda suddenly found themselves very much the centre of attention. The world's press were bowled over by what they saw.

The NSX was like no other Honda before it. This mid-engined, 3.0-litre monster was a stunning-looking creation. It was big in every sense, with a low-slung stance that gave it a clean, masculine appearance. It looked stunning from every angle, with hints of ultra-modern Ferrari around its rear end in particular. In fact, it was the enormous rear end of the NSX that gave it so much of its identity, housing both the mid-mounted 24-valve V6 powerplant and more storage space than most people would ever expect from a supercar.

In profile, the new NSX was amazingly evenly balanced, its front and rear ends extending seemingly similar lengths from the centrally located – and surprisingly spacious – cockpit. The beast actually measured six inches more in length than its Ferrari 348 arch rival – and it showed. This was a full-size supercar in every sense of the term.

But … and it was a big 'but', no matter how good the new NSX looked, its driving experience couldn't really be a match for any similarly-priced Ferrari, could it? Press and public alike would have to wait until early 1990 to find out, as the NSX wasn't scheduled to go on sale until at least then.

But the wait was well worthwhile. Any fears that a 'mere' a 3.0-litre V6 might be insufficient for powering what was meant to be a genuine supercar were unfounded, and that wasn't just because of the Honda's impressive power output, but also its groundbreaking construction. ▷

SPEC

1990 NSX 3.0

ENGINE: 2977cc quad-cam 24-valve fuel-injected VTEC V6

POWER: 274bhp @ 7000rpm

TORQUE: 210lb ft @ 5300rpm

PERFORMANCE: Top speed 165mph, 0–60mph 5.5 secs (manual transmission)

TRANSMISSION: Five-speed manual/ four-speed automatic

CHASSIS: Speed-sensitive power-assisted rack-and-pinion steering; independent coil-spring suspension with aluminium double wishbones and anti-roll bars front and rear; servo-assisted ventilated disc brakes all round with ABS

2002 NSX 3.2

ENGINE: 3179cc quad-cam 24-valve fuel-injected VTEC V6

POWER: 276bhp @ 7300rpm

TORQUE: 298Nm @ 5300rpm

PERFORMANCE: Top speed 168mph, 0–60mph 5.7 secs (manual transmission)

TRANSMISSION: Six-speed manual

CHASSIS: Speed-sensitive power-assisted rack-and-pinion steering; independent coil-spring suspension with aluminium double wishbones and anti-roll bars front and rear; servo-assisted ventilated disc brakes all round with ABS and EBD

▼ A fifteen-year production run is a serious achievement, as well as a fitting tribute to the all-round excellence of this most expensive Honda. (*Honda*)

WHAT WE LIKE...

When Honda do something, they do it brilliantly. Despite having never produced a genuine supercar before, the company's engineers came up with a genuine rival to any Ferrari or Porsche. For that they deserve every accolade going.

...WHAT WE DON'T

Some commentators criticised the NSX for being too bland and easy to drive – or was that just their way of saying a Ferrari was tricky? Well, if that's all they could come up with, it wasn't going to overly concern the management at Honda.

▼ The targa-topped NSX-T of 1995 was a popular version, offering open-air thrills in the world's easiest-to-drive supercar. (*Honda*)

A major manufacturer had never before released a production car with all-aluminium monocoque construction, a feature which provided a major saving in weight. Less weight equals better performance and improved fuel consumption; this was truly a win-win situation.

The downside of producing an all-aluminium car, of course, is that of cost. Everybody knew the NSX wouldn't be an inexpensive machine, but even Britain's *Car* magazine, hazarding a guess in April 1989, seriously under-predicted its eventual cost by the time it finally hit British streets in the summer of 1990. It was cheaper than a Ferrari 348, but it still cost a very large sum of money for any car wearing a Honda badge. This Japanese supercar had to be 'super' in every sense if it was to stand any chance of reasonable sales potential.

Happily, it was. As any first drive in the beast would confirm, Honda had managed to create a mid-engined two-seater with genuine supercar credentials and the performance and handling to match. Who cares that it didn't have a V8, a supercharger or twin-turbochargers providing the power? What it had was the very latest development of Honda's VTEC engine technology – and it was all the better for it.

From 'only' 2977cc of normally-aspirated V6 (albeit of quad-cam 24-valve design), Honda managed to extract a whopping 274bhp at a fantastic-sounding 7000rpm. Just as impressive was the torque figure of 210lb ft at 5300rpm, enabling enthusiastic drivers to really make the

most of this awesome engine's serious 'grunt'. To say magazine road testers of the time were impressed would be a massive understatement.

In 1991, Britain's *What Car?* magazine was full of praise for Honda's latest masterpiece of an engine: 'You can feel the tingle running down your spine the first time the rev counter needle sweeps past the 6500rpm mark and the sensual howl of the V6 fills the cabin – it's sheer magic.' It was true. Never before had any non-turbocharged V6 managed to provide such a heady mix of high-revving performance, adrenalin-pumping mid-range acceleration and impressive flexibility.

The excitement didn't end with the engine's power, either. Mounted transversely just behind the driver, it helped provide the NSX with near-perfect weight distribution. Mid-engined cars tend to handle impressively anyway, but the NSX's all-independent coil-sprung suspension with aluminium double wishbones and anti-roll bars

front and rear helped enormously. The result was an ultra-taut machine that remained flat and in control even when its handling capabilities were tested to the limit.

Speed-sensitive power steering provided ample feedback for the driver, ABS all-disc brakes made rapid stopping an easy affair, and a sophisticated traction control system helped to keep everything neat and tidy even in extreme circumstances. Don't forget, we're going back to 1990, a time when traction control system was considered revolutionary and only for the elite few. This was real headline-grabbing stuff back then.

As was the driving style of the NSX – although, remarkably, not everyone raved about every aspect of being behind the wheel. Almost absurdly, the NSX found itself criticised for being too easy to drive round town, lacking the idiosyncrasies that had dogged the likes of Ferraris for so many years.

Honda, it seemed, just couldn't win. If the NSX had been a tricky beast to handle, it would have been slated for just that. As it was, some onlookers were saying it was too dull in everyday situations. Still, at least *What Car?* saw the positive side, suggesting '...in traffic the NSX can be as docile as a kitten.' At last, somebody could see the point. Here was the world's first supercar that could be driven perfectly safely and easily by even the most unenthusiastic, inexperienced pilot when the need arose; but on the right road and with the right kind of petrolhead at the wheel, it would transform instantly into a fire-breathing dragon capable of eating Porsches for breakfast. ▶

▲ Many purists still prefer the Series I NSX's styling, its pop-up headlamps and impressive lines giving it real presence against its contemporaries. (*Honda*)

▲ Still instantly recognisable as an NSX, the new Series II was a cleverly updated and restyled version for 2002, giving this most desirable Honda a whole new lease of life. (*Honda*)

And how. The early NSX offered an incredible top speed of 165mph, taking just 5.5 seconds to reach 60mph. This was real supercar stuff, the kind of performance that any bright red machine wearing a prancing horse badge would have been proud of. For a Japanese-built Honda, it was nothing short of remarkable.

It wasn't just the performance that impressed; the sheer quality of the engine design was also a joy to behold. It's hard to believe that this ultra-powerful unit was derived from the V6 fitted to the Legend saloon of the time. That Honda managed to employ its own VTEC technology and transform it so effectively into a glorious-sounding, high-revving, 274bhp gem was something truly awe-inspiring.

The responsiveness of the engine, even by today's standards, is just phenomenal. So much power, so much flexibility under your right foot. And when linked to the super-slick six-speed transmission fitted to the NSX from 1998, it just

seems to get better and better the harder you work it.

It's typical of any Honda VTEC engine, of course – a series of powerplants that were making full use of variable valve technology well before it became fashionable elsewhere. It's what makes any decent Honda engine so instantly responsive and such a joy to listen to. Later-model NSXs came with a superb-quality Bose sound system fitted as standard; but why would you ever want to turn it on when an engine sounds this good…?

To their credit, Honda didn't neglect in-production development of the NSX, despite its being such an outrageously brilliant car to begin with. The first major addition to the range arrived in 1995 in the shape of the NSX-T, a targa-topped version offering ultra-fast wind-in-the-hair

▶ The instrumentation's digits provided a clue as to the NSX's fantastically high-revving nature. (*Honda*)

▶ The NSX was one of the few supercars of its era with genuine comfort and practicality designed in. (*Honda*)

motoring. The same year, too, the option of semi-automatic four-speed F1-style transmission – marketed by Honda as F-matic – was announced, subsequently a popular choice among NSX followers.

Three years later, a new manual-transmission 3.2-litre version of the NSX was launched, bringing with it 276bhp and up to 168mph. Fans of the semi-auto would still get 3.0-litre power, though anybody opting for the manual version also now got the six-speed set-up mentioned earlier.

The new 3.2-litre NSX went down well, with Britain's *Car* magazine rating it higher in their June 1998 group test than the Aston Martin DB7, BMW 840Ci, Nissan Skyline GT-R and Mercedes-Benz SL60 AMG; a remarkable result by any standards.

The biggest aesthetic change occurred in 2002 when the NSX's trademark pop-up headlamps were replaced with faired-in items with integral indicator units. These blended in beautifully with new, softer front-end styling, complemented by redesigned spoilers, new side body cladding and what Honda described as a new-look 'lateral air intake'. Although the overall shape of the car remained broadly the same as before, the change in appearance was surprisingly obvious – and successful, too. No longer did the NSX look like a product of the 1990s that was wearing its age well; suddenly it was as contemporary-looking as most of its new-generation rivals.

Interestingly, Honda also chose 2002 as the year when they would chop the NSX's UK list prices substantially. It has to be said that this was a necessary move, as the NSX-T was carrying a huge price tag for a car that had already been around for a dozen years. The price reduction for the 2002 model year still left the NSX as an expensive car, but just that bit more affordable than before.

All around the globe, the Honda NSX has a loyal band of admirers, owners and enthusiasts who adore its unique combination of attributes and capabilities, and that can only be a good thing. It was incredible that, way back in the 1980s, Honda's engineers managed to get the go-ahead for such a project. It's even more remarkable that the NSX managed to remain in production right through to late 2005, when Honda announced it had finally reached the end of the road. What an amazing career; what an incredible car. ■

TIMELINE

1984	Serious development of the NSX gets under way
1986	First recognisable prototypes espied under test
1989	Production-ready NSX unveiled in the spring
1990	NSX production finally begins
1991	*Autocar* describes NSX as '...a genuine marvel...'
1995	NSX-T 'Targa' version launched
1995	F-matic semi-auto transmission introduced
1998	3.2-litre version joins existing 3.0 model
1998	Six-speed manual transmission replaces five-speed
2002	Revised styling includes new headlamps, spoilers and more
2002	Stiffened suspension and wider track improved handling
2002	UK prices for NSX drop substantially
2005	Production of NSX ceases

▼ Fans were saddened when the end of NSX production was announced in 2005. It had been a long and successful career for what had been Honda's bravest ever new-car launch. (*Honda*)

ISUZU VEHICROSS

the maddest 4x4xfar

▲ Despite announcing some daring and interesting concept cars over the years, Isuzu's decision to put the unique VehiCross into production still came as something of a shock. (*Isuzu*)

It's a funny old world. At one time, it felt as though Isuzu were forever launching yet another concept vehicle at yet another motor show somewhere in the world, but their actual production vehicles seemed to remain permanently tedious.

Concepts? They've had them all: Deseo, VX2, KAI and other equally bizarrely-named SUV prototypes. Only one has ever made it into production, the Deseo finally evolving into the limited-production Isuzu VehiCross that attracted so much attention when it went on sale in Japan in 1998.

Then you look at what Isuzu actually produces today – and you despair. In the UK in particular, all you can buy brand-new with an Isuzu badge these days is a very ordinary pick-up truck, and what a great shame that is. I had high hopes for Isuzu when the Deseo concept was unveiled in 1993 and its production development, the Vehicross, was announced the following year.

Isuzu was finally waking up to the fact that 4x4 buyers were changing. There were now people who wanted funky, distinctive, trendy,

WHAT WE LIKE...

Crazy looks give the impression of some kind of moon buggy, which guarantees as many head-turning glances as a Ferrari. Meanwhile, the lusty V6 gives good performance by 4x4 standards.

...WHAT WE DON'T

An off-roader ... in a book like this? Well, yes. But the VehiCross is different. Very different. It's also more than a bit daft, which means you might just get laughed at.

head-turning SUVs, a contrast to the traditional farmer-type buyers of years gone by.

Sadly, British punters weren't given a chance to prove this to Isuzu, as the VehiCross was never offered as an official UK-spec model, although numerous 'grey' imports have since arrived.

Not everyone approved of the VehiCross when it first appeared as a production vehicle in 1998. One American road tester, commenting in the following year, said: 'So, what's the name of the funny SUV? VehiCross! Who sells it? Isuzu! Right. Now go buy an Amigo [Frontera]; the VehiCross is too damn weird for you.'

But then maybe this particular reviewer didn't recognise a good thing when he saw it. At least the VehiCross was different. It may not have been a major technological advance, but it certainly was different, and refreshing; and it brought focus back to the Isuzu brand name.

So what did Isuzu do to cash in on all this publicity? Nothing. Did it launch a VehiCross replacement for the 21st century? No. Did it follow it up with other 4x4s aimed at younger enthusiasts? No, again. It made the VehiCross in limited numbers and then ceased production, after which it carried on making Troopers (for a while) and pick-ups. And that was it.

It was a great pity, because the world of 4x4s certainly needs livening up style-wise. The VehiCross at least looked futuristic, a machine guaranteed to turn heads and attract attention in any crowded city street. The fact that it could also tackle the rough stuff when the need arose was an added bonus.

Under the bonnet of the VehiCross sat a 3.5-litre V6 lump linked to a four-speed automatic transmission and driven by a terrain-sensing automatic all-wheel-drive set-up. This constantly monitored the driving conditions of the VehiCross, adjusting the front and rear torque distribution levels every 20 milliseconds. It was all clever stuff, its entertainment value being increased by a dashboard read-out showing how much torque was being sent to the front axle at any one time.

But no amount of clever driveline or wacky looks could disguise the VehiCross's fairly lacklustre driving style, despite good performance by 4x4 standards. It wasn't a vehicle you yearned to drive more than once, and it wasn't a 4x4 many folk wanted to be seen in by the time production ceased. Still, it had been a seriously brave idea on the part of Isuzu. ▪

SPEC

ENGINE: 3494cc DOHC V6 petrol

POWER: 212bhp @ 5400rpm

TORQUE: 229lb ft @ 3000rpm

PERFORMANCE: Top speed 115mph, 0–60mph 10.5 secs

TRANSMISSION: Four-speed automatic

CHASSIS: Power-assisted steering; independent coil-spring suspension; automatic terrain-sensing four-wheel drive; servo-assisted disc brakes all round with ABS

◀ A 3.5-litre V6 powerplant endowed the VehiCross with good performance by 4x4 standards. But it wasn't enough to make this weird Isuzu a genuinely rewarding drive. (*Isuzu*)

TIMELINE

1993	Deseo concept 4x4 unveiled by Isuzu
1994	Go-ahead given for a production version
1998	VehiCross finally goes into limited production
1999	Exports to the USA get under way
2000	New colours and bigger (18-inch) wheels introduced
2001	VehiCross production ceases

LEXUS
IS200/IS300

the desirable compact

Nobody can accuse Lexus of not rising to a challenge. We all know that Germany rules the 'compact executive' class with the BMW 3-Series and Audi A4. So how did Toyota (or rather, Lexus) think they could take on such luminaries and maybe even beat them at their own game?

Well, they did it by following the successful formula of the much bigger LS400 model. The new compact Lexus had to be beautifully engineered, superbly built, great to look at and a joy to drive, and when the all-new IS200 finally arrived in 1999, few thought they'd failed.

Lexus followed the lead set by the 3-Series in adopting rear-wheel drive, creating a truly rewarding chassis along the way. This mini-Lexus had to be a real driver's car if it was to stand any chance of being taken seriously … and that's exactly what happened. The 153bhp IS200 may not have been the fastest kid on the block, but it was still a fantastic machine to pilot at speed.

The engine itself, a 2.0-litre 24-valve straight-six design with variable valve timing, was a gem. Power and torque were up to class levels, but the all-round refinement and quiet eagerness of the powerplant immediately impressed anybody who drove the Lexus. Link all that to a super-slick six-speed manual transmission and you had the ideal recipe for giving junior management a thrill on the drive to work each morning.

It wasn't just the way the car looked or drove that made it desirable. There was also its standard equipment to take into account, which managed to make many a German rival look positively spartan by comparison. As Lexus themselves said, 'These qualities have put the IS200 firmly on the wish list of many motorists who have become disenchanted with the over-familiar and more meagrely equipped models offered by rival manufacturers.'

Never ones to rest on their laurels, Lexus wanted to expand the IS200 line-up, a process that really got under way in 2001 with the launch

WHAT WE LIKE...

Sharp styling, fantastic engineering and good performance combine to produce a BMW-beating compact executive machine.

...WHAT WE DON'T

There'll always be someone in the pub who'll claim it's just a Toyota – but so what?

SPEC

ENGINE: 1988cc fuel-injected DOHC six-cylinder with VVT-i

POWER: 153bhp @ 6200rpm

TORQUE: 144lb ft @ 4600rpm

PERFORMANCE: Top speed 134mph, 0–60mph 9.5 secs

TRANSMISSION: Six-speed manual

CHASSIS: Rack-and-pinion power-assisted steering; double-wishbone independent coil-spring suspension all round; servo-assisted disc brakes (vented fronts) all round

TIMELINE

1999	Lexus IS200 unveiled; UK sales begin in May
2001	IS200 makes racing debut in BTCC
2001	IS200's specification mildly upgraded in September
2001	Bigger-engined IS300 on sale in UK from October
2002	IS200 SportCross announced with 'semi-estate' styling
2003	Limited number of Amarillo Yellow IS200s go on sale
2003	Limited Edition (LE) IS200 on sale from October
2005	New-look IS range unveiled in February

◄ It wasn't just the Lexus's driving style that won praise; it was also the sheer quality of the car, both inside and out. (*Lexus*)

of the logically named IS300. Powered by a 2997cc in-line six-cylinder lump, again with 24 valves, this latest version pumped out a useful 211bhp at 5800rpm – enough to increase top speed to 143mph (up from 134mph for the IS200) and reduce the vital 0–60mph time to a far handier 8.2 seconds. Not bad for a fully loaded four-door saloon.

The final major addition to the IS200/IS300 line-up arrived in 2002 with the launch of the SportCross, a five-door 'crossover' estate version aimed at buyers who craved a bit more space. It still looked great, thanks to its raked-back rear end, even if it wasn't the most spacious estate car on the market. Not that Lexus would ever admit to its being an estate, of course; oh no, this was a 'lifestyle vehicle'.

As if to expand the IS200's reputation as a driver's car, Lexus decided to go racing in 2001, the year the marque made its debut in the British Touring Car Championship. Well actually, it wasn't Lexus at all. In fact, a pair of IS200s was independently entered that year by ABG Motorsport, a company specialising in race-car modifications. But they certainly had the approval of Lexus, who were only too happy to benefit from all the publicity generated through the national press. And who could blame them? ■

▼ 2001 saw the Lexus IS200 competing in the British Touring Car Championship for the first time, thanks to major preparation and engineering work by ABG Motorsport. (*Lexus*)

LEXUS
SC430

seriously sophisticated

Major new car marques are a rare event these days, so when Toyota created the all-new Lexus brand for its most upmarket products at the end of 1988, pessimists predicted the company was taking a massive gamble. The Japanese had never competed successfully in Europe against the might of Mercedes-Benz, Jaguar and BMW – so why should Lexus be any different?

Because the brand new LS400 executive saloon of the time was so good, is the obvious answer. Here was a smoothly styled newcomer that more than matched the power, equipment levels and build quality of the most expensive Mercedes-Benz S-Class, all for significantly less cash.

That's not to say Lexus products are inexpensive. Plainly they're not. But in Britain, by 2005, the very latest Lexus SC430 executive coupé significantly undercut the price of both the Mercedes SL350 and the Jaguar XK8 Convertible.

But there's more – far more – to the sensational SC430, launched at Geneva in 2001,

than making its lucky buyers a useful saving. For a start, this is a stunning-looking addition to the ever-expanding Lexus line-up, with one of

WHAT WE LIKE...

Smooth styling, a clever roof arrangement, effortless V8 power and the best build quality in the business. No wonder the SC430 has been such a success in the 'executive convertible' market.

...WHAT WE DON'T

Some say it's a bit bland from certain angles; others say it only looks fantastic in particular colours. We say it's an engineering masterpiece.

the cleverest folding roof arrangements you'll find anywhere.

Electrically operated steel roofs that fold into the boot are nothing new these days, but the Lexus set-up is more intelligent than most. For a start, it's built from aluminium, which gives it a useful weight saving. Then there's its ease of operation, where everything is co-ordinated within 25 seconds at the single touch of a button. Best of all is the quality of the whole design which – compared with some on the market – makes it reliable, watertight and very snug indeed.

A deflector fitted behind the 2+2 SC430's rear seats helps to control airflow when the roof is lowered, reducing the buffeting sensation, and keeping the wind noise level to an absolute minimum. Those canny Lexus lads think of everything.

They certainly think of power and performance. That's obvious from the SC430's latest 4.3-litre V8 powerplant, an all-aluminium 32-valve DOHC design that pumps out a mighty 282bhp at 5600rpm. It's a V8 with grunt, but it's also exceptionally refined and one of the smoothest in the business.

The SC430 doubles up as a head-turning boulevard cruiser and, when the need arises, a real performance machine. Top speed is electronically limited to 155mph, while 60mph from rest is reached in a mere 6.2 seconds. All this is achieved without fuss or drama, thanks to Lexus's clever five-speed automatic transmission with what the company calls 'artificial intelligence', a shift control that can adapt gearshift patterns to suit both road type and individual driving style.

The cleverness doesn't end there, for the rear-wheel-drive SC430 also offers four-channel ABS, electronic brakeforce distribution, traction control, vehicle stability control and brake assist. Meanwhile, a tyre pressure warning system alerts the driver if there is a reduction in tyre pressures at any time.

You don't need to know how all this technology works in order to appreciate it. Anybody with a love of fine cars who drives an SC430 for the first time will be knocked out by the all-round sheer competence of this hugely understated machine. It's fast, it handles well, its brakes are stunningly effective and it covers long-distance mileage with consummate ease. Even better, compared with some other upmarket convertibles, the Lexus is refreshingly free of vulgar styling or unnecessary fashion statements.

It's little wonder the Lexus SC430 has been such a success throughout the world – not least in the USA and Europe – since its launch. That there was still a 36-month waiting list for the model in the UK, four years after its launch, says it all. ▨

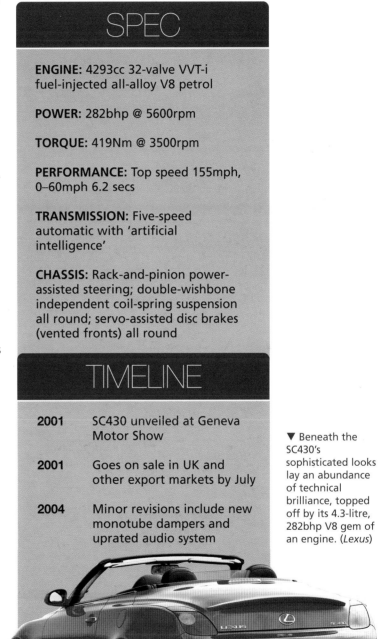

SPEC

ENGINE: 4293cc 32-valve VVT-i fuel-injected all-alloy V8 petrol

POWER: 282bhp @ 5600rpm

TORQUE: 419Nm @ 3500rpm

PERFORMANCE: Top speed 155mph, 0–60mph 6.2 secs

TRANSMISSION: Five-speed automatic with 'artificial intelligence'

CHASSIS: Rack-and-pinion power-assisted steering; double-wishbone independent coil-spring suspension all round; servo-assisted disc brakes (vented fronts) all round

TIMELINE

2001	SC430 unveiled at Geneva Motor Show
2001	Goes on sale in UK and other export markets by July
2004	Minor revisions include new monotube dampers and uprated audio system

▼ Beneath the SC430's sophisticated looks lay an abundance of technical brilliance, topped off by its 4.3-litre, 282bhp V8 gem of an engine. (*Lexus*)

MAZDA
323 1600 TURBO 4x4

family flier

When Mazda introduced a new-look front-wheel-drive 323 range in 1985, motoring enthusiasts yawned with indifference. The 323 had always been a rather dull Escort rival, and the latest incarnation was unlikely to be much different.

How wrong they were. Well, sort of. It's true that most versions of the 1985 Mazda 323 were about as exciting as an afternoon at a garden centre, but then along came the 323 1600 Turbo 4x4, a machine that made most other hot hatches seem puny by comparison.

This homologation special was the road-going version of Mazda's latest rally-challenging machine, as just a few minutes behind the wheel soon proved. With all-wheel drive providing class-leading traction, the Mazda's handling and roadholding took the hot hatch class a stage further, and with a twin-cam, 16-valve, turbocharged and intercooled version of Mazda's 1.6-litre four-pot throbbing away under the bonnet, there was all the power and performance to match.

In fact, there was 148bhp (developed at a heady 6000rpm), to be exact, which allowed a top speed of 125mph, hitting the 60mph mark

WHAT WE LIKE...

Raw and uncompromising hot hatch, so typical of the 1980s, was developed for rally success – and it showed. Rarity appeal makes it even more of a tempting proposition now.

...WHAT WE DON'T

There's plenty of turbo lag waiting to catch you out, and you might come unstuck through the lack of ABS, but for excitement behind the wheel, it's a cracker!

on the way in just 7.8 seconds. That may not sound spectacular by today's standards; but remember, we're going back to the mid-1980s, and we're talking about a hot hatch rather than some kind of semi-exotica. Back then, this was the kind of get-up-and-go guaranteed to attract the attention of performance enthusiasts.

Getting behind the wheel of a 323 1600 Turbo 4x4 was a surprising experience for most. They simply didn't expect a three-door Mazda hatchback to be a seriously desirable driver's car; but that's exactly what it turned out to be. Keeping the revs up meant that the turbo was working almost constantly, making the most of the gruff-sounding four-cylinder engine's capabilities. This high-revving powerplant was eager and willing to be worked hard, almost thriving on abuse. Turbo lag was a bit of a problem at times (a common complaint in the 1980s), but exploiting the revs meant it was less of an intrusion.

The Mazda offered raw, no-frills thrills and felt every bit the rally car out on the open road. It cornered in an impressively flat way, whilst grip in all weather conditions was just superb – no matter how hard and fast you were driving. Importantly, this rather special hot hatch was also enormous fun to drive, a feature that many cynics of the time just weren't expecting from a Japanese machine.

The 323 Turbo 4x4 enjoyed rave reviews in its day, as well as a fair chunk of success on the international rallying scene. But, despite appealing to an adventurous group of customers over its four-year production run, it never achieved the ultimate sales success it so rightly deserved.

Perhaps that was something to do with its pricing. By the time it disappeared from UK price lists in 1989, the well-equipped Lux version was selling for over 50% more than the (admittedly two-wheel-drive) Renault 5 GT Turbo. Meanwhile, the all-conquering all-wheel-drive Lancia HF Integrale, with 185bhp at its disposal, was only just over 20% more expensive than the poor little Mazda.

The fact that neither the Renault nor the Lancia would ever be as reliable or last as long as the 323 didn't seem to matter to most Brits. The all-wheel-drive Mazda remained a rare sight on UK roads, and enthusiasts everywhere missed out on a superb driving experience. ▪

SPEC

ENGINE: 1597cc fuel-injected 16-valve twin-cam four-cylinder with turbocharger and intercooler

POWER: 148bhp @ 6000rpm

TORQUE: 144lb ft @ 5000rpm

PERFORMANCE: Top speed 125mph, 0–60mph 7.8 secs

TRANSMISSION: Five-speed manual

CHASSIS: Rack-and-pinion steering; independent coil-spring suspension all round; disc brakes all round

▼ With 148bhp from its turbocharged and intercooled 1.6-litre lump, the 323 had all the right ingredients for the ultimate hot hatch recipe. (*LAT*)

TIMELINE

1985	1600 Turbo 4x4 launched, the fastest 323 ever seen
1988	Rod Millen's 323 Turbo takes second place in Monte Carlo Rally
1989	323 Turbo 4x4 production ceases
1990	Ingvar Carlsson's 323 Turbo takes second place in Monte Carlo Rally

MAZDA
MX-5

saviour of the soft-top

▲ It didn't take long for the first-generation MX-5 to establish its own cult following. Nowadays, it's seen as an all-time classic and is as popular as it's ever been. (*Mazda*)

When the wraps came off the all-new Mazda MX-5 in downtown Tokyo in 1989, it created an amazing reaction not just in its homeland but throughout the world. This wasn't just because the two-seater sports car market had been through such difficult times during the 1980s; it was also because the MX-5 marked such a massive change of direction for Mazda.

Here was a company better known for its dull but worthy family saloons and hatchbacks than for its out and out enthusiasts' cars, with only the RX-7 and all-wheel-drive 323 Turbo providing a welcome relief from such tedium throughout the 1980s. And now, just as that decade of conspicuous wealth was about to draw to a close, Mazda shocked the world by virtually reinventing the affordable two-seater sportster.

In truth, the exciting new MX-5 (better known in some markets as the Eunos or Miata) had been an open secret for some time, with heavily disguised prototypes being spotted by eagle-eyed

photographers during the late 1980s. Even so, once the official production version was unveiled in 1989, onlookers couldn't help being pleasantly surprised by just how 'right' the new MX-5 was.

This long-awaited little two-seater was curvaceous, cute and full of character, with styling that almost everybody fell in love with. From its simple pop-up headlamps to its rounded tail, the MX-5's proportions were so close to perfect they made every other rag-top sports car of the time look positively awkward.

The 1980s hadn't been a great time for traditional open-top sports cars, especially in the UK. The demise of the MGB and Triumph Spitfire had been particular low points, as had the failure of the promising but ultimately flawed Reliant Scimitar SS1. Britain desperately needed a brand new two-seater convertible to bring traditional fun back to motoring. That such a vehicle arrived with Mazda rather than MG badges – and happened to be built in Japan rather than Britain

SPEC

MX-5 SERIES I 1.6

ENGINE: 1598cc DOHC 16-valve fuel-injected four-cylinder

POWER: 114bhp @ 6500rpm

TORQUE: 100lb ft @ 5500rpm

PERFORMANCE: Top speed 121mph, 0–60mph 8.7 secs

TRANSMISSION: Five-speed manual

CHASSIS: Power-assisted rack-and-pinion steering; independent double-wishbone coil-spring suspension all round; disc brakes all round (ventilated fronts)

MX-5 SERIES I 1.8

ENGINE: 1839cc DOHC 16-valve fuel-injected four-cylinder

POWER: 128bhp @ 6500rpm

TORQUE: 110lb ft @ 5000rpm

PERFORMANCE: Top speed 123mph, 0–60mph 8.5 secs

TRANSMISSION: Five-speed manual

CHASSIS: Power-assisted rack-and-pinion steering; independent double-wishbone coil-spring suspension all round with Bilstein sports dampers; disc brakes all round (ventilated fronts)

– was seen as sad by some enthusiasts and inevitable by others.

In essence, Mazda took the concept of a conventional two-seater sports car, improved it massively without robbing it of its fun appeal, and launched it on an eager market with the promise of driver enjoyment, low running costs and, of course, reliability. And it was the latter point that especially marked the MX-5 out as something very different from Britain's sports car efforts.

The decision to make the MX-5 front-engined and rear-wheel drive was a vital one for the car's long-term appeal. Mazda certainly considered the logical option of front-wheel drive during the early days of the MX-5's development, a course of action pursued by Fiat for the subsequent launch of their Punto-based Barchetta. But Mazda's engineers were adamant that if the MX-5 was to have the traditional feel of a 1960s British sports car combined with the ease of ownership of a more modern machine, then rear-wheel drive was the only way forward.

It was one of the best decisions ever made by Mazda, and it's a philosophy that still stands today. What perhaps surprised some onlookers the most was that the MX-5 came with ▶

◤ The MX-5's snug-looking cabin was actually more spacious – and a whole lot more comfortable – than sports car fans had been used to prior to 1989. (*Mazda*)

▼ From day one, the MX-5 was praised for its lively driving styling and fun handling. Here was a brand new sports car that had learned its lessons from the old school. (*Mazda*)

nothing more powerful than a 114bhp, 1.6-litre engine upon its launch. Admittedly, it was an excellent engine: a 16-valve twin-cam four-cylinder design with a free-revving nature and an enthusiastic feel. But compared with some of the best performance cars which had already emanated from Japan, an output of 114bhp wasn't exactly spectacular.

Such criticisms faded as soon as you took to the wheel of one of those early MX-5s for the first time. These machines were all about fun rather than spectacular on-paper performance figures – and the MX-5 was soon acclaimed as one of the most fun-to-drive machines the Japanese had ever invented. Not the fastest, with a top speed of 121mph and 0-60mph in 8.7 seconds, but one of the most enjoyable, certainly. And, as a result of the MX-5's low-slung driving position, the eagerness of its engine and the slickness of its five-speed gear change, it actually felt a lot faster than its official figures suggested.

The world's motoring press were amazed by the MX-5's fun factor, something rarely associated with Mazda previously. They were equally full of praise for its handling and roadholding, two areas in which the MX-5 truly excelled. With independent double-wishbone coil-sprung suspension all round, tuned to offer just the right compromise between everyday ride quality and impressively flat handling, the MX-5 was tremendous fun when pushed to the limit, any rear-end breakaway being commendably easy to bring back under control with a touch of opposite-lock steering and an unfaltering right foot. Whether pottering through cities or making its way along winding A-roads, the MX-5 was one of those rare machines that made modern motoring such fun. No wonder MX-5 drivers were soon renowned for the size of their grins every time they took to the wheel.

Nor any wonder that the MX-5 generated such positive headlines throughout the world, with Britain's motoring press being particularly enthusiastic. *What Car?* magazine gave the MX-5 its Best Sports Car of 1991 award in October of that year, citing Mazda's finest as '…everything a sports car needs to be – fun to drive, good to look at and affordable.' They went on to say the MX-5 was '…huge fun to drive, with lovely

▲ The Series II MX-5 was a clever update of the original theme – a more grown-up offering but still with the same fun factor and similarly gorgeous looks. (*Mazda*)

▶ The fun of piloting an MX-5 came as a pleasant surprise to anybody used to Mazda's more mundane products of the time. (*Mazda*)

WHAT WE LIKE...

Mazda almost single-handedly reinvented the mass-produced two-seater soft-top sports car at the end of the 1980s, at a time when the breed was almost dead. For that, tens of thousands of enthusiasts will be eternally grateful. Of course, it helped that the MX-5 was also a cracking good car to drive and enormous fun into the bargain.

...WHAT WE DON'T

The 88bhp 1.6-litre MX-5 may not be the quickest thing on the street – but so what? These cars are all about open-top fun, and for that you don't need masses of power. Nimble handling helps the MX-5 to make good progress, in any case.

handling and good ride', a view echoed by just about every other British magazine of the time.

Such praise wasn't confined to the British press, with American journalists being just as vocal in their enthusiasm for the MX-5. Dennis Simanaitis, writing in *Road & Track* in March 1989, commented: 'Its combination of communication, responsiveness, predictability and forgiveness make it the best-handling two-seater I've driven in recent memory – and my memory for such things is good.'

Journalist Peter Egan, again writing for *Road & Track*, this time in November 1990, really enthused about the MX-5: 'Its quick steering, willing engine, short-throw gearbox, taut suspension and fits-like-a-glove driving position give it an instantaneous response that conjures up memories of the old Elan, only this time the headlamps work and the water pump lasts a bit longer.'

That last comment summed up perfectly the all-round appeal of the MX-5, for here was a delight-to-drive sports car that was also totally practical and reliable in day to day use. That was a combination that evidently suited whole swathes of buyers, for Mazda's inspirational creation soon found itself experiencing huge demand around the world.

The demand for the MX-5 almost caught Mazda off guard, for the company only ever ▶

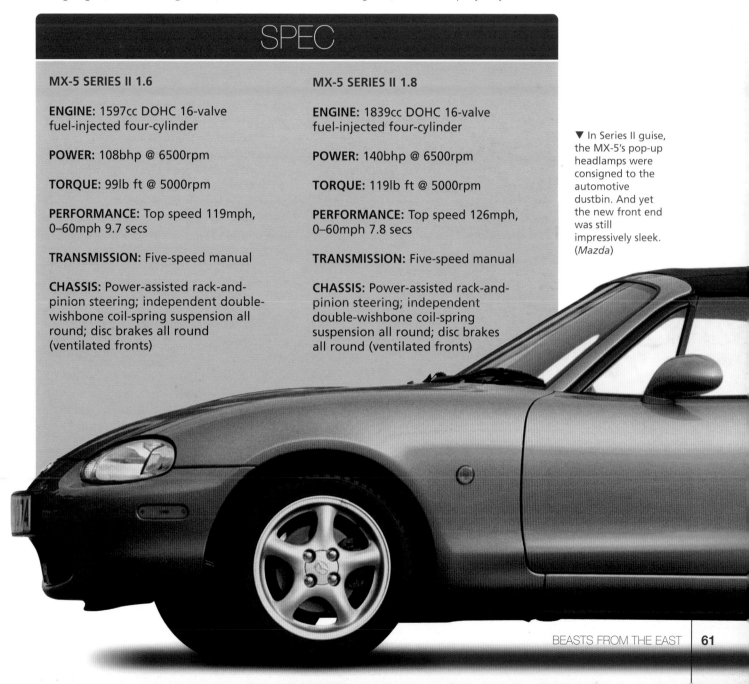

SPEC

MX-5 SERIES II 1.6

ENGINE: 1597cc DOHC 16-valve fuel-injected four-cylinder

POWER: 108bhp @ 6500rpm

TORQUE: 99lb ft @ 5000rpm

PERFORMANCE: Top speed 119mph, 0–60mph 9.7 secs

TRANSMISSION: Five-speed manual

CHASSIS: Power-assisted rack-and-pinion steering; independent double-wishbone coil-spring suspension all round; disc brakes all round (ventilated fronts)

MX-5 SERIES II 1.8

ENGINE: 1839cc DOHC 16-valve fuel-injected four-cylinder

POWER: 140bhp @ 6500rpm

TORQUE: 119lb ft @ 5000rpm

PERFORMANCE: Top speed 126mph, 0–60mph 7.8 secs

TRANSMISSION: Five-speed manual

CHASSIS: Power-assisted rack-and-pinion steering; independent double-wishbone coil-spring suspension all round; disc brakes all round (ventilated fronts)

▼ In Series II guise, the MX-5's pop-up headlamps were consigned to the automotive dustbin. And yet the new front end was still impressively sleek. (*Mazda*)

▶ The new MX-5 of '97 still offered a choice of 1.6- or 1.8-litre power, this time churning out 108 and 140bhp respectively. (*Mazda*)

▶ The Series II was a more sophisticated, better-equipped product than those early MX-5s, without losing any of the raw appeal so essential to the marque. (*Mazda*)

▼ With more balanced handling and less of a tendency to understeer, the second-generation MX-5 was almost foolproof. Amazingly though, its fun appeal was still intact. (*Mazda*)

intended its tiny sportster to be a niche vehicle. It was a way of bringing attention back to the Mazda marque, whilst also boosting company sales by a few thousand a year. But for an enthusiastic public, niche-market appeal just wasn't enough, which is why by 1992, less than three years after the MX-5 first went into production, the 250,000th example rolled down the line. It was a phenomenal achievement, the kind of success story that even the most optimistic of Mazda insiders never thought possible during the MX-5's gestation period.

Despite the tremendous competence of the MX-5, it was not immune to changing demands and the need for updates. By 1992 Mazda were fitting the MX-5 with a stiffer rear subframe to reduce motorway-speed vibrations, while the following year saw catalytic converters

installed on all UK-spec cars. The biggest change came in 1994 when the new 1.8-litre MX-5 was introduced to replace the 1.6. Offering 128bhp, the newcomer was a little more powerful than its predecessor, though in reality its performance was broadly the same thanks to the extra weight of the increasingly well-equipped MX-5.

The 1.8 was more expensive too, which meant a possible gap at the bottom of the MX-5 range that arguably needed filling. This occurred in 1995 when the 1.6-litre model was reintroduced, this time with a mere 88bhp to make it significantly different from the 1.8. Performance obviously suffered, but the new entry-level MX-5 still offered the same kind of fun appeal and countless smiles-per-mile, therefore proving a useful new addition to the range. It also offered terrific value for money in a market where fun cars seemed to be getting increasingly sophisticated and complex in design.

The original-style MX-5 was fast

GN52 UHU

becoming a timeless classic, a genuine legend in its own lifetime, but the day would eventually come when it would need replacing completely – and that was a real dilemma for Mazda's management and stylists alike. How do you replace something so loved, so uniquely styled and so utterly desirable? Very carefully, is the obvious answer.

The new Series II MX-5 took a bow at the 1997 Tokyo Motor Show, going on sale in the UK the following year. A first glance at photographs of the newcomer showed a car apparently little changed from its predecessor. But 'in the metal' the differences were immediately obvious, for the latest MX-5 was usefully larger than the old-style model and, most noticeably of all, did away with the original pop-up headlamps.

What the stylists did with the Series II was very clever, for some of the changes – such as the new-style headlamps – were dramatically different, and yet the car was still instantly recognisable as an MX-5 even with its telltale badges removed. Putting a Series I car alongside a Series II really emphasised this.

Under the bonnet of the Series II, there was still a choice of 1.6- or 1.8-litre power, this time offering outputs of 108bhp and 140bhp respectively. The latter allowed a top speed of 126mph, with 0–60mph in a healthy 7.8 seconds. And if that doesn't sound like much of an improvement over the Series I, bear this in mind: the newcomer was bigger, heavier and better equipped than its predecessor, so to maintain the same lively performance figures was a success in itself. In any case, this MX-5 was – as ever – about more than mere figures.

The latest version was much more about the driving experience, and some genuinely useful improvements had been made here. Although the previous MX-5 had offered terrific handling capabilities thanks to its superb chassis design and excellent weight distribution, the Series II was a further step forward. Where, for example, the old MX-5 had an occasional tendency to understeer when pushed to the limit, the latest model was better balanced and even more predictable. And yet, very cleverly, it was still just as much fun to drive.

Yasushi Ishiwatari, writing in *Top Gear* in 1998, claimed the MX-5 '…understeers less and … it's easier and more controllable to drift.' While David Vivian, no stranger to driving some of the ▶

TIMELINE

1989	Miata/Eunos/MX-5 range launched in Japan
1989	New MX-5 shown to British public at Earl's Court Motor Show
1989	*Car Australia* magazine awards MX-5 its Car Of The Year
1990	MX-5 goes on sale in the UK
1992	250,000th MX-5 is produced
1992	Rear subframe braced to reduce vibration at speed
1992	130bhp MX-5 M2-1001 launches in Japan in December; 300 produced
1993	Catalytic converters now fitted to UK-spec cars
1993	M2-1002 launches in February, but with standard 1.6 engine
1994	Minor MX-5 facelift includes launch of 1.8 version to replace 1.6
1994	Front and rear subframes stiffened and braced for extra rigidity
1995	MX-5 1.6 reintroduced, albeit with just 88bhp
1995	133bhp Japanese-spec 1.8 version introduced
1995	Limited edition 'Gleneagles' and 'California' launched in the UK
1996	Limited edition 'Merlot' and 'Monaco' launched in the UK

▶

▲ By 2005, Mazda had achieved the seemingly impossible yet again: a brand new third-generation model that was still instantly recognisable as an MX-5, despite its cutting edge design and up-to-the-minute specification. (*Mazda*)

world's greatest supercars during his journalistic career, wrote of the new MX-5 in *Autocar* the same year: 'There's nothing small or dainty about the driving experience any more. It's fast, focused and fun.'

Mazda's engineers, it seemed, had achieved the near impossible. They had come up with a replacement for a nine-year-old design classic – and it was still great to look at, even better to drive and just as much fun as any other four-wheeled machine of the time. The old-style MX-5 was dead, but the mourning was generally short-lived; its successor was just as much of a design masterpiece.

Part of the reason for the new MX-5's superlative handling and roadholding was Mazda's latest development of its double-wishbone independent suspension set-up, as well as its uprated anti-roll bars and sports dampers, aided along the way by near-50/50 weight distribution. No wonder the whole thing felt so good and seemed so well balanced in all conditions.

So would the new MX-5 continue for as long as its predecessor with little in the way of major

updates? Apparently not, for as early as 2000 the Series II MX-5 received its first round of revisions, including modified front-end styling and what's now referred to as the 'sharknose' look. It was a fairly subtle change but effective nevertheless, and it involved reshaping the MX-5's 'mouth' and giving a more chiselled look to the styling around and beneath the headlamps. There was thus more of a family link with the forthcoming RX-8, as well as a bit more attitude out on the street. But this latest look wasn't the only change to occur in 2000.

Mazda also took the opportunity to boost the 1.8-litre version's output to 145bhp at a heady 7000rpm thanks to the adoption of S-VT (sequential valve timing), as well as offering a six-speed transmission for the first time ever. Uprated ABS brakes with electronic brake-force distribution, stiffened suspension, the option of Bilstein dampers, a more rigid bodyshell and a whole host of other changes helped keep the MX-5 ahead of the game, essential in a market where new rivals were fast appearing.

The Mazda MX-5 found itself up against the successful new Toyota MR2 Roadster, and would

▶ A better-finished, better-equipped, better-built interior than ever before was part of the 2005 model's impressive package. (*Mazda*)

also face fresh competition with the launch of the MG TF – now with coil-sprung suspension instead of the old MGF's Hydragas set-up. The pressure was on Mazda to maintain the MX-5's dynamics and driving style, a challenge to which the company's engineers rose admirably.

If the Series II was going to be as long-lived as the original-style MX-5, it would have needed to stay in production through to the end of 2006. But that was not to be. In fact, another new-generation MX-5 was unveiled to an expectant audience at the Geneva Motor Show of March 2005, the newcomer going on sale in most export markets by the end of that year.

And the verdict? Another clever reinterpretation of the MX-5's timeless styling, this time with bulging wheel arches, a dramatic new front air dam and a new look of sophistication about the whole stance. The MX-5's DNA was recognisable even at first glance, but this time in a style far more in tune with 21st century tastes.

Beneath the skin too, new developments had taken place, most noticeable of which was a choice of 1.8- or 2.0-litre power, the latter offering a highly useful 156bhp at 6700rpm. Transmission options included five- and six-speed manual or six-speed automatic, while new suspension design (double wishbone front with a multi-link rear) resulted in even more impressive handling and roadholding to cope with the extra power.

Thanks to the clever use of ultra-high-tensile steel, the new MX-5 offered more bodyshell rigidity and strength than just about any rival, while still managing to weigh in at barely more than the Series II model of the late 1990s. This was an MX-5 driving experience that was just as much fun as before, but this time with the rigidity and safety you'd expect from a modern-day design.

The sports car market has changed immeasurably since 1989, and the MX-5

has changed along with it. That the very latest version retains the same principles and appeal as the first MX-5 ever built says it all. Mazda truly understands what makes a great sports car. And the MX-5 simply goes from strength to strength. ■

TIMELINE

1997	New 'Series II' MX-5 launches at Tokyo Motor Show in October
1998	Latest MX-5 range goes on sale in the UK
2000	Revised MX-5 launched with restyled front end and six-speed gearbox
2002	201bhp MX-5 SP developed and launched in Australia
2002	Limited edition 'Phoenix' launches in Europe
2005	Preview shots of disguised new MX-5 released by Mazda in January
2005	'Series III' MX-5 unveiled at Geneva Motor Show in March
2005	New MX-5 range on sale in most export countries by late summer

▼ Even before the third-generation MX-5 officially went on sale, most export countries saw record numbers of advance orders. The newcomer – like its predecessors – had got off to a flying start. (*Mazda*)

MAZDA RX-7

rotary revolutionary

▲ Final incarnation of the RX-7 line was a stunning looking machine, its curvaceous looks oozing sexiness and desirability. (*Mazda*)

When a company launches a car that it claims is unique, motoring pundits tend to treat it with suspicion. 'Unique' is a big boast, and one that few cars can genuinely get away with. But for the Mazda RX-7 of 1978, it was the most obvious adjective to use. There was no other machine on sale quite like this.

It wasn't the RX-7's smart coupé styling that set it apart from other 1970s offerings, such as the Datsun 260Z and Porsche 924; it was what lay under the Mazda's bonnet: a power unit so alien to most potential buyers, it would prove to be the RX-7's biggest marketing challenge.

We're talking rotary power, an invention of German engineer Felix Wankel in the early years of the twentieth century. By 1961, Mazda had acquired the rights to produce Wankel-style rotary engines and eventually a whole family of rotary-propelled Mazda vehicles was on offer, but it wasn't until the RX-7 came along 17 years later that a proper rotary-powered sports car was created.

Here was an impressive looking, all-new coupé – and it deserved an engine that would really do it justice. That arrived in the shape of a twin-rotor version of the Wankel lump, and every rival manufacturer throughout the world was looking on in interest. Could the RX-7 achieve what other rotary-powered models had failed to deliver: sales success?

A rotary engine works in a completely different way from a conventional piston engine. In a piston engine, the same volume of space (the cylinder) alternately does four different jobs: intake, compression, combustion and exhaust. A rotary engine does these same four jobs, but each one happens in its own part of the housing. It's a bit like having a dedicated cylinder for each of the four tasks, with the piston moving continually from one to the next.

As in a piston engine, a rotary unit uses the pressure created when a combination of air and fuel is burned. But in a rotary engine, the pressure of combustion is contained in a chamber formed by part of the housing and sealed in by one face of the triangular rotor, which is what the engine uses instead of pistons. The rotor follows a path which keeps each of the three peaks of the rotor in contact with the housing, therefore creating three separate volumes of gas.

It might sound complicated, but the whole principle of a rotary engine is remarkably straightforward. And, in theory, if there are fewer moving parts in an engine, there's less to go wrong.

So here, in the shape of the new RX-7, was a Japanese sporting coupé with style, performance and a vital unique selling point. From its pop-up headlamps to its gently sloping rear end, this latest Mazda looked great by late 1970s standards. Beneath its svelte good looks sat a super-smooth, free-revving rotary engine that provided a top speed of 117mph and 0–60mph in less than ten seconds – not fast by today's standards, but very quick for 1978.

In fact, so high-revving and smooth was the rotary engine that Mazda had to fit a warning ▶

SPEC

FIRST GENERATION

ENGINE: 2292cc (equivalent) twin-rotor unit

POWER: 105bhp @ 6000rpm

TORQUE: 106lb ft @ 4000rpm

PERFORMANCE: Top speed 117mph, 0–60mph 9.9 secs

TRANSMISSION: Five-speed manual

CHASSIS: Worm and nut steering; independent coil-spring front suspension; front disc and rear drum brakes

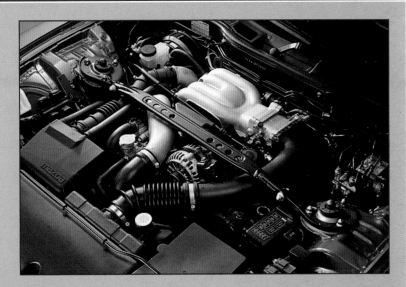

SECOND GENERATION – TURBO II

ENGINE: 2354cc (equivalent) '13B' twin-rotor engine with turbocharger

POWER: 200bhp @ 6500rpm (by 1991)

TORQUE: 195lb ft @ 3500rpm

PERFORMANCE: Top speed 143mph, 0–60mph 6.5 secs

TRANSMISSION: Five-speed manual

CHASSIS: Rack-and-pinion power steering; independent coil-spring suspension all round; disc brakes all round

THIRD GENERATION

ENGINE: 2616cc (equivalent) triple-rotor unit

POWER: 237bhp @ 6500rpm

TORQUE: 218lb ft @ 5000rpm

PERFORMANCE: Top speed 156mph, 0–60mph 5.8 secs

TRANSMISSION: Five-speed manual

CHASSIS: Rack-and-pinion power steering; independent coil-spring suspension all round; disc brakes all round

▲ Mazda's use of Felix Wankel's rotary engine design reached a new level of success throughout the long career of the RX-7 family. (*Mazda*)

buzzer for when the revs reached 7000rpm. This car just wanted to run and run.

Available in the USA as a two-seater and in some other markets – including its homeland – as a 2+2, the RX-7 fitted in with the needs of many of the coupé buyers of the late 1970s. That its front end was reminiscent of the three-year-old and increasingly popular Porsche 924 was perhaps no coincidence.

Where the Mazda left the Porsche standing, though, was in its sheer energy and its remarkable driving style. First-time drivers were amazed at just how rev-happy the RX-7's rotary engine was, and this helped to make the car feel a lot faster than its figures suggested. While a Porsche 924 pilot was busy changing up the gears as its red-line limit was reached in all too short a time, the RX-7 would speed past, rotary engine spinning wildly right up to its motorbike-like maximum.

Tie all that in with a super-slick manual gear change (typical of the Japanese at this time) and the kind of fun but predictable handling that such a vehicle deserved and you had the recipe for real sporting success.

Various upgrades and minor restyles took place during the eight-year production run of the first generation RX-7, including the introduction to some markets of the RX-7 Turbo in 1983. But the model really came into its own in 1986, when the second generation RX-7 took a bow. Suddenly, Mazda's headline-grabbing sports car had grown up.

The RX-7 now looked more masculine, many onlookers suggesting its styling influence was the latest Porsche 944. Well, if it worked for the Germans, why not the Japanese? The RX-7 suddenly seemed bigger and a tad more butch,

WHAT WE LIKE...

A revolutionary engine and fantastic styling came together to make one of the world's all-time-greatest long-distance coupés. A truly unique sports car that enjoyed 24 years of sales success.

...WHAT WE DON'T

Well, it was always the thirstiest car in its class. But with such a high-revving, gorgeous sounding rotary engine under the bonnet, who cares?

▶ Early RX-7 interiors were very much 'of their time'; check out that amazing upholstery! (*Mazda*)

▼ By the standards of 1978, the first-generation RX-7's styling was ultra sleek and very distinctive. (*Mazda*)

having grown biceps in all the right places; and it looked set to re-ignite the rotary flame.

This time the RX-7 boasted a much-improved rotary engine, known as the 13B and pumping out 146bhp in standard form. The year after the newcomer's unveiling in 1986, Mazda reintroduced the idea of a turbocharged RX-7 in the shape of the Turbo II. And this 182bhp beast really knew how to perform.

Remember, we're going back to 1987 here, a time when the Escort XR3i and Golf GTi ruled the enthusiasts' highways. Then Mazda came along with a turbocharged rotary-engined coupé that managed a top speed of 148mph, hitting 60mph in an amazing-for-the-time 6.5 seconds. This was bordering on supercar territory then, yet the RX-7 continued to offer good value for money.

The second generation RX-7 can also claim to be the only member of the Mazda rotary family available as a convertible, introduced in 1988 to cash in on renewed interest in the rag-top market worldwide. It made a massive difference, transforming the attractive but fairly blunt-looking RX-7 coupé of the time into a sexy, head-turning, boulevard cruiser – albeit one with a rather impressive turn of speed. By the time of the model's demise in the early 1990s, the RX-7 Convertible Turbo II was pumping out 200bhp with acceleration and top speed to match. Mazda had managed to bridge the gap beautifully between poseur's good looks and enthusiast's performance. ▶

TIMELINE

1978	First generation RX-7 goes into production in March
1978	On sale in the USA (as a 1979 model) from April
1980	Front and rear tail lights and front bumper and spoiler redesigned
1981	Rear-end restyle arrives, referred to as Series II
1982	Improved engine with greater fuel efficiency announced
1983	Turbo version goes on sale in Japan
1983	New 13B 1.3-litre engine introduced for Series III model
1986	Second generation RX-7 announced, known as Series IV

▶

▲ Lift-up glass tailgate gave the early RX-7 a degree of practicality, even though this machine was more about performance and driver thrills. (*Mazda*)

Even so, the good-looking second generation RX-7 couldn't last forever, although its seven-year production run was almost a match for that of the first. As the early 1990s dawned, curvaceous car styling became very much in vogue and Mazda knew the RX-7 was in need of a complete restyle.

Yet few people were prepared for just how radical the third generation RX-7 would actually be. It was rotary powered (of course); this time, though, by a triple-rotor unit with twin turbochargers, creating an awesome 237bhp combined with 218lb ft of all-torque pulling power.

But it wasn't just the new RX-7's powerplant that was creating so much attention by 1993. It was also the car's sensuous new look, an amazing amalgam of curves, swoops and dramatic statements. This two-seater-only newcomer was as much of a contrast with the original RX-7 as it was possible to be, with all the latter's purity and simplicity replaced by a testosterone-fuelled overdose of masculine magic.

The RX-7 was once again generating vital publicity for its maker – and, happily, the all-new third generation model was being well received everywhere. In fact, in the vital American market, the motoring press just couldn't get enough of the Mazda's dramatic new capabilities, with *Motor Trend* magazine commenting: 'The RX-7 redefines road manners for its class, the handling feels nimble and natural … no sports car in its price range delivers the same level of sensory gratification for the enthusiastic driver.' High praise indeed.

In fact, so impressed were *Motor Trend* with the latest RX-7's performance, handling, value for money and general desirability, they awarded it their accolade of Import Car Of The Year 1993. The RX-7 was back on a roll.

Even before the third generation model's power output was subsequently increased to a whopping 255bhp, its performance was phenomenal for such a relatively affordable machine. A top speed of 156mph was attainable, assuming the driver could find a length of road long enough and with no speed limits to worry about. And en route, 60mph was achieved in around 5.8 seconds. The RX-7 was now without doubt one of the most desirable enthusiasts' cars on the planet.

But not one of the most expensive. During the twin-turbo RX-7's relatively brief career on sale in the UK, its list price was around 30% less than that of the 250bhp Porsche 911 Carrera or the 264bhp Lotus Esprit S4. The Mazda's power and performance matched those of the German and British products, while its list price was no more than you'd pay for a rather dull executive saloon from BMW or Mercedes-Benz.

The third generation RX-7 remained in production right through to 2002, though the second half of the 1990s onwards saw its export markets dwindling. New emissions legislation meant it was no longer economically viable to offer the outrageous RX-7 as an official import, particularly throughout Europe. Fans of the rotary concept went into immediate mourning.

Fortunately, 'grey' imports of late-model RX-7s have been a feature of the British scene in particular for some time now, which has helped to keep the model's reputation intact and its long-term appeal as strong as ever. Nowadays, a secondhand 'grey' RX-7 offers spectacular value for money – 'the most bangs for your buck', as the Americans might say. And what could be better than that? ■

TIMELINE

1987	Turbo II version goes into production
1988	RX-7 Convertible launched
1989	Series V models launched with extra power and minor restyle
1991	Mazda brand name changed to Efini for Japanese-spec RX-7s
1993	Third generation twin-turbo RX-7 unveiled, known as Series VI
1994	Australian-modified RX-7 SP launched, for local sale only
1995	Efini name dropped for Japanese-spec RX-7s, reverting to Mazda
1996	Series VII unveiled with modified ECU and new-look rear spoiler
1999	Series VIII arrives with redesigned turbos and intercooler
2002	RX-7 production ceases

▼ New European emissions legislation saw exports of the RX-7 seriously dwindle towards the end of its life. It was a great shame, for this was still a machine with real potential. (*Mazda*)

MAZDA
RX-8

return of the rotary

▲ Unique new styling and the finest ever interpretation of the Wankel rotary engine concept marked the RX-8 out as an instant hit. (*Mazda*)

If Mazda was going to replace the iconic RX-7 with something even more exciting and revolutionary, the company's designers and engineers were going to have a tough task on their hands. Undeterred, they set to – and the result is what you see here. The all-new and unique RX-8 had arrived.

The newcomer officially took a bow at the Detroit Motor Show at the start of 2003, bringing glamour and excitement back to the Mazda marque after an unexciting few months. The fact that Mazda chose the USA as the launch country of its most daring sporting coupé to date was an indication of just how seriously the company viewed its export potential.

The announcement of the RX-8 came 25 years after the original rotary-engined RX-7 had gone on sale, during which time Mazda had become the unrivalled king of rotary engine technology. The previous chapter dealt with the uniqueness of the rotary concept and how Mazda used it to

great effect in the RX-7. Let's just say then, that the RX-8's version was even more radical.

This 1.3-litre normally-aspirated powerplant was available from launch in two states of tune, offering either 192bhp or 231bhp, which means that no RX-8 is exactly a slouch, although the 231bhp version is a very rapid machine indeed. That's thanks to what Mazda calls its RENESIS engine, a bizarre acronym of rotary engine genesis.

Mazda's brief to its engineers was to create an engine with the same kind of power as the previous-generation twin-turbo RX-7 but in normally-aspirated guise. It also had to be more fuel efficient and less polluting than the RX-7, the latter two factors being particularly important if the newcomer was to realise its export potential.

Where RENESIS differed from previous rotaries was in its side intake and exhaust porting layout, enabling greater efficiency throughout the enormous rev range and, partly aided by its light

ENGINE: 1308cc twin-rotor 'RENESIS' rotary unit

POWER: 231bhp @ 8200rpm

TORQUE: 211Nm @ 5500rpm

PERFORMANCE: Top speed 146mph, 0–60mph 6.4 secs

TRANSMISSION: Six-speed manual

CHASSIS: Rack-and-pinion electric power-assisted steering; independent double-wishbone front and multi-link rear coil-sprung suspension; vented disc brakes all round with ABS and EBD

weight and compact design, lowering fuel consumption too. The idea worked brilliantly, and the result was a remarkably small power unit with an impressively large output.

So would this new-design rotary really work, or would previous reliability issues rear their ugly head again? Happily, it worked, and the most extensive testing ever undertaken by Mazda also suggested this would be a long-lasting and reliable powerplant. Indeed, since its launch the RX-8 has undergone – and passed with flying colours – numerous reliability and durability trials, and has rarely put a foot (wheel?) wrong. The rotary engine had finally come of age.

But it's not just the RX-8's power source that makes this different from any other Japanese performance coupé. Mazda decided to go one step further and create a coupé with four doors and proper seating for two pairs of adults. The designers cleverly employed a couple of rear-hinged doors behind the two front doors, enabling back seat passengers to climb aboard with impressive ease. The resultant huge access area that appeared when all four doors were open instantly made the RX-8 the most practical coupé on the planet; and with a decent boot bringing up the rear, too.

The combination of innovative design, practicality, performance and sheer driver appeal led Britain's influential *Top Gear* magazine to

name the RX-8 'Best Coupé' in its Car Of The Year 2004 awards. Richard Hammond admitted to being rather surprised by the RX-8's all-round excellence:

'It could have gone oh so wrong, the Mazda RX-8. It's a coupé with twice as many doors as it should have, it's not German and it's got a rotary engine that's about as easy to fix as it is to gift-wrap a pineapple. Mazda really didn't make it ▶

▲ With up to 231bhp available from the RX-8's RENESIS powerplant, this latest upmarket coupe from Mazda was no slouch. (*Mazda*)

◀ Well-designed, well-finished interior was more than a match for the RX-8's natural opposition. (*Mazda*)

▲ Four doors and four seats in such a sexy looking coupe? Oh yes. The fact that the back doors were rear-hinged made the whole thing even quirkier. (*Mazda*)

▶ The RX-8's performance, handling and driver appeal were enough to see it winning *Top Gear* magazine's Coupe Of The Year award in 2004. (*Mazda*)

WHAT WE LIKE...

Unique engine design and equally innovative four-door concept make this one of the world's most fascinating coupés of the 21st century. That it's also a fabulous driver's car is the icing on the automotive cake.

...WHAT WE DON'T

The styling can look a little fussy in some colours – but perhaps that's nitpicking. This remains a hugely desirable and iconic performance machine.

easy for itself. It's like when that bloke combined surfing and roller skates to come up with the skateboard. He could so easily have come up with underwater skating, which would have been rubbish. He could have drowned. And so could Mazda. But it's OK, because Mazda has come up with something every bit as revolutionary as the skateboard.'

It had indeed. And the revolution started as soon as you took to the wheel for the first time. Like every previous rotary-engined Mazda before it, the RX-8 boasts one of the highest-revving engines in the business, achieving its peak output at a mighty 8200rpm. Blip its throttle and you'll see what I mean. Then there's the ultra-slick six-speed transmission fitted to the most powerful version of the RX-8 – it really is a joy to use, as is the Mazda's sharp steering and its stupendously efficient braking set-up.

The RX-8's handling and roadholding are just as accomplished, its multi-link independent coil-sprung suspension proving remarkably roll-free even when pushed to the limit. This is aided by the RX-8's limited-slip differential (which Mazda prefers to call Super LSD), a torque-sensing set-up that dramatically improves the car's smoothness and stability under hard cornering or on particularly smooth road surfaces. It helps to make the RX-8 a predictable but enormously enjoyable driver's car, one that thrives on hard work and high revs.

of character and charisma – has helped ensure serious sales success. Even before the RX-8 went on sale in most export markets, orders were being placed and waiting lists were starting to build. The momentum has scarcely slowed since then.

If you've never driven a rotary-engined car in general or a Mazda RX-8 in particular, I suggest you go out tomorrow and do just that. With so much power and performance lurking under your right foot, you'll be in for a terrific ride. And with four seats and four doors at your disposal, you can even take the kids along with you; which is nice. (Or not.) ▨

As if the RX-8's driver appeal and unique four-door layout weren't enough to win it friends, Mazda then decided to cram it full of goodies and still manage to sell it at a bargain price when it went on sale in Britain, in spite of its extensive list of standard equipment, including climate control, 18-inch alloys, traction control and, of course, that oh-so-lovely six-speed transmission. That's a phenomenal package for such a competitively priced coupé.

Raw performance alone doesn't make any coupé a great drive, of course. That's where the RX-8's unique personality scores even more points. As *Top Gear*'s Richard Hammond put it, 'In sticking doggedly to its rotary engine formula, Mazda has created a car that manages to bring all the expected Japanese reliability, but still has the charisma that comes with being different from the rest.'

Different doesn't always mean better, but in the case of the Mazda RX-8 it certainly does. The Nissan 350Z may win in the styling stakes, perhaps; and there might be a few German coupés knocking around with more prestigious badges. But the RX-8's uniqueness – its amazing rotary engine, four-door layout, four-seater accommodation and overdose

TIMELINE

2003	**Production-ready RX-8 unveiled at Detroit Motor Show in January**
2003	**UK sales begin by the end of October**
2004	**RX-8 named *Top Gear* magazine's 'Coupé Of The Year' in April**
2004	**100,000th RX-8 rolls off the production line in October**
2004	**Dual-fuel RX-8 Hydrogen RE concept begins extensive testing**

▼ It didn't take long for the RX-8's unique mix of attributes to smash through Mazda's original sales expectations for the model. (*Mazda*)

MITSUBISHI STARION

the turbo warrior

▲ Even by 1980s standards, the Starion was an angular looking beast that, by the time production ceased, was starting to look its age. More important though, was the terrific performance potential of its 2.0-litre turbo, churning out 177bhp by 1985. (*LAT*)

If ever a Japanese performance coupé was underrated in its day and continues to be now, it's the Mitsubishi Starion. Whether it was its angular styling or Mitsubishi's relatively lacklustre marketing that was the problem, the Starion never achieved the kind of export sales success it truly deserved. After all, when the Starion 2000 first appeared in 1982, this was a very rapid machine.

Here we had a fairly traditional front-engine, rear-drive, four-seater coupé in a similar mould to Europe's Ford Capri and Opel Manta of the time. In fact, the Starion's engine was nothing spectacular – just a straightforward 2.0-litre single-overhead cam four-cylinder from elsewhere in the Mitsubishi line-up. Here, though, Mitsubishi decided to strap on a mighty turbocharger, transforming what could have been a fairly ordinary machine into a tyre-shredding monster.

Early Starions pushed out a highly impressive 168bhp to begin with, boosted to an even more useful 177bhp (at a screaming 6000rpm) by 1985. And this was when Mitsubishi's fastest coupé really came of age, scorching its way to a top speed of 134mph, with 60mph going by in just 6.8 seconds. This was the mid-1980s, remember – and that kind of performance from a fairly affordable coupé was spectacular.

Not everyone liked the Starion; they criticised its fast-dating looks, its hard ride and its excess of turbo lag. But those who knew better soon loved the Starion for what it excelled at: providing real-life thrills every time it took to the streets.

Excitement was what the Starion was all about, and once the turbo was on full boost, that's exactly what it provided by the bucket load. Acceleration was real push-you-back-in-your-seat stuff, with a slick five-speed gear change enabling you to make the most of every bit of horsepower lurking under the lengthy bonnet. With the revs high and the turbo spinning merrily, progress by Starion was very rapid indeed.

ENGINE: 1997cc turbocharged OHC four-cylinder

POWER: 177bhp @ 6000rpm

TORQUE: 214lb ft @ 3500rpm

PERFORMANCE: Top speed 134mph, 0–60mph 6.8 secs

TRANSMISSION: Five-speed manual

CHASSIS: Power-assisted steering; independent coil-spring suspension all round; disc brakes all round

TIMELINE

1982	Starion launches in Japan
1982	Export sales follow almost immediately
1985	Power boosted to 177bhp and ABS becomes standard
1987	Wide-body Starion goes on sale worldwide
1987	Starion wins Group A World Rally Championship
1988	4x4 developed for rallying but never homologated
1989	Bigger-engined 2.6 model finally launched in UK
1990	Starion production ceases

The handling was fun too, the conventional rear-drive set-up providing just enough grip even when the Starion was working overtime. When that rear end did break away a touch, it was soon brought back into line, the experienced fun-loving driver grinning ear to ear for the rest of the journey.

The Starion's fairly narrow stance was done away with in 1987 when the wide-body version went on sale, its blistered wheel arches and enlarged proportions giving it a more grown-up, more attractive appearance. Even so, the still-angular styling was starting to date, and more modern rivals were appearing.

The final major change for the Starion occurred in 1989, when Mitsubishi's 2.6-litre four-pot turbo replaced the 2.0-litre in every market. But this brought bad news, because the fitting of a catalytic converter and other anti-pollution equipment saw the Starion's power drop to just 153bhp – a fall of 24bhp; not what performance fans wanted to see.

The ultimate Starion would be a 2000 Turbo from 1988, by then with ABS brakes and limited-slip differential as standard. And what a bargain it was, too, its list price undercutting the non-turbo Porsche 944 by a massive amount. The Starion had it all: power, performance and value for money. And it still does – assuming, of course, you're patient enough to hunt down an excellent example of what is now a fairly rare beast. ∎

WHAT WE LIKE...

The angular styling may look dated now, but the Starion 2000 still goes like a bomb and offers spectacular value on the used market – assuming you can find a good one, of course.

▼ Lots of cheap looking plastic could be found inside the Starion; but then, this wasn't a machine bought for the quality of its fixtures and fittings. (*LAT*)

...WHAT WE DON'T

Low-volume sales mean this isn't the easiest modern classic to pick up in the 21st century. Engine is low-tech by Japanese standards.

MITSUBISHI 3000GT

technology to die for

▲ Mitsubishi's eventual replacement for the Starion couldn't have been more of a contrast, its curvaceous styling and supercar looks hiding a wealth of hi-tech engineering. (*LAT*)

With the ageing Starion requiring replacement for the 1990s, Mitsubishi needed to come up with an outstanding up-to-the-minute design if it was to woo fans of performance coupés all over again. The Starion had been successful in its day, but its styling was starting to date and its dynamics were beginning to lag behind those of its rivals as the 1980s drew to a close.

Mitsubishi needed to do something pretty drastic if they were to regain lost ground, so whatever coupé they launched had to be very special indeed. There was also the added complication of a collaboration deal signed with America's mighty Chrysler concern, which meant that any new coupé developed for use by both companies had to appeal to American buyers as much as it did to Japanese or European. With tastes varying so much between such disparate markets, it wouldn't be an easy task.

This was an area of the market in which Mitsubishi had struggled to excel during the late

1980s, with rivals such as the twin-turbo Nissan 300ZX and Toyota Supra Turbo gaining valuable publicity – and sales – as a result of their exciting specifications and driver appeal. By comparison, the poor old Starion 2.6 was just too much of an old-timer by then, and its replacement couldn't come a day too soon.

Whether the resulting Mitsubishi 3000GT – unveiled at the Tokyo Motor Show in 1990 – could truly be considered a replacement for the Starion is debatable, for the two machines were a world apart in both style and technological ingenuity. But whatever Starion fans thought of the newcomer, everybody seemed knocked out by its stunning style and the promise of the most advanced technology in its class.

The 3000GT – known in Japan as the GTO – went into production in 1991, and officially arrived in the UK the following year, albeit in just a single power/trim level. Interestingly, American buyers were offered both the 3000GT and its restyled but otherwise identical brother, the Dodge Stealth – a wise move, as anybody seeking an American badge on their coupé could opt for the Dodge, while those with a penchant for anything Japanese would choose the Mitsubishi. But what, exactly, would the latter group be getting for their money?

A lot of car, is the simple answer, for the 3000GT was a full six inches longer than the Honda NSX and was therefore among the largest coupés in its class. But it's what lay beneath the skin of the most powerful version available that made it a true leviathan. Known in some markets as the VR-4, this most exciting of all 3000GTs ▶

SPEC

3000GT SL

ENGINE: 2972cc quad-cam 24-valve fuel-injected normally-aspirated V6

POWER: 218bhp @ 6000rpm

TORQUE: 205lb ft @ 4500rpm

PERFORMANCE: Top speed 139mph, 0–60mph 6.5 secs

TRANSMISSION: Five-speed manual (four-speed automatic optional)

CHASSIS: Power-assisted rack-and-pinion steering; independent coil-spring suspension all round; ventilated disc brakes all round with ABS

3000GT VR-4

ENGINE: 2972cc quad-cam 24-valve fuel-injected V6 with twin turbochargers and dual intercoolers

POWER: 320bhp @ 6000rpm (1994-on)

TORQUE: 315lb ft @ 2500rpm

PERFORMANCE: Top speed 155mph, 0–60mph 5.2 secs

TRANSMISSION: Six-speed Getrag manual (five-speed pre-1994)

CHASSIS: Power-assisted rack-and-pinion steering with four-wheel steering; independent coil-spring suspension all round; permanent four-wheel drive with viscous coupling; ventilated disc brakes all round with ABS

◀ With the VR-4 version of the 3000GT pumping out up to 320bhp, aided by twin turbochargers and dual intercoolers, there was no shortage of performance. Top speed was artificially limited to 155mph. (*Mitsubishi*)

WHAT WE LIKE...

Technically advanced superstars like this don't come along every day, which makes the 3000GT one of the most desirable choices for anybody with a love of gadgets, gizmos and mind-boggling technology. That it also looks fabulous and goes very fast indeed is an added bonus.

...WHAT WE DON'T

When new, this amazing machine was reckoned by some testers to be so advanced that it lacked any real charisma or driver feedback. And second-hand? Well, like any other Mitsubishi, the 3000GT has a great reputation for reliability – but if something does go wrong, it's likely to be complicated and expensive.

▼ The 3000GT was such a competent high-performance machine, some critics suggested it lacked any kind of charisma or soul. In many ways, it was almost too good. Mitsubishi must have felt as though they couldn't win... (*LAT*)

came complete with a 3.0-litre quad-cam 24-valve V6 with twin turbochargers and dual intercoolers, a magnificent beast of an engine that had no trouble developing 300bhp. This improved still further in 1994 when output was increased to 320bhp, by which time the car's 0–60mph sprint had been reduced to a minuscule 5.2 seconds and its top speed was resolutely (and artificially) stuck at 155mph.

It wasn't just the engine that set the VR-4 version aside from the competition, for Mitsubishi's finest also offered permanent four-wheel drive, four-wheel steering, speed-activated spoilers, an adaptive suspension system and, by 1994, a six-speed German-built Getrag manual gearbox.

Interestingly, the twin-turbo 3000GT was the only version offered by Mitsubishi in the UK, although the VR-4 badges were conspicuous by their absence. British buyers, it was assumed, wouldn't be interested in a normally-aspirated 3000GT, even if second-hand 'grey' imports in more recent times have suggested this wasn't actually the case. Still, as always, Mitsubishi insisted they knew best!

It didn't take long for the 3000GT VR-4 to start generating excited headlines around the world, putting Mitsubishi firmly back on the map of desirable performance car manufacturers. Britain's *What Car?* magazine described the 3000GT as a '...technical showcase in Ferrari-crib body.' But it was America's *Road & Track* that,

◀ In keeping with the 3000GT's highly developed specification, its interior was a top-quality, pleasing place to be. (*Mitsubishi*)

◀ By 1994, the twin-turbo 3000GT's standard transmission had been upgraded to a six-speed manual. (*Mitsubishi*)

even in the 3000GT VR-4's twilight years, truly enthused about this Japanese masterpiece:

'Grab the short gearshift and throw it into first. Feel a little daring? Keep your foot on the throttle so the six-cylinder powerplant teeters around 3500rpm, on the verge of getting a shot of air-forced testosterone from the twin turbochargers. Make a rapid scan of the road ahead and behind to make sure there are no bogeys hidden in your launch path… then drop the clutch.

'The VR-4 first hunkers down as the twin turbos inhale a big gulp of fresh air and exhale in the form of a deep growl. Power is split between the front and rear wheels as they fight to grab hold of the asphalt. The center-mounted viscous coupling in the all-wheel-drive system sends more torque to the tires with the best grip, ensuring very little tire chirp or wheelspin during launch. And as you make your way through the shift gates, the horsepower continues to surge on with very little lag…'

All sounds very exciting, doesn't it? And it was. The main problem was that some testers throughout the 1990s insisted on criticising the 3000GT for being almost too good. It was technologically advanced, incredibly sophisticated and almost completely foolproof to drive. It did everything so well that even the most inept driver could probably pilot this beast both quickly and safely. It was a performance car without drama – and for some critics, this meant a performance car without soul, quirkiness, or any real character.

Personally, I admire the 3000GT for that very reason. It proves beyond all doubt that it is possible to have a very high performance machine that's also safe and practical in anybody's hands. And while it may not have been the most charismatic coupé ever to come out of Japan, it

was one of the fastest, most advanced products of the 1990s.

Or rather, the VR-4 version was; as well as the model known in Britain simply as the 3000GT. But for Japan and key export markets, there were more affordable variations on the same theme available, offering less power and performance.

Standard versions of the 3000GT were relatively straightforward compared with the VR-4, lacking the latter's all-wheel drive, four-wheel steering and twin turbochargers. Even so, the 'base' and SL models still produced a healthy 218bhp at 6000rpm, an excellent figure for any 3.0-litre normally-aspirated powerplant. They also came as standard with five-speed manual transmission, although a large proportion of American and Japanese buyers opted for the extra-cost four-speed automatic instead.

Out on the open road, these cheaper 3000GTs behave differently from the VR-4, as you'd expect. They don't feel as direct in their steering, and their handling isn't as impeccable at the limit. Neither is there that sudden acceleration boost that only a decent turbo or twin-turbo machine can provide. But as a good-looking, reasonably fast and easy-to-live-with alternative to the Supras of this world, any 'grey' import version of a 3000 GT SL makes an interesting and very affordable choice these days.

Inevitably, it's the twin-turbo 3000GTs that enthusiasts hanker after, whether that's an officially imported version from 1992–98 or a well-maintained 'grey' example. No other Japanese coupé offers quite this level of ultimate grip, and few others compare in terms of outright performance at what are now bargain basement prices.

The 3000GT wasn't always easily affordable. In 1996, a new UK-spec example would have set ▶

▲ Its only major restyle helped to give the 3000GT more of a contemporary look, its original pop-up headlamps disappearing and its general lines softening for the late '90s. (*Mitsubishi*)

you back a hefty sum, even if it was cheaper than the entry-level Honda NSX of the time. But the Mitsubishi was also dearer than a new BMW M3 Coupé and, even more crucially, the same price as the latest twin-turbo Toyota Supra. In an era when enthusiastic drivers were demanding real feedback and the most adrenalin-pumping thrills for their money, the Supra was almost without compare.

The 3000GT and Supra may have been the same price and offered the same kind of performance as each other, but there was no doubt which machine appealed to petrolheads the more. That was a real shame for Mitsubishi, because their product was a technological marvel that did just about everything superbly well, albeit in a slightly clinical manner, and this, I'm afraid, would be its ultimate downfall.

Even by the 3000GT's final year of production, it still had a lot going for it. Britain's *World Car Guide 1999*, published by Express Newspapers, was particularly enthusiastic about its almost

foolproof driving style, no matter what the road or weather conditions:

'As a showcase for automotive technology, the 3000GT is undeniably impressive. Four-wheel drive, active speed-sensitive spoilers, a twin-turbo 24-valve V6 engine and six-speed gearbox all feature in this big, brash GT. They all work efficiently and the car is endowed with huge reserves of performance, grip and traction. On a wet road it will leave many a pure sports car a long way behind.'

High praise; but the same publication went on: 'Yet there are those who criticise the 3000GT precisely because it is so competent, complaining that the challenge and excitement of driving a high performance car is lost.'

Mitsubishi, it seemed, just couldn't win. They had created a monster that was too competent for the very people it was supposed to be aimed at. But that didn't deter its maker from giving it a healthy eight-year production run, as well as a host of useful improvements along the way.

The rarest 3000GT of all (and, again, one never offered in the UK) was the Spyder, a hard-top convertible with an electrically folding roof, introduced in 1995 to considerable critical acclaim. America's *Motor Trend* magazine was particularly impressed: 'For the convertible fan, this isn't a compromise, it's nirvana', they insisted. Even so, the Spyder remained very much a niche model, attracting only 1,618 buyers before it faded away.

By the time the 3000GT ceased production, it had received various minor front and rear end restyles, including having its original pop-up headlamps replaced by fixed units, plus leather upholstery being fitted as standard in the VR-4 from 1993, dual airbags from 1994 and, as mentioned earlier, up to 320bhp available the same year. Perhaps the most bizarre change occurred in 1997 when a new, cheaper, entry-level 3000GT hit the streets of Japan, offering a mere 161bhp from its single-cam V6. It was an obvious attempt to boost sales of the 3000GT in the autumn of its life, yet if anything it probably managed to dilute the model's high-tech image a fraction.

Inevitably, the twin-turbo version of the 3000GT line-up was always the most desirable model on offer, and it still holds the most appeal now. Our advice? Ignore those critics who moan about the 3000GT's lack of charisma or its absence of thrills and spills. Focus instead, on the fact that with a 3000GT you can go very, very fast indeed without feeling as though you have to battle against any automotive forces beyond your control.

This machine is blisteringly quick, utterly predictable and, as a result, still makes a fantastic everyday cut-price second-hand supercar. It is still one of Japan's most underrated performance machines, as well as being a technological marvel. Surely all that makes it well worth a second look? ▪

TIMELINE

1990	Mitsubishi/Chrysler joint-project models (3000GT and Stealth) unveiled
1991	3000GT goes on sale in Japan
1992	Sales in most export markets (including UK) get under way
1993	Minor equipment updates include standard leather upholstery in VR-4
1994	Upgrade sees dual airbags fitted and VR-4's engine boosted to 320bhp
1995	3000GT Spyder unveiled in spring (not for UK sale)
1997	Dodge Stealth discontinued but 3000GT lives on
1997	New entry-level GT launches with single-cam 3.0 V6
1999	Latest update sees huge rear spoiler for VR-4 and minor style changes
1999	3000GT production ceases by year's end

▼ The 3000GT was a big car with huge performance and monstrous cornering power. Sadly though, that didn't ensure immunity from criticism by the world's motoring press. (*Mitsubishi*)

MITSUBISHI FTO

the 'grey' best-seller

With the upmarket 3000GT settled in the Mitsubishi line-up and taking the company further upmarket than ever before, there was an obvious gap below it for a more affordable sporting machine aimed at the less affluent enthusiast. It was logical thinking like this that saw the arrival of the new Mitsubishi FTO range in 1994.

The FTO was something of a styling masterpiece, looking bang up to date in a chunky, brutish kind of way. Its curvaceous, three-box shape was swoopy, almost sensuous, while clever use of spoilers front and rear gave it just the right amount of youth appeal. It was a sporting coupé aimed at just about anybody who wanted to bring some fun back to their motoring. All except for the British, that is.

For reasons best known to themselves, Mitsubishi decided the FTO wasn't to UK tastes and made it quite clear from the beginning that official imports wouldn't be offered. It was a

bizarre decision, given the popularity of other Japanese coupés in Britain at the time, and it was a decision that would soon be undermined thanks to the determination of large numbers of enthusiasts in the UK. But more of that later.

From its launch, the FTO was designed to appeal to as broad a spread of prospective buyers as possible, which helps explain why the entry-level model offered a mere 125bhp from its 1.8-litre single overhead-cam four-cylinder engine. Known as the GS, this particular FTO was hardly a speed demon, thanks to its top speed of 120mph and the fairly leisurely 9.2 seconds it took to reach 60mph from standstill, but it filled a useful niche in the Mitsubishi line-up, keeping happy those buyers who wanted coupé looks but who weren't too bothered about power and performance.

The FTO started getting interesting when you looked at the next model in the range – the GR, renamed the GX by 1997 as part of a general minor facelift. This version featured a sensationally smooth 2.0-litre quad-cam 24-valve V6 lump that pumped out a far healthier 178bhp in this guise, endowing the GR with up to 137mph flat out, taking a far more exciting 7.9 seconds to hit 60mph. Things were looking up for the FTO!

At the top of the tree was the most desirable FTO of all – the GPX, a model that used the same 2.0-litre V6 as the GR but, in this instance, retuned and equipped with variable valve timing to give a whopping 200bhp. That was an extraordinary output for a fairly compact coupé, so it's little wonder the FTO GPX was impressively quick. In fact, it would just about hit 149mph if the (derestricted) road was long enough, and would take a mere 6.3 seconds to pass the 60mph mark. ▶

SPEC

FTO 1.8 GS

ENGINE: 1834cc OHC 16-valve fuel-injected four-cylinder

POWER: 125bhp @ 6000rpm

TORQUE: N/A

PERFORMANCE: Top speed 120mph, 0–60mph 9.2 secs

TRANSMISSION: Five-speed manual/four-speed Tiptronic

CHASSIS: Power-assisted rack-and-pinion steering; independent coil-spring suspension with MacPherson front struts and multi-link rear; disc brakes all round

FTO 2.0 GPX

ENGINE: 1999cc quad-cam 24-valve fuel-injected 'MIVEC' V6

POWER: 200bhp @ 7500rpm

TORQUE: 20.4kgm @ 6000rpm

PERFORMANCE: Top speed 149mph, 0–60mph 6.3 secs

TRANSMISSION: Five-speed manual/four-speed Tiptronic

CHASSIS: Power-assisted rack-and-pinion steering; independent coil-spring suspension with MacPherson front struts and multi-link rear; disc brakes all round (ventilated fronts)

◀ A good range of specification and trim levels was offered during the FTO's career, ensuring there was at least one version to suit most potential buyers. (*LAT*)

▲ The FTO's distinctive profile and – in top-spec guise – its healthy performance ensured no shortage of converts to the marque. This was a model with real enthusiast appeal. (*LAT*)

WHAT WE LIKE...

One of the most popular 'grey' imports of all time, the FTO continues to make sense now, offering a terrific driving style and real value for money. Styling still looks great, despite the age of the design.

...WHAT WE DON'T

With just 125bhp to play with, the entry-level FTO GS isn't exactly a ball of fire. But if performance isn't your top priority, it might make economic sense; maybe.

Comparing the GPX with the entry-level FTO was as much of a contrast as it was possible to imagine within a single model line-up. But to have three very distinct FTOs available made perfect economic sense for Mitsubishi, providing a vital boost to sales over several years.

Inevitably, the driving styles of the different FTOs were very ... well, very different indeed. The GS was competent and likeable, the GR was usefully quick and a lot more fun, while the GPX was an absolute sensation on any open road.

Maximum power in the GPX was developed at a heady 7500rpm, although it would happily rev to 8000rpm-plus – and this engine really enjoyed working hard. It thrived on being pushed to the limit, and the harder it worked the better it sounded. It had an almost Honda VTEC quality to

it, and was perfectly placed to make the FTO a seriously desirable machine.

A great engine alone doesn't make an outstanding car. Happily though, the FTO's chassis was well up to the job, its all-coil (MacPherson struts up front) suspension being taut enough to keep the handling flat, combined with more than enough grip to give overwhelming confidence without reducing the vital fun factor. Keep those revs high, keep your foot to the floor and you'd find an FTO GPX (or even GR) one of the most exciting experiences in its class.

Adding to the excitement was the availability of Tiptronic-style transmission in place of the standard five-speed set-up, which gave quick clutchless changes up and down the 'box via the stubby gear lever that simply rocked back and forth. Not every FTO fan chooses this feature, but those who have lived with it for a while generally love it. For a machine launched as early as 1994, it was certainly something of a novelty in the affordable sports car class.

With so much going for this car, why did Mitsubishi decide not to allow the UK and other key export markets the opportunity of officially imported examples? It's a mystery and will surely go down as one of Mitsubishi's biggest marketing mistakes. It was great news, however, for Britain's specialist 'grey' importers, most of whom soon found the FTO was outselling just about every other 'grey'. With or without Mitsubishi's help, British petrolheads were really taking to the FTO – in a big way.

The most popular imports by a long way were the V6-engined FTOs, and a ready market for these was soon established. Mitsubishi did their best to dissuade buyers from going 'grey' by suggesting problems with parts supplies, insurance and vehicle specifications, but British buyers were having none of it. They wanted their FTOs, and not even the car's manufacturer was going to stop them.

By 1999, Mitsubishi did one of the biggest about-turns in its history when it announced that a limited number of 'official' UK-spec FTOs would indeed by allowed into Britain via the specialist Ralliart set-up. This, though, was too little too late. The chance to cash in on the FTO's popularity had passed, as by then the model was a full five years old and was facing competition from newer, often cheaper rivals. Second-hand 'grey' FTOs would continue to sell in healthy numbers, but a brand new example of a car whose initial excitement factor had started to fade was no longer hot property.

Even so, the FTO still had a lot going for it, and Britain's *World Car Guide 1999* praised its driving style: 'This 2.0-litre V6 has variable valve timing which gives it a Jekyll and Hyde character. Below 6000rpm it feels pretty ordinary, but take it through to 8000rpm and 200bhp is unleashed.'

The same publication also said the FTO '…combines distinctive styling with some real technical interest', going on to describe it as 'stunning'. Despite being a five-year-old design, the FTO still had fans.

And it continues to attract them today. Older examples of the FTO now offer spectacular value for money compared with some of their more commonplace

rivals, as well as being genuinely exciting and thoroughly competent driver's machines. Grab a GPX with Tiptronic transmission and you've got one of the finest affordable coupés to come out of the1990s.

The FTO finally faded away in 2001, but its army of fans worldwide is still as enthusiastic and dedicated as ever. This fantastic machine became a modern classic in its own lifetime, an accolade it truly deserved. That its near-legendary status in the UK was achieved without the help of Mitsubishi themselves is quite remarkable; indeed, almost laughable. ▦

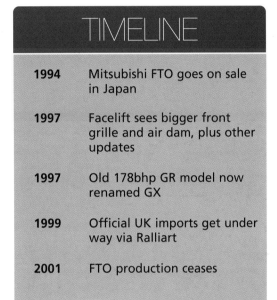

TIMELINE

1994	Mitsubishi FTO goes on sale in Japan
1997	Facelift sees bigger front grille and air dam, plus other updates
1997	Old 178bhp GR model now renamed GX
1999	Official UK imports get under way via Ralliart
2001	FTO production ceases

▼ By the time limited numbers of official British imports arrived in 1999, the FTO was a full five years old and its initial novelty value had waned. Now though, it still makes a superb secondhand buy. (*LAT*)

MITSUBISHI GALANT 2.5 VR-4

the big evo

▲ It may look like an ordinary Galant, but the VR-4's 150mph top speed and 0-60mph time of just 5.9 seconds suggest otherwise. This ultra-fast Japanese saloon was determined to take on the toughest competition from Germany. (*LAT*)

The Galant range of family saloons had hardly been Mitsubishi's most thrilling products over the years. From the model name's debut in 1969, via numerous incarnations and redesigns and through to the launch of the eighth-generation line-up in 1996, each Galant had been a worthy but unexciting addition to the Mitsubishi family, so when the VR-4 version first hit the streets, it's little wonder it caused raised eyebrows.

Here was a Mitsubishi Galant (or Legnum, as it's known in Japan) like no other. Beneath its four-door saloon or five-door-estate bodywork sat an EVO-style all-wheel-drive set-up and racing-type suspension, both deemed necessary thanks to the VR-4's amazing powerplant.

Like various other Galants, this one boasted a 2.5-litre V6 under its bonnet – but that's where any similarities ended. Mitsubishi's engineers had radically changed the lump into a 24-valve, quad-cam, twin-turbocharged gem capable of pumping out a mighty 276bhp.

That was the same kind of output as was being churned out by the 2.0-litre EVO VI at the time, so comparisons were inevitable. But where the no-compromise EVO was an outrageous road-going rally car in almost every aspect, the Galant VR-4 was an entirely different kind of beast.

Make no mistake, this was a quick motor. A top speed limited to 150mph and 0–60mph in a neck-snapping 5.9 seconds confirmed that. But the VR-4 delivered its power in a subtly different way from the all-conquering EVO – and it all started with its fantastic V6 growl. This machine boasted some of the best sound qualities of any Japanese performance saloon, enough to get a red-blooded driver lusting after it. But the real experience started as soon as right foot made contact with accelerator.

There's something very special about a twin-turbo V6 that a more conventional four-cylinder turbocharged machine can't quite match. Yes, power outputs can be the same, as can torque figures. But the lusty, throaty nature of a V6, combined with the adrenalin rush stimulated by two eager turbochargers, creates a driving experience never to be forgotten.

Turbo lag was rarely a problem for the VR-4, with performance and acceleration almost seamlessly available by the bucket load. Coupled with Mitsubishi's extensive knowledge of four-wheel-drive engineering, this most exciting of all Galants offered handling and roadholding to match. In fact, for what was a fairly large family saloon (or estate), the VR-4 boasted almost unrivalled agility and driving appeal, combined with simply sensational grip no matter what the road conditions.

When the VR-4 went on sale in the UK in 1999 through the specialist Ralliart concern, it retailed at a price which placed it well and truly in BMW and Mercedes-Benz territory. But no German saloon of similar value could hope to offer the Galant's ultimate combination of power, performance, handling and grip. The fact that it was also available as a highly practical estate car was enough to make it a truly unique proposition.

Official imports to the UK would always be limited, for the VR-4 was a highly specialised car, and no matter how fast or exciting it was, there would always be a huge proportion of British luxury car buyers who wouldn't dare be seen in something so radical or so exciting. A BMW was a far more sensible choice – and a far duller one, too.

The Galant VR-4 still ranks as one of the finest performance cars ever created by Mitsubishi, and that's quite an accolade. ▨

WHAT WE LIKE...

You want a fantastically powerful, ultra-quick Mitsubishi that's less raw and more practical than an EVO? The Galant VR-4 fits the bill perfectly. And with twin-turbo V6 power at your disposal, family-style motoring has rarely been so exciting.

...WHAT WE DON'T

If you like in-your-face performance cars, you will always consider the Galant to be second best to an EVO. For everyone else it's well-nigh perfect.

SPEC

ENGINE: 2498cc fuel-injected 24-valve quad-cam V6 with twin turbochargers and intercoolers

POWER: 276bhp @ 5500rpm

TORQUE: 268lb ft @ 4000rpm

PERFORMANCE: Top speed 150mph, 0–60mph 5.9 secs

TRANSMISSION: Five-speed manual

CHASSIS: Power-assisted rack-and-pinion steering; independent coil-spring suspension all round with permanent four-wheel drive; disc brakes all round (ventilated fronts)

TIMELINE

1996 Eighth generation Galant/Legnum range launched in Japan

1998 Twin-turbo VR-4 unveiled in saloon and estate forms

1999 Limited UK imports of VR-4 get under way via Ralliart

2002 Final UK-spec VR-4s are sold

▼ A big saloon with so much performance potential and such astonishing cornering characteristics will always be seriously desirable. (*Mitsubishi*)

MITSUBISHI EVO

an unstoppable performance

▲ One of the greatest all-rounders was the Evo VIII MR. It may not have been as powerful or as ultra-quick as the awesome FQ-400 version, but it was still a seriously capable beast. (*Mitsubishi*)

Mention the name Mitsubishi Evo in any crowded bar just about anywhere in the world and you'll find few enthusiasts with a bad word to say about one of the most amazing rally-developed super saloons ever created. And it's easy to see why, simply by looking at the power and performance figures on offer and by reading the countless road tests that have been published over the years.

But to get a genuine feel for what makes any Mitsubishi Evo truly special, you'll need to get behind the wheel and go for one of the craziest drives of your life. I promise you, it will change the way you think about four-wheel-drive saloons and high-performance road cars in general.

It's an obvious and well-known fact that the Mitsubishi Evo was created to take on the world's toughest rallying circuits. In fact, its very existence is down to Mitsubishi's desire to succeed in the World Rally Championship. Not unexpectedly, the road-going production versions were simply a by-

product of the homologation rules of the time.

In the early 1990s, any rally car that was to compete in the WRC's Group A required a homologation of 2,500 production versions, and it's for this reason alone that a road-going derivative of the Mitsubishi Evo was created. That the newcomer went on to become a highly revered icon of its time, a masterpiece that would be developed and upgraded to near-perfection over many years, is an indication of just how right Mitsubishi got the Evo from day one.

In reality, developing the all-wheel-drive Lancer Evolution wasn't the trickiest of tasks, as Mitsubishi already had extensive experience of designing and producing go-faster four-wheel-drive versions of various Galant models. Applying the same theories and logic to the smaller Lancer platform wasn't too difficult, and the result would be a usefully more compact, agile machine with bucket loads of rallying potential.

Producing 2,500 examples of the exciting new

Lancer Evolution wasn't difficult either, but would there be that many buyers willing to spend a not inconsiderable sum on such an uncompromising rally-inspired super saloon? With the benefit of hindsight, that seems a ridiculous question, such has been the Evo's amazing success over many years. And, in the end, no fewer than 5,000 examples of what we now refer to as the Evo I were snapped up between September 1992 and December 1993.

The most basic of the EVO offerings was the ultra-spartan RS, a version sold with steel wheels, manual windows, standard seats and an almost alarming lack of equipment. Its main appeal was about saving weight and making the most of the 247bhp (at 6000rpm) available. Buyers who demanded a few extra goodies could spend more on the Evolution GSR and enjoy a slightly more cosseting experience.

No Evolution would ever be luxurious or refined, for this car was all about power, performance, thrills, adrenalin, grip, handling, excitement and exhilaration. All those attributes were provided in full, thanks to the Evo's fantastic-sounding, high-revving turbocharged and intercooled 1997cc twin-cam lump with an amazing-for-the-time torque output of 228lb ft at a mere 3000rpm. Linked to a 4x4 drivetrain that distributed torque 50/50 front to rear in normal conditions but which had the ability to reallocate it according to what was happening at any particular time, the whole set-up was incredibly efficient and startlingly successful. Here was a performance car with just about all its power and torque being useable in real-life conditions.

The Evo's subsequent successes on the world rallying stage have become the stuff of legends, particularly with Finnish supremo Tommi Makinen at the wheel. The fact that Makinen won no fewer than four consecutive World Rally Championship driver's titles by the time the 1990s drew to a close reveals a great deal about the man himself – and the awesome machines he ended up piloting. These were the halcyon days of Mitsubishi's rallying exploits, and it was largely thanks to the all-round competence and near-perfection of the Lancer-based Evo.

Throughout the 1990s, of course, the Mitsubishi Evo was changed, upgraded, updated and made ever more exciting. Its makers knew they couldn't sit back and wait for rivals to catch up, so the Evo became the subject of a ▶

◀ Originally designed as a homologation special for worldwide rallying success, the Evo's subsequent career has been much more far-reaching than most pundits could ever have predicted. (*Mitsubishi*)

SPEC

EVO VI

ENGINE: 1997cc DOHC 16-valve fuel-injected turbocharged and intercooled four-cylinder

POWER: 276bhp @ 6500rpm

TORQUE: 274lb ft @ 3000rpm

PERFORMANCE: Top speed 150mph, 0–60mph 4.4 secs

TRANSMISSION: Five-speed manual

CHASSIS: Power-assisted rack-and-pinion steering; independent coil-spring suspension all round with MacPherson struts, lower wishbones, front and rear anti-roll bars and active yaw; permanent four-wheel drive; ventilated disc brakes all round with ABS

▼ The road-going Evo's looks have always been dramatic, purposeful and more than a bit mad. Subtlety is not one of its strong points! (*Mitsubishi*)

seemingly continuous series of modifications, each major round culminating in another numerical addition to its moniker, which is why the upgraded version that appeared in 1993 was officially christened the Evolution II – and why, twelve years later, the Evo IX was taking a bow.

Untangling the complicated web of modifications can be … well, complicated. What's important is that each successive generation of Evo offered at least one of the following: more power, even better handling, superior braking, extra downforce at speed – or, if you were lucky, elements of all four. And it all started with that Evo II, unveiled at the end of 1993, with its more powerful 256bhp engine and extra torque. As with the Evo I before it, the newcomer's all-coil independent suspension, all-wheel drive, front and rear anti-roll bars (and a lot more) endowed it with the kind of grip and handling unprecedented in the world of high-performance saloons. It's no wonder Mitsubishi had little difficulty finding buyers for every Evo II they produced.

By January 1995 the Evo III was ready for launch, bringing with it a larger rear spoiler and a dramatic new front air dam for extra downforce, as well as enlarged brake cooling vents for even swifter stopping

capabilities. Power was up again, this time to 266bhp at 6250rpm (with torque remaining the same as before at 228lb ft), thanks largely to turbo and exhaust mods. It's not surprising that 7,000 Evo IIIs were quickly snapped up by performance-hungry fanatics.

The new 276bhp Evo IV of 1996 saw the biggest change of all, resulting in a completely new platform thanks to the launch of a new-generation Lancer. There was a bigger bodyshell, more room inside, a little more equipment and new technological wizardry. A twin-scroll turbo kept exhaust pulse energy high all the way to the turbine wheel, improving boost so effectively that the size of the turbine housing had to be increased. Mitsubishi's much-vaunted inclusion of active yaw control (AYC), which adjusted rear torque split to minimise understeer and improve the car's turn-in, helped to keep things under even greater control, aided by a new torque-sensing limited-slip front differential on RS versions. Not only that, buyers were also offered a super-close-ratio five-speed transmission at extra cost, as well as a choice of final-drive ratios. The Evo series had, as its name suggested, evolved into a seriously well-endowed piece of equipment.

How could the Evo V top all that? It managed to do so upon its debut in January 1998, by featuring increased front and rear track, enlarged flared wheel arches, new 17-inch wheels and reconfigured suspension geometry. The car's official power output remained at 276bhp, although independent experts suggested the real figure was nearer the 280bhp mark.

▼ The Evo: dramatic stuff from any angle. (*Mitsubishi*)

By the following year, the new Evo VI was on the scene, bringing with it improved cooling and – according to Mitsubishi – greater engine durability. Interestingly, a new addition to the range appeared in the guise of the RS2, combining the RS's utilitarian specification with just a few of the GSR's extra touches.

In August 1999, it was a UK-spec Evo VI that *Autocar* magazine pitched head to head against the new R34-series Nissan Skyline GT-R, a comparison that seemed a little odd at first glance. After all, here we had the very latest Nissan super-coupé that retailed in Britain at nearly 80% more than a Mitsubishi Evo VI, yet at least one magazine thought it fair to compare the two in action against each other. It seemed almost ludicrous, but it also showed up some fascinating results.

There was no denying that the Skyline was an awesome beast; its combination of performance, handling and driver feedback placing it at the top of many a road tester's wish list. But the fact that a machine costing so much less could provide such close competition was little short of remarkable. When it came to comparing performance, *Autocar* seemed amazed by the closeness of the two: 'All out against the stopwatch, there is never more than a tenth or two in it on acceleration'. In fact, the magazine's testers went a step further when they explained the '…shorter geared and lighter Evo VI initially feels more explosive, hence its marginal superiority up to about 80mph.'

What really came to the fore during the comparison was just how different the two cars were in their style of power delivery, with the ▶

WHAT WE LIKE...

Taking the Impreza principle a stage further, the Mitsubishi Evo always managed to be more powerful, more exclusive and arguably more exciting than its Subaru rival. Although not as financially accessible, either new or second-hand, the Evo remains one of the ultimate 'must-haves' of the Japanese performance car scene.

...WHAT WE DON'T

Critics of the Evo always reckon it looks like a normal car covered in glue that has ram-raided Halfords. We think that's a cheap jibe. Any Evo will always remain a seriously desirable (and seriously fast) choice when funds allow.

▲ By the time the Evo concept had evolved into the Evo VIII 260, Mitsubishi's record-breaking rally star was an astonishingly capable machine by any standards. (*Mitsubishi*)

▲ Right-hand drive Evos for UK consumption have never had trouble finding buyers eager to experience the unique thrills on offer. (*Mitsubishi*)

▲ 410bhp from only a 2.0-litre four-pot? That's the Evo VIII MR FQ-400 for you, one of the most incredible official-spec versions ever offered for sale. For many, it marked the pinnacle of the Evo's road-going success story. (*Mitsubishi*)

Evo offering a far rawer, much less refined feel at all speeds, as *Autocar*'s testers were keen to point out:

'What is most fascinating is the different approaches they employ in order to obtain almost identical results. The Evo is noisier and more frenetic, and suffers from more turbo lag than the Skyline. But when it goes, it goes even harder than the Nissan. Its mid-range pick-up is eye-watering once the turbo is at full pressure beyond 2700rpm. And although the Skyline feels ludicrously rapid by ordinary standards, beside the Evo its acceleration never feels quite as dramatic.'

The Evo's acceleration not only felt dramatically quicker than just about anything else in its class, the figures achieved supported this impression. Top speed was a frantically fast 150mph, with 0–60mph in a stunning 4.4 seconds. A 30–50mph overtaking time (in third gear) was achievable in an amazing 2.7 seconds, while 0–100mph could be yours in a mere 11.2 seconds – just 0.4 of a second behind the arguably more sophisticated Skyline.

In the end – and rather understandably – *Autocar* insisted both cars were winners, each one exceptionally desirable by any standards. But it was the magazine's wake-up call to other manufacturers that made the most fascinating reading when they said: 'Fact is, these are two of the finest enthusiast's cars we've ever encountered, and the knowledge that they both

come from Japan should be carefully noted by anyone currently developing a European sports car.' Britain was suddenly in no doubt at all that Japanese performance cars meant business.

No matter how brilliant the Evo VI was, Mitsubishi couldn't leave their rally-winning star alone for long. The inevitable Evo VII came along in 2001, and it was significant for two reasons. Firstly, it marked Mitsubishi's decision to leave the Group A rally stage and concentrate on the WRC class instead, which meant an end to limited-production homologation requirements. And, secondly, it saw the arrival of another all-new platform, this time based on the latest Lancer Cedia. It was a bigger car than before and, some felt, lacked some of the outright straight-line antics of its predecessors; but the quality of its chassis and the fascination provided by its technological cleverness more than made up for that.

With the introduction of a new active centre differential, further improved active yaw control and a torque-sensing new limited-slip diff up front, the Evo's driving characteristics were even more mind-blowing than before. The way this all-wheel-drive legend now gripped, combined with some of the flattest handling we'd ever seen at the price, astounded everybody lucky enough to get behind the wheel. And with the same 276bhp available as before, there was simply no stopping the Evo bandwagon. ▶

SPEC

EVO VIII 260

ENGINE: 1997cc DOHC 16-valve fuel-injected turbocharged and intercooled four-cylinder

POWER: 265bhp @ 6500rpm

TORQUE: 261.6lb ft @ 3500rpm

PERFORMANCE: Top speed 152mph, 0–60mph 6.1 secs

TRANSMISSION: Five-speed manual

CHASSIS: Power-assisted rack-and-pinion steering; independent coil-spring suspension all round with front MacPherson struts and stabiliser bar, limited-slip front differentials, active centre differential and super active yaw control; permanent four-wheel drive; ventilated Brembo disc brakes all round with ABS and EBD

EVO VIII MR FQ-400

ENGINE: 1997cc DOHC 16-valve fuel-injected turbocharged and intercooled four-cylinder

POWER: 410bhp @ 6400rpm

TORQUE: 350lb ft @ 5500rpm

PERFORMANCE: Top speed 157mph, 0–60mph 3.5 secs

TRANSMISSION: Five-speed manual

CHASSIS: Power-assisted rack-and-pinion steering; independent coil-spring suspension all round with front MacPherson struts and stabiliser bar, limited-slip front differentials, active centre differential and super active yaw control; permanent four-wheel drive; ventilated Alcon front/Brembo rear disc brakes with Sports ABS and EBD

▼ Whichever Evo you're able to afford to buy and run, you'll find it one of the most exciting automotive experiences of your life. And that's a promise. (*Mitsubishi*)

Standard Mitsubishi Evos have always been awe-inspiring machines, of course; but in the same way that factory-spec Subaru Imprezas just aren't exciting enough for some people, there has always been a demand for Evos with even more power and thrills. Over the years this has been provided by independent modifiers and specialists all over the world, but it has also fallen on Mitsubishi themselves to take the Evo theme a stage further and provide even more amazing performance.

Perhaps the ultimate example of this occurred when the Evo VIII was unveiled in 2003, a range of models with as 'little' as 265bhp available – or, if the bank account permitted, a whopping 405bhp thanks to the amazing new Evo VIII MR FQ-400 derivative. To get such an animal parked in your garage, you'd first need to find a substantial amount of money; once you'd managed that, however, you were assured of 405bhp at 6400rpm, with a monstrous 350lb ft of torque also on tap. The chassis and drivetrain had been uprated to correspond, with super active yaw control now a feature, not to mention special Bilstein monotube shock absorbers and the latest Alcon front and Brembo rear ventilated disc brakes.

The result of such a combination was shocking, not just because of how fast this incredible machine was, but also just how accomplished it felt at all times. Its 400-plus horsepower takes a lot of keeping under control, and the car's suspension, steering and braking systems have to be incredibly highly developed to handle it with such consummate ease. That the Evo VIII MR FQ-400 provided as much feedback and rawness as any of its predecessors, whilst remaining almost absurdly poised and completely controllable, even when pushing it right to the limits, was a real tribute to Mitsubishi's engineers and their dedication to the Evo cause.

So just how fast are we talking here? Amazingly, this most highly developed official version of the Evo VIII would hit 60mph from standstill in an almost unmatched 3.5 seconds, prior to propelling itself on to a top speed of 157mph. That made it faster accelerating than most supercars costing two or three times as much, as well as a far more thrilling drive into the bargain. By Japanese four-door saloon standards, it was simply unprecedented.

Yet Mitsubishi still weren't resting on their laurels, which is why the latest Evo IX was unveiled to the world in March 2005. Sadly, there would be no official replacement for the awesome MR FQ-400, with power outputs now ranging from 280 to 'only' 340bhp depending on which variation was chosen. The new-generation range went on sale in the UK in June of the same year, providing the usual tough competition to the likes of Subaru's most exciting Imprezas, and, as before, they received a hugely positive reaction

▼ The Evo success story runs and runs, with increasingly more exciting, more thrilling versions being announced by the factory during the model's amazing career. Just how far can the concept be taken? Watch this space. (*Mitsubishi*)

from press and enthusiasts alike. But their arrival also marked the end of an era, for this was the last generation Evo to be based on the then current Lancer platform.

By the spring of 2005, Mitsubishi were making no secret of the fact that an all-new Evo series was being planned for a 2007 launch, based on yet another new generation of Lancer saloon, itself the product of a joint platform venture with DaimlerChrysler. Would the newcomer retain the previous Evos' rawness, sharpness and almost unrivalled levels of driver feedback and response? Time would tell. But one thing is for sure: the Mitsubishi Evo is now firmly placed as one of Japan's all-time greats. It is a car that has single-handedly done more to boost Mitsubishi's reputation worldwide than just about anything else before, or since. ■

TIMELINE

1990	Mitsubishi begins development of rally-inspired Lancer Evolution
1992	Lancer Evolution launched in RS and better-equipped GSR guises
1993	Evolution II launched in December; power up from 247 to 256bhp
1995	Evolution III arrives in January with more power and styling mods
1996	New Evo IV launched in August; brand new platform and up to 276bhp
1996	Tommi Makinen wins the first of four consecutive World Rally Drivers' Championship titles piloting an Evo
1998	Evo V announced in January; revised suspension and bigger brakes
1999	Evo VI brought better cooling and improved power delivery
2001	Latest Evo (VII) now based on new and bigger Lancer Cedia platform
2003	Evo VIII on sale; 265–405bhp available through different variants
2004	Evo VIII MR special edition introduced
2005	Evo IX announced in March; variable valve timing among improvements
2007	All-new Evo X based on latest Lancer platform due to arrive

NISSAN 200SX

the smooth operator

▲ Svelte, sexy styling, turbocharged performance and entertaining rear-wheel-drive handling marked out the original 200SX as one of the finest Japanese coupés of the late 1980s. (*LAT*)

What most Europeans know as the 200SX is better known in Japan as the Silvia, in Australia as the 180SX and in America as the 240SX, which inevitably means its background is a complex one. Don't let that deter you, because the 1989–94 version of the 200SX is a particularly fine driver's car; and while its restyled replacement of 1994-onwards may not have looked as exciting, it was, in turn, an impressively fast performance machine.

Prior to the launch of the 200SX in 1989, most markets had seen the rather square and ugly Silvia selling in reasonable numbers. When the time came to replace it, Nissan knew it had to come up with something a lot sexier, faster and more desirable. The latter inevitably meant changing the model name from Silvia, a moniker that had been used on sporty Nissans since the start of the1970s.

Quite why most of Europe got to know the newcomer as the 200SX is a bit of a mystery, as its engine was based on the same 1809cc four-

pot that had given good service in the Silvia. Surely the Australian tag of 180SX would have been more appropriate? Well, maybe, but that didn't stop this being a superb powerplant, its twin-cam 16-valve layout – with turbocharger and intercooler for good measure – leading to an impressive output of 171bhp at 6400rpm. Even better was that it suffered the least obtrusive turbo lag in the business, which allowed an impressively smooth and drama-free band of power right through the rev range.

Not that this wasn't a machine to push you back in your seat, of course. Flat out it would top 140mph, with the vital 0–60mph dash coming in at under 7.0 seconds. By the standards of the late 1980s, that was pretty rapid – and made even more entertaining by the 200SX's delightful rear-drive handling.

This was a model with all the best positives of an 'old school' performance machine and none of the negatives. Press it into a tight corner at speed and the rear end maintained its highly impressive grip, coming slightly unstuck only when really pushed to the limit. Even then, adopting the opposite-lock technique and keeping the power high soon brought the rear end neatly into line once again, providing enthusiastic drivers with some of the most entertaining experiences of any high-powered coupé.

Rapid progress was made even easier by the 200SX's ultra-slick and quick five-speed gear change, complemented by all-disc braking (ventilated up front) when the need came to stop in a hurry. The only real downside was the disappointingly vague and light steering, which made on-the-limit antics marginally less rewarding than they could have been. ▶

SPEC

RS13

ENGINE: 1809cc DOHC 16-valve fuel-injected four-cylinder with turbocharger and intercooler

POWER: 171bhp @ 6400rpm

TORQUE: 168lb ft @ 4000rpm

PERFORMANCE: Top speed 140mph, 0–60mph 6.9 secs

TRANSMISSION: Five-speed manual

CHASSIS: Power-assisted rack-and-pinion steering; independent coil-spring suspension all round with MacPherson front struts and multi-link rear; disc brakes all round (ventilated fronts)

S14

ENGINE: 1998cc DOHC 16-valve fuel-injected four-cylinder with turbocharger and intercooler

POWER: 197bhp @ 6400rpm

TORQUE: 195lb ft @ 4800rpm

PERFORMANCE: Top speed 142mph, 0–60mph 6.5 secs

TRANSMISSION: Five-speed manual

CHASSIS: Power-assisted rack-and-pinion steering; independent coil-spring suspension all round with MacPherson front struts and multi-link rear; disc brakes all round (ventilated fronts)

◀ There was never any shortage of power or excitement from under the 200SX's bonnet, with even the earliest 1.8-litre versions offering 171bhp. This twin-cam 16-valve four-cylinder with turbo and intercooler was an absolute gem. (*Nissan*)

To most Europeans, this was the first time they'd ever seen the 200SX badge on a Nissan, although in some markets the tag had been used on a two-door version of a very dull saloon going by the name of Sentra. Don't confuse the two, because they have about as much in common as chicken and cod. Remember this when boasting internationally that you drive a 200SX, or they might just assume you're the proud owner of a sadmobile. And if you're wondering why the

Americans called 'our' 200SX the 240SX, it's because their version came with a normally-aspirated 2.4-litre engine instead of the 1.8 turbo.

In the UK at the start of the1990s, the new 200SX was busy catching the imagination of enthusiasts everywhere, its combination of fast, smooth performance, great handling, sexy looks and sheer value for money, winning it many friends from day one.

The motoring press couldn't get enough of it either, with Britain's *What Car?* magazine awarding the 200SX its 'Coupé Of The Year' title in 1990, beating such luminaries as the Porsche 944, Toyota Celica and VW Corrado.

In typical style, Nissan didn't leave the 200SX to its own devices for too long. By 1991 Nissan had designed a smoother and better-looking front end for the 200SX, as well as making a few minor engine tweaks and some trim changes here and there. But the interior remained largely the same, which meant it was fairly plain, grey and unsophisticated. But so what? This most exciting of all coupés of the early 1990s was all about the driving experience. The fact that the upholstery was nasty and the back seats were absurdly cramped would be taking criticism a bit too far.

With most Japanese makers still adopting a four-year model programme back then, it was probable that a brand new 200SX would be appearing by 1994 – and that's exactly what happened. Understandably, enthusiasts were eager to see how the original could be improved upon. Even more power? That would be good. Even sleeker, sexier looks? That was almost inevitable. So by the time the wraps came off the company's latest creation, anticipation was high.

WHAT WE LIKE...

Sensationally svelte styling of the original 200SX hides a car with stunning performance, terrific rear-drive handling and a real fun factor. This was far and away the best affordable coupé of the 1990s.

...WHAT WE DON'T

Second-generation 200SX of 1994 lacked the original's wow factor in its styling, and sales dipped as a result. In this market, good looks and image are essential.

▶ Despite controversy over its styling, the new-for-1994 2.0-litre 200SX was still an enormously entertaining machine for the enthusiastic driver. (*LAT*)

▼ Classic tail-out, rear-drive handling was always a hallmark of the 200SX, making it one of the finest drivers' cars of its era. It offered an abundance of good old-fashioned fun – and was all the better for it. (*LAT*)

◀ A minor restyle for 1996 saw the 200SX receive new-shape headlamps and a longer bonnet in an effort to make it sleeker and sexier. It was a reasonable success, despite so many fans still mourning the original-shape version of 1989-94. (*Nissan*)

Oh dear. Where the 'old' 200SX (known internally as RS13) was curvaceous, sleek and almost as coupé-like as it's possible to be, the latest model (codenamed S14) looked rather square. Gone were the pop-up headlamps. Gone was the gradual slope to the rear end that epitomised the coupé style. This was almost a three-box shape, more reminiscent of a low-slung two-door saloon than a proper coupé.

It was a controversial move, and one that Nissan would come to regret in terms of export sales. But you know, beneath its deliberately understated styling the new 200SX was a very fine car; yet again, its success story started under the bonnet.

This time round, engine size had increased to 1998cc, which meant a boost in power to a whopping 197bhp. That was enough for 145mph flat out, with 0–60mph in a mere 6.5 seconds. Again, traditional rear-wheel drive was the dish of the day, giving yet more fantastic handling and serious entertainment value. It was as fun to drive as the old-style 200SX but with more power, just as much grip, and brought even more of a grin to the face of every one of its owners.

But by 2000, the 200SX concept was getting just a bit too dated for sophisticated European tastes of the 21st century, which meant it had to go. More technologically advanced coupés were now becoming the norm, so that by the time the new millennium dawned, magazines such as *What Car?* were led to describe the 200SX as '...crude by today's standards'. The end was nigh.

These days, a late-model version of the early-shape 200SX makes a fantastic introduction to Japanese performance motoring. Get a low mileage example with a healthy turbo and it'll prove immensely reliable, too. With values as low as they're ever likely to get, it's an experience just about everyone can afford. Sometimes, you know, life is just so great. ■

TIMELINE

1989	RS13 version of Silvia launched, known in Europe as 200SX
1991	Update includes smoother-looking restyled front end and extra power
1994	S14 version of Silvia launched with new body but same 200SX tag
1996	Facelift includes restyled headlamps and longer bonnet
1999	RS13 finally ceases production, five years after S14's arrival
1999	New-look S15 arrives but export sales are restricted
2000	S14 production ceases and the 200SX name dies with it

NISSAN 300ZX
supercar saviour

▲ At long last, the Z-series of Nissans was back on track following the launch of the latest 300ZX in 1989. This was a real driver's car, with an image to match. *(LAT)*

With the arrival of the 1990s just around the corner, it was obvious to even the most sympathetic Nissan fan that the company's Z-series line was in serious trouble. From the day the original 240Z was replaced by the bigger, heavier, less powerful 260Z, the rot had set in, and by the time such atrocities as the 280ZX and original-style 300ZX had appeared, the Z-line was seen as too heavy, cumbersome and well past its prime. It kept thousands of overweight middle-aged Americans happy, but that was about it.

Drastic action was called for, and Nissan gave the go-ahead for a new Z-series model for the new decade. It had to be a real driver's car, with performance, handling and desirability to rival the best on the market. It had to be a machine for getting the Z brand back on track; and it had to be phenomenally competent if it was to achieve such a major feat.

Like its predecessor, the newcomer was also called the 300ZX. And like the one before, it

shared the same basic 2960cc V6 motor. That, however, is just about where the similarities ended, for the new 300ZX was a revelation. In fact, it took the Z brand further upmarket than it had ever dared go before and was soon being hailed as a genuine Japanese supercar.

The old 300ZX's 3.0-litre powerplant had been upgraded for use in this latest model, incorporating a 24-valve set-up and new technology such as variable valve timing – a common feature these days, but a real innovation in the spring of 1989. It helped to boost the V6's output to a very healthy 222bhp, enough for a top speed in excess of 140mph.

The new 300ZX really came of age six months later with the arrival of the turbo version. In fact, this was a twin-turbocharged machine, with twin intercoolers too. Suddenly, this most powerful Z-series car found itself with a mighty 280bhp (at 6400rpm) at its disposal, which meant an artificially limited top speed of 155mph. It was the newcomer's through-the-gears acceleration that really set the performance car world alight, with the 0–60mph dash being completed in an adrenalin-surging 5.6 seconds. This was real supercar stuff by the standards of the late 1980s, and it helped to put Nissan well and truly back in the camp of performance car manufacturers.

Yet speed and acceleration alone don't make a great performance car, as Nissan knew only too well. That's why the new 300ZX's independent coil-sprung multi-link suspension (with electronically adjustable shock absorbers) was tuned to perfection. Front and rear stabiliser bars and a limited-slip differential completed the standard handling package. And the result? A hard ride, but handling that was ▶

SPEC

300ZX

ENGINE: 2960cc 24-valve DOHC V6

POWER: 222bhp @ 6400rpm

TORQUE: 197lb ft @ 3500rpm

PERFORMANCE: Top speed 140mph, 0–60mph 7.4 secs

TRANSMISSION: Five-speed manual

CHASSIS: Power-assisted rack-and-pinion steering; independent coil-spring suspension all round; disc brakes all round (ventilated fronts) with ABS

300ZX TURBO

ENGINE: 2960cc 24-valve twin-turbo V6 with twin intercoolers

POWER: 280bhp @ 6400rpm

TORQUE: 274lb ft @ 3600rpm

PERFORMANCE: Top speed 155mph, 0–60mph 5.6 secs

TRANSMISSION: Five-speed manual

CHASSIS: Power-assisted rack-and-pinion steering with four-wheel steer; independent coil-spring suspension all round; disc brakes all round (ventilated fronts) with ABS

◀ Whether the 300ZX buyer chose normally-aspirated or twin-turbo power, the same 3.0-litre V6 gave effortless performance and plenty of feedback. (*LAT*)

▶ 280bhp from the most powerful 300ZX was an impressive achievement at the end of the '80s. It wouldn't take long for the newcomer to gain cult status worldwide. (*LAT*)

WHAT WE LIKE...

If ever there was a relatively affordable supercar from Japan, it was the awesome twin-turbo Nissan 300ZX, a brutal machine with scorching performance and handling to match.

▶ The driver of the twin-turbo 300ZX was treated to four-wheel steering as standard, making for a more responsive and dynamic experience. (*LAT*)

...WHAT WE DON'T

The classic simplicity of the original Datsun 240Z had been lost forever. But when a performance car is this good, it's not exactly a disaster ... is it?

impressively flat, enabling even the most critical of enthusiasts to really have fun – and feedback – behind the wheel.

The driving experience was made even more special by the four-wheel steering (officially known as high capacity actively controlled steering) fitted as standard to the 300ZX Turbo, a system that allowed the rear wheels to turn a subtle but vital two degrees in unison with those at the front. It made for a more dynamic, responsive and exhilarating drive when the Nissan was really pushed to the limit, and it helped to make the standard car's enormous rear-drive level of grip feel even more impressive.

Not content with creating a near-300bhp masterpiece, Nissan looked at other ways of expanding the line-up as sales of the 300ZX started taking off, and the most obvious result of this came along in 1993 with the launch of the convertible model, a handsome beast by any standards. It helped to soften the 300ZX's brutal styling, while also expanding the model's appeal in that most vital of export markets, the USA.

By now the 300ZX range was complete, with buyers able to choose from normally-aspirated or twin-turbo powerplants, standard or Targa roofs, two-seater or 2+2 layouts or, of course, the two-seater convertible – the first time ever that a full convertible version had been officially available in the Z-car family.

Not every export market was treated to the full

range, with the UK in particular being offered just the 2+2 Targa Turbo version between the model's British debut in April 1990 and its demise in September 1994. By 1991, in the UK, this solo model undercut in price both the drastically less powerful Porsche 944 S2 and the cheapest Lotus Esprit by a considerable amount, offering seriously good value, and the 300ZX soon found itself with a niche following among hardcore enthusiasts who knew a good buy when they saw one.

The motoring press also fell for the 300ZX's charms, impressed by its heady cocktail of power, handling and sheer brute force. Britain's *Autocar* magazine extolled its virtues with eagerness, describing it as '…proof that Nissan has its heart in the right place' and 'Japan's best GT'.

But the 300ZX's success in Britain was fairly short-lived, and by the end of 1994 it was no longer an official import. New European emissions regulations meant it would be both difficult and expensive to reconfigure the 300ZX in order to comply; the model's overall sales volume didn't justify that. And so, not for the first time, British enthusiasts found themselves robbed of a truly exceptional piece of engineering.

History repeated itself two years later in the USA, when new extra-stringent emissions regulations saw the 300ZX failing to keep up on the 'green' front once again. And so, despite the impressive size of the American sports car market, Nissan reluctantly withdrew its cut-price supercar and focused instead on more-mainstream models.

That wasn't the end of the 300ZX altogether, as production continued – mainly for homeland consumption – right through to 1999, when the very last example of Nissan's then most upmarket Z-car finally rolled off the production line, a full decade on from its original unveiling.

As with so many other Japanese performance cars, more examples of the 300ZX found their way to the UK unofficially than they did through Nissan themselves. It's been a popular 'grey' import over the years, and still has its own cult following now. But make sure you're aware of differences in specification before you take the plunge; you wouldn't want to end up with a normally-aspirated example with automatic transmission by mistake if it's a turbocharged manual you're after…

That it was bureaucracy and regulations that killed the 300ZX in its key export markets says a lot about the appeal of this twin-turbocharged monster. It wasn't that buyers weren't willing to invest in a high-performance Nissan; they just weren't allowed to in the end, thanks to changes in legislation. Exactly how long this behemoth could have remained on sale if it had been left alone is anyone's guess. That it lasted a whole ten years before having to be killed off completely is an indication of what an amazing machine it was – and how determined Nissan were to exploit its full potential. ■

TIMELINE

1989	New 300ZX (Z32) unveiled in the spring
1989	300ZX Turbo introduced six months later
1990	2+2 Targa version on sale in the UK from April
1993	300ZX Convertible goes into production
1994	British imports of 300ZX cease
1994	Series II model launched in Japan with styling upgrades
1996	V6 engine detuned to meet new Japanese smog regulations
1996	American imports of 300ZX cease
1999	300ZX production discontinued

▼ The Z32-series 300ZX enjoyed a healthy decade-long career, although in later years its export potential was killed by various changes to anti-emissions legislation. (*Nissan*)

NISSAN
SUNNY GTI-R
monster hatch

▲ Humble Nissan Sunny origins hid a machine of awesome talent, with 220bhp on tap from the GTI-R's 16-valve twin-cam turbo. (*LAT*)

As four-wheel-drive 'superhatches' were grabbing so much publicity in the 1990s, it was inevitable that at least one major Japanese manufacturer would want to jump on the very same bandwagon as the Ford Escort Cosworth and Lancia Delta Integrale. With their world-beating rally successes and simply outrageous performance capabilities, both these European models were attracting a dedicated following, as well as generating more positive publicity for their respective makers than any multi-million dollar advertising campaign.

The recipe was straightforward enough: take one standard hatchback, transform it into a world-class rally car, develop a homologated version for the road and then sit back and enjoy many months – even years – of glorious publicity. Simple.

Well, maybe not; but it was certainly a worthwhile enough cause for Nissan to want to give it a try, a decision that eventually led to the

launch of the Sunny (known in Japan as the Pulsar) GTI-R. And what an incredible machine this was.

The basis for the GTI-R was, logically enough, the three-door derivative from the new-for-1990 Pulsar/Sunny line-up – the fourth generation of this successful model range. But as even the most optimistic Nissan fan can confirm, it was hardly the most exciting of beginnings. In the UK, in particular, the Sunny had always been seen as a car that hat-wearing septuagenarians would drive to church on a Sunday morning. So why should the latest models to wear the Sunny badge be any different? This left Nissan with a major image problem when it came to developing a 'superhatch' version.

Undeterred, Nissan continued with development of what was to become the GTI-R, and when the time came to unveil their new fire-breathing monster to the outside world, they made no attempt to hide its Pulsar or Sunny badges. Almost inevitably, fans of the model would come to refer to it simply as 'the GTI-R', though officially it was indeed a Nissan Sunny.

The contrast with the rest of the Pulsar/Sunny range couldn't have been more obvious, for here was a machine that, in specification, was more than a match for the finest homologation specials available from Ford and Lancia.

Most important was the adoption of Nissan's new ATTESA four-wheel-drive set-up for the GTI-R's hugely modified chassis, endowing it with the same levels of grip and handling we'd come to expect from the likes of the Lancia Integrale. All that grip was useless, though, if there wasn't a powerplant up front capable of really doing it justice. And once again, Nissan truly excelled here.

Using as a base the same 1998cc 16-valve twin-cam engine that would also go on to power the forthcoming Pulsar/Sunny GTI, the GTI-R got off to a promising start. But once a custom-built turbocharger and intercooler had been installed, Nissan had managed to extract an incredible 220bhp from the lump. Not only that, but the GTI-R was also boasting 196lb ft of all-torque pulling power at a respectably low 4800rpm. Such a combination was surely a recipe for success?

It certainly compared well with the 200bhp (later upped to 210bhp) being coaxed out of the Lancia Integrale in 1990. Meanwhile, the Escort Cosworth would manage anything up to 227bhp in standard form; but as this fastest of all Fords was still two years away from launch when the Sunny GTI-R was unveiled, it was hardly a fair comparison. Nissan unashamedly had Lancia in their sights when working on the GTI-R – and, rather impressively, they managed to trounce the Italians with relative ease.

A specially uprated five-speed transmission was also developed for the GTI-R, as well as quick-rack power steering for instant response even at high speed. Braking power was assured thanks to ventilated discs up front and ABS as standard, while suspension was taken care of via a fairly uncomplicated independent coil-sprung affair. A limited-slip differential completed the package, helping to ensure the GTI-R was as foolproof as possible, even in relatively inexperienced hands.

The looks department of the GTI-R hadn't been forgotten either – which is just as well really, as the 1990–94 Pulsar/Sunny was never what ▶

▼ No other Pulsar/Sunny looked quite the same as this under the bonnet! Throw into the equation Nissan's new ATTESA four-wheel-drive set-up and you had a heady cocktail of talent at your disposal. (*LAT*)

▶ Work the GTI-R hard and you could see 60mph from standstill in a fraction over six seconds. (*LAT*)

▶ The GTI-R's superb all-wheel-drive system endowed the car with fantastic handling and roadholding capabilities. (*LAT*)

WHAT WE LIKE...

Often overlooked by fans of Escort Cosworths and Lancia Integrales, the GTI-R did everything just as well but with reliability and value for money thrown in for good measure. How many other hot hatches offered 220bhp at such a reasonable price?

...WHAT WE DON'T

It's not unusual for a GTI-R to have been thrashed, trashed or abused during its career. That's why you should buy only the very best example you come across.

you'd call a stunning-looking device. That's why the standard three-door's unadventurous styling was enhanced by a less-than-subtle air scoop on the bonnet and very in-your-face front and rear spoilers. Add into the equation a set of smart 14-inch alloys and you ended up with a Sunny that looked like no other.

Onlookers expecting such an outrageously powerful rally-developed special to be bargain-basement when it came to interior creature comforts were also in for a shock. It's true that this was an Integrale rival, which meant that weight needed to be kept down in order to extract the best performance figures. But even a standard GTI-R would come with electrically-adjustable colour-coded door mirrors, air conditioning and electric windows.

All of which was very nice, but unless the GTI-R drove in a way that would genuinely impress previous pilots of an Integrale, it would be widely considered that Nissan had wasted their time. Happily, this was far from being the case, and that became immediately obvious as soon as the wonderfully throaty 2.0-litre DOHC engine burst into life.

Nissan did an excellent job of keeping turbo lag as minimal as anyone could expect at the start of the1990s. That meant near-instant power at

the driver's disposal, with the kind of acceleration worthy of a performance machine twice as expensive. With 220bhp propelling a hatchback that weighed a mere 1200 kg, it's no wonder the GTI-R was such a road rocket.

Flat out would see 134mph, with 60mph passing by in a shade over 6.0 seconds; and with a few minor mods and tweaks that GTI-R owners are renowned for carrying out these days, it's perfectly possible to get that figure well below the six-second mark. Not bad for a three-door Nissan Sunny hatchback.

Even reading those figures can't fully prepare you for the GTI-R driving experience. It's not just the power at your disposal or the incredible rate at which the thing accelerates; it's the precision and nimbleness of the beast that impress just as much. The super-sharp steering endows the driver with confidence, boosted even more by the astonishing levels of grip on offer.

Point the GTI-R at your favourite bend on your favourite road and just hang on in there. This car will take you round faster, safer and with more driver feedback than anything else you can buy for reasonable money these days. There's no need to slow down or to brake in preparation; you've got all the handling and roadholding capabilities at your disposal that other hot hatch drivers usually only dream of. And unlike so many of the more fragile offerings designed by other

companies, the GTI-R will do all this reliably, dependably and uncomplainingly.

How sad then, that the Sunny GTI-R never created the niche for itself in the UK that the Escort Cosworth subsequently enjoyed. The GTI-R wasn't even an expensive car in its day, being quite a bit cheaper than the Lancia Integrale at the time. Maybe in the end, 'Nissan' and 'Sunny' badges just hadn't got the same level of exciting appeal to punters as 'Integrale' or 'Cosworth'. Yes, perhaps that's it.

Ridiculous, isn't it? So many people missing out on such a superb driving experience, simply because Nissan wasn't an iconic manufacturer of 'superhatches' in the same way as Lancia or Ford. Well, it was Joe Public's loss. And all these years on, it's a major gain for anybody lucky enough to have snapped up a bargain-priced 'grey' import GTI-R. It's one of the finest ways of having fun without being naked. ∎

TIMELINE

1990	Outrageous GTI-R version of Pulsar/Sunny launched
1994	Production ceases

NISSAN
SKYLINE GT-R
the outrageous one

Road testers of the 1990s often referred to the Skyline GT-R as the very best performance car ever to come out of Japan. And when you bear in mind that such a claim placed it ahead of such luminaries as the Honda NSX and Toyota Supra Twin Turbo, this must have been a very special beast indeed.

Well, of course it was. In R33 V-spec guise, the few official UK imports of the GT-R produced from 1997 onwards managed to pump out a mighty 277bhp at 6800rpm, which translated into an artificially limited top speed of 155mph and a background-blurring 0–60mph time of under five seconds. This placed the Skyline GT-R well and truly in the supercar performance league, a previously undiscovered sector of the market for Nissan in the UK. Some stunning performance machines and desirable coupés had been launched by Nissan over the years, but nothing to compare with the all-conquering capabilities of the Skyline GT-R.

What many followers of Japanese fashion don't realise is that the Skyline name dates right back to the beginning of the 1960s and, even more surprisingly, the very first high-performance version appeared as early as 1964. That model, known as the S54 2000GT-B, was developed primarily for competition use and proved a formidable challenge to the purpose-built Porsche 904GTS race cars of the time.

The GT-B's successor (known officially as the 2000GT-R) saw the arrival of the now famous GT-R badge for the first time. Again, it was an awesome machine, its 160bhp straight-six engine endowing it with enough testosterone to guarantee no fewer than fifty outright wins in various Japanese saloon car races by the time production ceased in 1972.

Rather bizarrely, the highly successful GT-R moniker then went into hibernation for a disappointing seventeen years, finally re-emerging in 1989 for the all-new R32 series

R33 GT-R V-SPEC

ENGINE: 2568cc DOHC fuel-injected 24-valve straight-six with twin Garrett T25 turbochargers and dual intercoolers

POWER: 277bhp @ 6800rpm

TORQUE: 271lb ft @ 4400rpm

PERFORMANCE: Top speed 155mph, 0–60mph 4.9 secs

TRANSMISSION: Five-speed manual

CHASSIS: Speed-sensitive power-assisted rack-and-pinion steering with super-HICAS four-wheel steering; independent multi-link coil-spring suspension all round with front and rear anti-roll bars; ATTESA ET-S PRO part-time electronically-controlled four-wheel drive with active LSD; ventilated disc brakes all round

Skyline. The power source this time was a 2.6-litre twin-cam straight-six with twin turbochargers and an intercooler, linked to a superbly sophisticated chassis that incorporated electronically-controlled four-wheel drive and four-wheel steering. The result was a Nissan coupé with the kind of performance normally associated with products from Stuttgart or Milan. The GT-R had really come of age.

Things improved still further in 1995 when the new R33 series Skyline appeared – and it's this model that most enthusiasts think of when they conjure up images of a Skyline GT-R. The R33 was bigger than its predecessor, boasting an altogether larger bodyshell and longer wheelbase. But with more power on tap than before, the newcomer had no problem offering even more tremendous performance, and one of the most exhilarating driving experiences of the decade.

It didn't take long for unofficially imported examples of the R33 GT-R to start appearing on British roads (and elsewhere in the world), despite this being a model developed primarily

for its home market. UK-based enthusiasts who could afford one of the most exciting production cars of the mid-1990s were soon queuing up for a chance to get behind the wheel of their own example; yet the response from Nissan GB was to wait until 1997 for the GT-R to become available as an official UK import.

Even then, it was announced that a mere 100 examples would be brought to Britain, a figure that seemed absurdly small even when the fairly high official list price was taken into account. Exclusivity would be guaranteed, it seemed. ▶

▲ The GT-R's specification sheet makes for a complex read – and it all starts with the twin-turbocharged 2.6-litre straight-six motor, kept under control by the Skyline's four-wheel drive system with active LSD. (*Nissan*)

◀ A brace of Skylines battling it out on the track always makes for an entertaining experience. (*Zoë Harrison*)

UK-spec GT-Rs were all V-spec versions, offering stiffened suspension and an even more sophisticated all-wheel-drive system. And in *Autocar* magazine's first official road test of the UK-spec GT-R in October 1997, testers were overwhelmed by what they experienced: 'What distinguishes the Skyline from most other ultra-quick transport is that it successfully blends a huge amount of technological achievement with an even bigger level of tactile communication. And in doing so it ends up offering the best of both worlds on the road: titanic speed and peerless all-weather stability mated to exquisite feel and supreme driver involvement.'

At the heart of such praise was the cleverness of the new GT-R's technology, an impressive gathering of some of the most sophisticated ideas in the business. Not that there was anything particularly sophisticated about the Skyline's powerplant, for this was an engine that relied on massive Garrett T25 twin turbochargers and dual intercoolers for its sheer brute force. Even so, it was – and still is – a hugely efficient engine, its DOHC 24-valve straight-six design being a great base to work from. It was always

an engine that relied on good-old-fashioned turbochargers to achieve its awesome true potential – but there's absolutely nothing wrong with that.

It was the Skyline's chassis that really created the unique driving experience, and it all started with what Nissan referred to as its ATTESA ET-S PRO part-time electronically-controlled four-wheel-drive system with active LSD. This was a fully automatic all-wheel-drive set-up that directed all the GT-R's drive to the rear wheels under normal conditions. Electronic sensors would then monitor individual wheel speed, longitudinal and lateral acceleration, throttle opening and brake-light activation to give a clear idea of wheelspin, stability and driver intention. When the need arose, the whole system could then transfer anything up to half the engine's torque at any one time directly to the front wheels for the ultimate in stability, particularly when accelerating out of corners.

Then there was the Skyline's impressive four-wheel steering, referred to as super-HICAS by Nissan, a system that involved various high-tech sensors to deduce whether a driver's steering input matched what the car was actually doing. Any discrepancies would bring the electronically-controlled rear-wheel steering into play, via a small electric steering rack. In a corner, the rear wheels would initially steer in the opposite direction to the front wheels, to create oversteer and to sharpen the initial steering response; on sensing that the car had responded, the rear wheels would then steer the same way as the fronts, creating understeer and helping to bring the machine safely out of the corner, almost irrespective of its speed at the time.

Such technological advances were great news for Nissan, as they created headline-grabbing credentials for its awesomely quick new flagship. But for Skyline owners, surely some of the thrills of on-the-limit driving had now diminished? Could the GT-R V-spec really be so exciting and rewarding to drive when it came laden down with technology, gizmos and gadgets?

Yes, without a doubt. In fact, in their in-depth road test in 1997, *Autocar* magazine's testers were astonished at the brilliant feedback provided by the incredibly quick newcomer: 'Given the amount of technology that's bubbling away beneath the Skyline GT-R's skin, it might be asking too much for it also to be one of the great communicators. Not so. By painstaking development of the chassis around the Nürburgring, Nissan has somehow managed to create a car that will not only astound drivers with its outrageous objective handling capabilities but also one that is bursting with feel and feedback.'

Autocar seemed particularly impressed with the Skyline's steering and sophisticated all-wheel-drive system: 'Although there can be drive to the front to theoretically corrupt the flow of information, not to mention an extra electronic steering rack at the rear, the relationship between tarmac, wheel rim and driver's ▶

WHAT WE LIKE...

Often described as Japan's best-ever performance car, and justifiably so. Road testers of the time reckoned there was nothing of comparable price that could outperform a Skyline GT-R point-to-point in any road conditions, and we're inclined to agree. That this is probably still the case all these years on is little short of remarkable.

...WHAT WE DON'T

Fail to make use of the Skyline's amazingly slick gear change and you might find turbo lag a bit of a pain. The solution? Change down a cog, keep the twin turbos working overtime and concentrate on making very, very rapid progress.

▼ Three letters guaranteed to get any Japanese petrolhead's pulse quickening! (*Zoë Harrison*)

▲ Fully equipped interior was what you'd expect – and what you got – from such an upmarket Japanese super-coupé. (*NISMO*)

◥ Lower yourself into the superbly contoured driver's seat and ready yourself for one of the most mind-blowing experiences of your automotive life… (*NISMO*)

fingers is as intimate as it is in any Porsche currently on sale.'

The key to such feedback lay in the fact that the Skyline's four-wheel drive managed to completely disengage drive to the front wheels under normal conditions, thus endowing the GT-R with all the feel of a big, traditional and very responsive rear-drive monster. *Autocar* called all this a '…unique combination of grip, body control, handling stability and plain-old seat-of-the-pants communication.' And it all worked brilliantly.

Even the shortest of enthusiastic test drives in a GT-R V-spec would demonstrate these attributes perfectly, for no other machine existed in the mid-1990s that managed to offer quite such an amazing mix. The excitement started as soon as the good-old straight-six powerplant rumbled into life, a blip of the throttle giving an aural clue as to what was about to happen. Bigger, more powerful engines existed in other Japanese cars back then, of course, but there was something very special about this Nissan lump. And something very thrilling about the way it propelled the Skyline so brilliantly.

A standard 277bhp from the R33 GT-R V-spec may not have been much more impressive than the Honda NSX's output, despite the Nissan's prodigious use of twin turbochargers. But its torque figure of 271lb ft at a commendably low (by turbo standards) 4400rpm provided great acceleration. And the fact that the all-wheel-drive set-up and active LSD combined to reduce standing-start wheelspin to an absolute minimum meant there was little else

on the road that could compete with a GT-R away from the line.

In mid-range too, the Nissan's acceleration was simply astonishing. A 155mph top speed and 0–60mph time of under 5.0 seconds are all well and good, but it's overtaking-style acceleration that's particularly useful. And here again, the GT-R didn't disappoint, achieving a 30–70mph time through the gears of just 4.7 seconds, with 30–50mph in second gear taking a mere 2.3 seconds.

To achieve such impressive figures it was essential to keep the revs high and ensure the twin Garrett turbochargers were working overtime. Fall into the trap of remaining in too high a gear when you needed extra oomph and you'd find the GT-R suffering from disappointing turbo lag and a drastically

less exciting feel to the whole experience. But by making full use of the slick five-speed transmission, dropping down a cog or two when the need arose for the most rapid acceleration available, progress Skyline-style was quicker than in anything else at anywhere near the price.

Speed and power alone don't automatically make a car fun to drive, but the Skyline still ranked as one of the most thrilling, exhilarating, and communicative performance machines ever created, because, for much of the time, it didn't behave like a four-wheel-drive machine at all. It felt exactly like a monstrous-engined rear-drive behemoth, almost in the old American muscle-car mould of the 1960s, which meant that despite being just about as high-tech as it was possible to be in the 1990s, the GT-R never felt clinical, anonymous or characterless.

It was a knack that other manufacturers hadn't quite understood prior to this, with the Mitsubishi 3000GT springing to mind as an obvious example. Like the Skyline, it also offered four-wheel drive, four-wheel steer and oodles of adrenalin-pumping power. Unlike the Nissan, the Mitsubishi felt almost bland by comparison. The Skyline was the most exciting thing to come out of Japan in a very long time, insisted its growing army of fans around the world.

Even so, how many enthusiasts would be able to afford a UK-spec Skyline GT-R, complete with its official new three-year warranty? In reality, of course, Nissan had no trouble selling its allocation of one-hundred GT-Rs to fanatical British buyers, and the car was soon being regarded as an absolute legend in its own lifetime. Even so, could its high price tag actually be justified?

To put it into perspective, let's not forget that the cheapest Honda NSX on offer at the same time cost almost 40% more than the Nissan, and the most affordable Porsche 911 of 1997, the Carrera, offered an impressive 285bhp but cost over 20% more in the process.

Perhaps the closest on-paper rival to the GT-R was the Jaguar XK8 coupé, retailing at the same price in 1997 – but with an output of 290bhp, exceeding the Skyline's figure by a healthy 13bhp. But in reality the two machines could scarcely be compared, for the Jaguar was a smooth and sophisticated grand-touring coupé for the managing director, while the Nissan was an ▶

▼ Serious upgrades have been a major part of the Skyline's following over the years – hence the NISMO-developed GT-R Z-Tune, a 500bhp monster based on the late-model R34 series. Even more highly developed Z-Tune versions have been known to develop 600bhp-plus, especially in competition use. (NISMO)

uncompromising performance machine for the hardened petrolhead. They may have boasted not dissimilar power outputs, but it was the way in which that power was delivered that proved the XK8 and GT-R could scarcely be considered true rivals.

In that sense, the arrival of the British-spec Skyline GT-R in the autumn of 1997 meant the launch of a genuinely unique machine that didn't fall into any particular category or market sector. It had few, if any, real rivals and it had an appeal that couldn't truly be compared with any other performance car of the time. Nissan had achieved the seemingly impossible; and all that from a company more used to the British buying Micras and Primeras.

Hardened enthusiasts didn't need to wait for the arrival of the officially-imported Skyline, of course, in order to get their hands on one. This was a car that was soon making a name for itself as a 'grey' import, creating a strong but niche following among fanatics bored with what else was around at the time. Of course, they also had

to be the kind of enthusiasts who could afford a Group 20 insurance rating.

Development of the Skyline GT-R didn't end with the R33, of course, for 1999 saw the arrival of the extensively new R34 series, a marginally smaller car complete with engine upgrades, new-style ceramic twin turbochargers designed for a sharper, almost instantaneous response and – crucially – a slick six-speed gearbox. The new V-spec version also included in its standard equipment front and rear diffusers to create extra downforce at speed, adding to the car's stability and even its cornering prowess. And it was needed, for despite an official power output of 276bhp (all part of a gentleman's agreement at the time to artificially limit the power from Japanese performance cars), an unofficial reality of 320bhp was nearer the mark.

It was enough for *Autocar* magazine, in a back-to-back comparison between the new R34 GT-R and the substantially cheaper Mitsubishi Evo VI in August 1999, to explain '…there is, in the end, no real loser in a showdown like this, despite the fact that everyone involved in the test thought the Skyline to be the superior machine.' As with the R33, just 100 examples of the new R34 would be officially sold in the UK.

By the beginning of 2002, the R34 was nearing the end of its very successful production run, which was followed by the launch of a run-out limited edition model known as the GT-R Nur. With a more accurately balanced engine design based on Nissan's N1-specification powerplant used in the Nürburgring's 24-hour race and Japan's own Super Taikyu series (at both of which the Skyline had traditionally excelled), the GT-R Nur was instantly hailed as one of the most desirable Skylines ever produced.

It was a fitting end for a machine that had changed Nissan's image in such a major way, a car that had proved beyond all doubt that Japan could indeed produce machinery to rival the very best supercars in the world. The only downside was that, as the very last Skyline GT-R rolled off the line in August 2002, it was made clear by Nissan that a replacement for this modern legend was far from imminent.

In fact, at the time of writing it's thought that an all-new Skyline GT-R won't be bursting onto the world stage until 2007, ready for the 2008 model year. The good news is that the newcomer may well end up being sold officially in the USA for the first time, albeit badged as an Infiniti.

That doesn't stop the R33 and R34 GT-Rs from continuing to enjoy their legendary status today, as well as offering immense potential to fans of modified cars. It's a relatively easy procedure for a replacement engine-management chip to push a GT-R's output close to the 500bhp mark, while seriously reworked examples have been known to pump out almost twice that amount. But even a standard GT-R V-spec will provide the most amazing spread of performance across its extensive rev range, its twin turbochargers, four-wheel drive and four-wheel steering all combining to produce some of the greatest driver thrills you're ever likely to experience.

It's no wonder so many fanatics remain convinced that this is the very best high-performance Japanese car of all time. ∎

TIMELINE

1989	GT-R version of then-current R32 Skyline launches in Japan in August
1991	Safety improvements included fitment of side door beams
1993	V-Spec GT-R with Brembo brakes and 17-inch wheels introduced
1995	GT-R version of new R33 Skyline launches in January
1995	New V-Spec version incorporates ATTESA E-TS PRO four-wheel drive
1997	Xenon headlamps and passenger airbag added to GT-R's spec
1999	GT-R version of new R34 Skyline announced in January
1999	V-spec version launches to include active LSD
2000	V-Spec Grade 2 brings bigger brakes and carbon fibre bonnet
2002	Final-edition GT-R Nur launches in Japan in February
2002	Skyline GT-R production ceases in August

▼ With the last Skyline GT-R produced by the end of 2002 and no immediate replacement in sight, it was the end of an era for fans of the Nissan supercar. (NISMO)

NISSAN
350Z

return of a legend

▲ A stunning looking creation from any angle, the new 350Z blended contemporary style with influences from the original and still stunning 240Z. It was a recipe that worked brilliantly. (Nissan)

If Nissan was to stand out in the 21st century as more than just a manufacturer of worthy but dull saloons, estates and MPVs, it had to grab back some of the limelight it had lost over the years. The logical solution to that lay in exploiting the legend of the 'Z cars' all over again. What Nissan needed was a new Z, the kind of performance machine that would generate as much excitement in the early years of the new century as the original Datsun 240Z did at the start of the 1970s.

The result was the amazing Nissan 350Z, a 276bhp V6-powered rear-wheel-drive two-seater coupé with scorching performance, impressive handling and looks to die for. Nissan's legendary Z series was back on the automotive map at long last. For fans of high-performance coupés throughout the world, this could only be good news.

Near-production-ready examples of the 350Z were seen as early as the beginning of 2001,

when Nissan took the wraps off its exciting newcomer at the North American International Auto Show in Detroit. It was predicted the Z would be on sale in the USA and Canada by mid-2002, going on to join other export markets throughout the subsequent twelve months or so.

To say the new 350Z took the show by storm would be a major understatement. Here, at last, was a successor to the old 300ZX, itself a brutal looking machine that was also a bit of an unpredictable beast in the wrong hands. Would the all-new 350Z be any different, whilst still being exciting enough to do the Z brand justice?

Of course it would. How could any car that looked so stunning and with such pedigree behind it not be a world-beater? The biggest challenge to face Nissan was making sure the 350Z appealed in equal measures to all the world's major markets.

Naturally, the new 350Z had to be a success in its homeland. Equally, it needed to establish

SPEC

ENGINE: 3498cc quad-cam fuel-injected all-alloy 24-valve V6

POWER: 276bhp @ 6200rpm

TORQUE: 363Nm @ 4800rpm

PERFORMANCE: Top speed 155mph, 0–60mph 5.9 secs

TRANSMISSION: Six-speed manual

CHASSIS: Rack-and-pinion power-assisted steering; double-wishbone multi-link independent coil-spring suspension; Brembo disc brakes all round (front: vented discs with four callipers) plus ABS and EBD

◀ Three-and-a-half litres of V6 power gave the 350Z superb performance and a thrilling driving style, both essential ingredients if the newcomer was to be a success. *(Nissan)*

strong sales in the USA, Canada and throughout Europe if it was to make financial sense for its Japanese maker, so the car's final specification was tweaked slightly for each market, particularly in Europe. Nissan's own research showed that nearly 60 per cent of European upmarket coupé owners used their cars every day for commuting, unlike in the USA and Japan. This meant carrying out work to improve the ride quality of the 350Z for European consumption, as well as reducing its NVH (noise, vibration and harshness) effect.

Whatever the minor differences between the different export markets, some things were destined to remain the same across the board – and that included the 350Z's amazing 3.5-litre all-alloy 24-valve V6. This impressive unit was a development of Nissan's VQ engine series, of which more than half a million are produced each year at the company's Iwaki plant, renowned as one of the most advanced engine assembly facilities in the world. To fit in the 350Z, the VQ engine was the subject of serious modifications; in particular, changes to its intake and exhaust systems allowed better breathing, resulting in higher power and torque figures across the broad rev band. ▶

◤ Every detail of the 350Z suggested mean and purposeful. *(Nissan)*

▼ Fantastically styled dashboard was both ergonomically brilliant and exciting to look at. *(Nissan)*

▲ In side profile, the 350Z's influences from earlier Z-series models are obvious. It was a clever job, and one that proved immediately popular with potential buyers. (Nissan)

▶ An exciting place to find yourself, given the 276bhp that lay under the long bonnet, stretching away in front of you. (Nissan)

WHAT WE LIKE...

Nissan's legendary Z series deserved a makeover for the 21st century, but few pundits were prepared for just how amazing the new 350Z would be. Fantastic styling, scorching performance and a glorious V6 that just howls its way up to 155mph flat-out. Nissan's Z is back with a bang.

...WHAT WE DON'T

It's so good looking, so fast and so very desirable, traffic cops will hate you and BMW drivers will see you as a challenge. Just let them try...

It is the power of the 350Z that makes itself immediately obvious as soon as you lower yourself into the driver's seat and fire up the 276bhp that lies ahead of you. Maximum power is generated at 6200rpm, so there is a lot of adrenalin-pumping action when you make the most of this rev-happy engine's playful nature. But it's not just the power at your disposal that thrills;

it's also the magnificent sound quality of the engine that sends a tingle down your spine. There's nothing quite like the sound of a really well-sorted V6 to get things off to a flying start – and without doubt, the 350Z has one of the finest V6s you're likely to find in any car at any price.

Britain's *Top Gear* magazine, on awarding the 350Z its Car Of The Year title in 2004, had nothing but praise for the Nissan's powerful heart: 'The 350Z has a fruity rasp, hinting at the fun to be had from its 3.5-litre V6 engine. From standstill to 60mph takes just 5.9 seconds and top speed is 155mph. No, it hasn't rewritten the record books, but those figures are pretty respectable. None of us have found the 350Z wanting

when it comes to enjoying it on the road. The 276bhp goes through a six-speed gearbox with a precise short-throw action. Racing changes? Easy.'

Top Gear was right to heap so much praise on to both the 350Z's engine and its transmission, the latter being notable for its amazingly slick action and the speed with which gear changes can be accomplished. All this helps to make the most of every single horsepower burbling away under the Nissan's bonnet.

The engine itself is situated well back in the 350Z, a substantial way behind the front axle, in fact, leading Nissan to describe it as 'front/mid-mounted'. That's probably a bit of an ambitious description, although it does help to explain the 350's impressive 53/47 per cent front-to-rear weight distribution, aided by a particularly low centre of gravity. This all gets even better when you realise that the extra weight over the front wheels helps provide better traction for sharper turn-in. Then, as the driver accelerates out of the apex, the weight distribution transfers towards the rear, helping to create a 50/50 balance when it's needed most.

The 350Z's wide-track chassis houses a sophisticated and effective multi-link independent suspension all round, while class-beating stopping power is catered for by Brembo discs front and rear. Yet there's more to creating a top-handling, super-fast coupé than simply equipping it with all the latest technology ▶

▼ The NISMO-concept 350Z of 2004 showcased a number of upgrades available for the model, including a sports exhaust, deeper front spoiler, dramatic 19-inch five-spoke alloys and a whole lot more. And you thought the standard 350Z looked cool... *(Nissan)*

▶ To celebrate 35 years of the Z-series, Nissan launched this very special version of the 350Z in January 2005. Launched in conjunction with Sony PlayStation's Gran Turismo 4, the 300bhp creation was limited to a mere 176 units and was an almost immediate sell-out. *(Nissan)*

under the skin; the bodyshell itself also needs to be exceptionally rigid if it is to do the potentially promising handling capabilities full justice.

Happily, the 350Z excels in this area too, its torsional rigidity being almost as impressive as it's possible to be. At the rear, a complex A-shaped subframe is augmented by a substantial bracing tower which runs the full width of the luggage area and is visible through the rear tailgate. Meanwhile, a hollow steel strut bracing bar, filled with reinforced urethane for optimum strength and weight, runs across the engine bay. Extra strength also comes from reinforced joints in the floorpan and a double floor structure above the mid-mounted fuel tank. The result is an exceptionally rigid bodyshell, adding hugely to the confidence-inspiring and unusually 'flat' handling experience.

But no matter how fantastic the 350Z is in terms of its performance, driver appeal and excitement levels, all this would be irrelevant if it didn't look right; if its styling wasn't spot on; if the car didn't ooze sex appeal from every automotive pore. And let's face it; some of Nissan's previous sporty offerings were a bit weak in these areas.

Remember the 280ZX of 1978 and its direct replacement, the first-generation 300ZX of 1983? If not, you're lucky. Fans of the original 240Z treated them with disdain, so overgrown and bloated had the Z-series become by the late 1970s. And if the all-new 350Z was being designed to appeal to all potential buyers in all markets, surely the marketing and design boffins at Nissan could well have made the same mistake all over again.

They could have; but they didn't. The 350Z was an astonishingly good-looking machine, one that managed to combine a contemporary, almost brutal style with architectural overtones of the classic 240Z. In the cold light of day it hardly resembled the 240Z at all, and yet in its detailing and its overall stance it was an obvious descendant.

Inside the 350Z, the dramatic styling theme continued. The compact cabin featured an attention-grabbing, almost triangular roofline which rose quickly to a peak and then fell equally rapidly to a wraparound C-pillar, reminiscent in shape of that of the best of the previous Z-series models. This fusion of soft curves and geometric angles – typified externally by the 'free-form' Xenon headlamps – really set the 350Z apart from the crowd, an effect completed by a number of subtle design touches that included large aluminium-finish door handles and extensive use of the new geometric Z emblem.

The dashboard continued the 350Z's no-compromise sports theme, with a centrally-mounted tachometer dominating the three-instrument binnacle directly facing the driver. For the perfect driving position, the binnacle was attached not to the dashboard but to the steering column, moving with the wheel when the latter was adjusted for height and reach.

In the centre of the dashboard was another reminder of the 350Z's heritage: three small instruments in individually cowled clusters, angled acutely towards the driver. Showing volts, oil pressure and the trip computer, they echoed the style and positioning of three similar dials found in the original 240Z; pretty cool.

With so much going for it, combined with relatively affordable prices for a sporting coupé of such outstanding capabilities, it's not surprising the 350Z got off to such a flying start in every market it entered. Never ones to rest on their laurels, Nissan knew they couldn't leave it untouched forever, so by 2004, some minor modifications had been carried out to the Z's suspension settings and dampers to soften the ride somewhat, without compromising the roll-free handling and impressive grip.

The biggest news of all came the same year when the 350Z Roadster took a bow, a stunning-looking convertible version that had been a twinkle in the eye of Nissan's chief designers from the outset. What a machine! With the same 276bhp V6 powerplant, six-speed super-slick transmission and grin-inducing handling as its coupé brother, how could the Roadster possibly fail? Orders started flooding in, with deliveries in most markets beginning in early 2005. As with the launch of the 'standard' 350Z before it, a waiting list for the Z Roadster was building within just a few days of the order book opening.

So where else could Nissan take the 350Z now that the coupé and Roadster versions were both on sale? Even faster, is the obvious answer – hence the arrival of the 350Z Gran Turismo 4 (in association with Sony PlayStation) at the beginning of 2005. This near-300bhp limited-edition model, of which just 176 examples would be sold in the UK, managed to knock 0.1 of a second off the 350Z's already impressive 0–60mph time of 5.9 seconds, as well as featuring lacquered 18-inch alloys and a choice of special yellow or black paintwork. The ultimate 350Z had arrived. And like every other 350Z before, it was an immediate sell-out. ∎

TIMELINE

2001	350Z announced to rave reviews worldwide
2002	Japanese and American sales begin by June
2003	350Z goes on sale in UK in October
2003	GT pack option features part-leather interior and upgraded sound system
2004	UK's *Top Gear* magazine hails 350Z its Car Of The Year
2004	Modification to shock absorbers improves ride quality
2004	UK orders begin for 350Z Roadster in October
2005	300bhp 350Z Gran Turismo 4 launched at UK's Autosport International
2005	350Z Roadster goes on sale in most export markets

▼ Perhaps it was only a matter of time before the stunning 350Z coupé evolved into an equally impressive full convertible. By 2005, the 350Z Roadster was proving yet another sales success for the Z line. (Nissan)

SUBARU
IMPREZA TURBO
the new power generation

Before the now legendary Impreza Turbo burst onto the performance car scene for Subaru's 1993 model year, such levels of power, performance and grip had only ever been available to drivers of far more expensive machinery. That in itself was remarkable. But what really made the 'blown' Impreza stand out was that it came from a company historically renowned for all-wheel-drive workhorses, the kind of vehicles that farmers swore by and the vast majority of townies ignored.

By the time the Impreza Turbo (available as a four-door saloon or five-door semi-estate) went on sale in the UK in the early part of 1994, anticipation was high among enthusiasts that here was a car worth taking very seriously indeed. You had only to look at the power output of 208bhp from its 2.0-litre turbocharged 'flat-four' engine to realise it held promise. But at the price it went on sale in the UK, the whole thing seemed almost too good to be true.

To put it into perspective, cast your mind back to 1994, a time when rally-inspired classics such as the Ford Escort Cosworth and Lancia Delta HF Integrale were still around. The products from both the Blue Oval and the Italian stallion cost a hefty sum more than Subaru's impressive new arrival.

The Impreza may have lacked the attention-grabbing monstrous rear spoiler of the Cosworth and the classic Italian lines of the Integrale; but it still managed to make both of its major European rivals look horrendously overpriced. In fact, the Subaru cost about the same to buy in Britain as a brand new and extremely dull Ford Mondeo 1.8 Ghia – a comparison that soon had petrolheads everywhere laughing all the way to the bank.

Despite the value for money on offer, Impreza drivers found themselves making very few compromises when investing in a Turbo of their own. From about 75mph upwards, the Subaru's mid-range acceleration would lag marginally ▶

1994 IMPREZA TURBO FOUR-DOOR

ENGINE: 1994cc fuel-injected 16-valve horizontally-opposed DOHC four-cylinder with turbocharger and intercooler

POWER: 208bhp @ 6000rpm

TORQUE: 201lb ft @ 4800rpm

PERFORMANCE: Top speed 137mph, 0–60mph 5.8 secs

TRANSMISSION: Five-speed manual

CHASSIS: Rack-and-pinion power-assisted steering; transverse-link independent coil-spring suspension with rear trailing arms and front/rear anti-roll bars; permanent four-wheel drive with viscous coupling; ventilated disc brakes all round with ABS

2005 IMPREZA WRX FOUR-DOOR

ENGINE: 1994cc fuel-injected 16-valve horizontally-opposed DOHC four-cylinder with turbocharger and intercooler

POWER: 221bhp @ 5600rpm

TORQUE: 221.3lb ft @ 4000rpm

PERFORMANCE: Top speed 144mph, 0–60mph 5.6 secs

TRANSMISSION: Five-speed manual

CHASSIS: Rack-and-pinion speed-sensitive power-assisted steering; transverse-link independent coil-spring suspension with rear trailing arms and front/rear anti-roll bars; permanent four-wheel drive with viscous coupling; rear LSD; ventilated disc brakes all round with ABS

▼ Whichever Impreza Turbo or WRX you choose, you'll find the flat-four turbocharged and intercooled powerplant an absolute revelation compared with some of the less entertaining high-performance offerings from elsewhere. *(Subaru)*

2002 IMPREZA STi PRODRIVE 305PS

ENGINE: 1994cc fuel-injected 16-valve horizontally-opposed DOHC four-cylinder with turbocharger/intercooler and uprated ECU

POWER: 300bhp @ 6000rpm

TORQUE: 299lb ft @ 4000rpm

PERFORMANCE: Top speed 155mph, 0–60mph 4.6 secs

TRANSMISSION: Six-speed manual

CHASSIS: Rack-and-pinion speed-sensitive power-assisted steering; transverse-link independent coil-spring suspension with inverted suspension struts and front/rear anti-roll bars; permanent four-wheel drive with viscous coupling; front and rear LSDs; Brembo ventilated disc brakes all round with ABS

▲ The first-generation Impreza Turbo was at its best looking in four-door saloon guise, though most fans were inevitably more attracted by its class-leading levels of performance and handling. (Subaru)

▶ Impreza interiors were never the most exciting of styling exercises; but that wasn't a major issue for most buyers. (Subaru)

WHAT WE LIKE...

The Impreza Turbo changed the way we thought about affordable high-performance motoring, offering Cosworth-like levels of performance and grip at a fraction of the cost. For those on an even tighter budget, a second-hand Impreza still offers sensational driver appeal without breaking the bank. It's arguably the most practical high-performance saloon of the last twenty years.

...WHAT WE DON'T

Styling of the five-door Impreza has never been exactly inspirational, and interiors have always seemed a bit drab. But such things are purely subjective. The Impreza Turbo and WRX remain two of the finest performance buys of their time.

behind the Cosworth and the Integrale, but its 137mph top speed meant it was soon catching up. Also, the Impreza's 0–60mph time of just 5.8 seconds saw it absolutely up there with the best of them, while its 30–70mph overtaking time of a mere 6.6 seconds was a match for anything genuinely comparable.

But the Impreza Turbo was about so much more than mere performance figures, for this awesome newcomer was one of the most characterful performance cars to come out of Japan in recent times. Its unique charisma started as soon as you opened the bonnet and took a look at what lay beneath. Like so many other high-performance saloons, the Subaru relied on a 2.0-litre turbocharged and intercooled four-cylinder lump for its rapid propulsion. What made the Impreza different was that it used a 'flat-four' design, often referred to as a Boxer engine, with its cylinders horizontally-opposed rather than working in the traditional vertical style. And, like every other Boxer-engined car ever created, it gave the Impreza a distinctive and very likeable driving style.

Fire up an Impreza engine and you'll revel in what you hear. A Boxer engine will delight anyone within earshot with its burbling, growling note and its eager-sounding nature. When you learn to make the most of the Impreza's high-revving nature and keep the turbocharger working flat out whenever you can, you quickly realise just what a cracking good design it really is.

Happily, the Impreza's delightfully powerful, impressively enthusiastic powerplant is linked to an all-wheel-drive system that handles it all with ease. It's a permanent all-wheel-drive set-up, with torque distributed between the wheels that can use it most via a highly effective viscous coupling. As the system detects loss of traction or a building of wheelspin anywhere, it apportions more of the torque to those wheels with most grip – and it works brilliantly. In normal dry-road conditions, the torque is split almost equally front to rear; but as conditions change and the car gets pushed increasingly harder into corners, the proportions of power distribution vary widely.

It all came together to create a high-performance road-going rocket that could be driven quickly and safely by just about anyone, while still being a machine that oozed character and individuality. Unlike so many other easy-to-drive performance cars over the years, there was nothing clinical or bland about the Impreza Turbo's driving style.

Any owner's first drive in a new Impreza confirmed this. Making the most of the Boxer engine's high revs meant the turbocharger was always on tap, providing a smooth and consistent level of turbo rush from about 3500rpm right up to the 7000-revs red line. It was all so beautifully easy that making the most of an Impreza's surging acceleration inevitably became addictive. No other rally-inspired performance machine of the time sounded quite like an Impreza Turbo or offered quite the same combination of feedback, exhilaration and useable acceleration.

It was enough to make *Autocar* magazine enthuse about Subaru's amazingly quick newcomer in no uncertain terms, describing its 0–60mph dash as '…one that tops the Escort Cosworth, Integrale and, just to shut the snide boys up, the Porsche 968 as well'. And while ▶

TIMELINE

1992	Impreza announced in Japan in October; turbo four-door goes on sale
1993	UK imports of non-turbo models get under way
1993	Five-door turbo goes on sale in Japan in September
1994	245PS WRX STi series launched in Japan in January
1994	UK sales of Impreza Turbo four- and five-door begin in April
1994	WRX STi power increased to 275PS in November
1995	WRX STi-2 launched in August with limited-edition '555' blue colours
1996	STi-2 V-Limited launched with gold wheels and sports-blue paint
1996	All Impreza Turbos now feature restyled bumpers and bigger intercooler
1996	STi-3 introduced with 280PS engine
1997	WRX Type-R STi two-door launched in Japan in January
1997	Limited edition Impreza Turbo Catalunya goes on UK sale in March
1997	STi-3 V-Limited launched with WRC emblem and other features
1997	Suretrac rear LSD now fitted to all Impreza Turbos

▶

◀ Various UK police forces experimented with the Impreza Turbo, its useful mix of compact dimensions and outrageous performance making it ideal for high-speed pursuits. *(Subaru)*

▶ Impreza interiors have improved over the years, with more recent versions offering drastically higher standards of quality and a tad more style. (Subaru)

▶ The Impreza WRC 2003 rally machine lines up alongside its UK-spec STi stablemate. (Subaru)

▼ Subaru's various WRC offerings have enjoyed fantastic success over the years, adding hugely to the Impreza's publicity machine and the car's fanatical following. (Subaru)

the magazine lost no time in criticising the Impreza for its fairly drab cabin and its unimpressive fuel consumption, its testers knew a bargain when they saw it: 'An enthusiast with less than £18,000 could never hope to find himself behind the wheel of a sophisticated four-wheel-drive chassis backed by Cosworth levels of performance,' they claimed. 'Not until the Impreza Turbo 2000, that is.'

It was great news for performance car buyers everywhere, and even better news for followers of the world's rally scene. The Impreza lost no time in establishing itself as a rally-winning legend, setting new standards and grabbing the limelight in the World Rally Championship series. Who could forget the images of Subaru winning the Manufacturer's Title in the 1995 and 1996 WRC, for starters? With Colin McRae at the wheel and the might of Subaru's all-wheel-drive technology at his disposal, it seemed there was no stopping the amazing Impreza Turbo.

As with any car developed for rally success, road-going versions of the Impreza benefited hugely from the lessons learned, leading to the Impreza being acclaimed as one of the most finely-balanced, impressively developed performance machines of its generation. But even that wasn't enough for some buyers, and it wasn't long before highly modified Impreza Turbos were hitting the streets, via both Subaru themselves and scores of independent specialists.

By the beginning of 1994, a 245PS-powered Impreza WRX STi was available in Japan, a car that started the trend for super-performance Subarus. And by the end of that year, the STi's output was increased to 275PS, rising to a heady 280PS by 1996. The following year, all Impreza Turbos and WRX models were fitted with Subaru's new Suretrac limited-slip rear differential for even greater grip and handling, while 1998 saw the arrival of the Impreza's new Phase 2 engine complete with new intake manifold,

redesigned camshafts and, it was claimed, even greater responsiveness.

Certain go-faster Imprezas have achieved cult status over the years, of course, not least the WRX 22B STi two-door coupé of 1998 and the awesome limited-production P1 of 1999. That very same year was when the 236bhp version of the new Prodrive-developed RB5-series Impreza was launched, proving beyond all doubt this specialist company's prowess and understanding of Impreza DNA.

Prodrive had established a name for itself in the world of Subarus by providing the expertise behind the company's world-beating rally machines. So when Prodrive turned its unrivalled attention to road-going Imprezas aimed at people for whom a standard machine just wasn't enough, it's no surprise that every fast-car-loving enthusiast in the land sat up and took notice.

In more recent times, this has culminated in the launch of various Impreza performance packs developed by Prodrive, with up to 265bhp readily available by 2003. Although output remained the same as a standard Impreza STi, the modified version's higher torque figure of 257lb ft at 3500rpm contributed towards the drastically reduced 0–60mph time of just 4.8 seconds, with 0–100mph available in an amazing 14.1 seconds.

The 305PS Performance Pack announced by Subaru the previous October – and again developed by Prodrive – was even more astonishing, its 300bhp capability adding only modestly to the Impreza WRX STi's list price in 2002/03. Not only was power drastically increased but a new torque figure of 299lb ft (up from 253lb ft) at 4000rpm delivered an even higher level of thrills. Zero to 60mph was now ▶

TIMELINE

1998	STi-4 V-Limited launched with more equipment and faster steering rack
1998	WRX 22B STi two-door coupé launched in Japan; just 400 produced
1998	Phase 2 engine arrives with new intake manifold and redesigned camshafts
1998	STi-5 goes on sale in Japan
1999	214bhp RB5 goes on sale in UK in April
1999	236bhp Prodrive version of RB5 also appears
1999	Limited-production P1 on sale in UK from December

▲ The 2004-model WRX five-door – just like its predecessors – combined near-supercar performance with estate car practicality; a rare combination of talent in the market back then. *(Subaru)*

◀ Specialist versions like the WRX 22B STi two-door and the limited-production P1 have helped lift the Impreza's excitement factor to an all-time high over the years. *(Subaru)*

achievable in a blindingly quick 4.6 seconds, with just 12.2 seconds taken to reach 100mph from rest. Subaru's family-friendly performance machine was getting even more serious.

Modified Imprezas are all well and good when it comes to generating headlines around the world, of course, but it's always been the standard Turbo models that have been the mainstay of the range in terms of overall sales figures. And as the latter half of the 1990s began drawing to a close, it was inevitable that Subaru would be bringing out an all-new Impreza for the turn of the century. The original-style model was still doing well, but its styling was starting to date and its novelty factor had waned slightly. The time had come for a freshen-up.

But what actually arrived in 2000 sent a shockwave through Subaru's fan base, for the brand new Impreza line-up announced by the company was more than a bit bizarre looking. As before, it was available in both four- and five-door guises, and from the side and rear views was a perfectly handsome design, its simple lines, blistered wheel arches and smart spoilers endowing it with an effective new look and a lot more attitude. But moving round to the front of the new-style Impreza, most people considered its 'face' to be disastrous.

The Impreza had suddenly become goggle-eyed, its oval headlamps and wide-mouthed grille giving it something of a shocked expression. Subaru hoped Impreza buyers would look beyond the newcomer's odd front, but that was expecting way too much. No matter how powerful, fast or superbly handling a car is, if it possesses looks that are almost laughable

it stands little chance of building on its predecessor's success.

It was a great shame, for in every other sense the turbocharged versions of the new Impreza – now sold in the UK as the WRX – were superb machines. Power output wasn't dissimilar to before at 218bhp from Subaru's highly-praised four-cylinder Boxer engine; but with higher torque levels and a bigger turbo, there was now a far more rapid response to any right-foot antics.

The Impreza's all-wheel-drive chassis was similarly upgraded, the new-look models now offering even higher levels of grip whilst also benefiting from an improvement in ride quality – an important aid to giving the Impreza WRX a more refined, substantial feel than before. Indeed, Subaru's engineers had worked hard on stiffening the Impreza's bodyshell, making it appear more spacious, improving the quality of the car's gear change and generally bringing down noise levels – all in an effort to make the car seem, if anything, a little more Germanic and a touch less raucous and frantic. The Impreza WRX needed to grow up a little, thought Subaru.

The power, performance, handling and roadholding the Impreza had become renowned for were still there, of course, but this time wrapped up in a slightly more sophisticated package. Even so, it was still considered ugly. And that's what would always hold it back.

As soon as the new-for-2000 Impreza range was announced, detrimental comments about its looks were being made by press and public alike – and last-of-the-line examples of the old-style model soon found themselves in greater demand

▼ The Impreza STi 'WR1' of 2004 was a fantastic looking machine with performance and grip to match. Just 500 examples made it to the UK, all of them snapped up by eager enthusiasts. *(Subaru)*

than before. It's little wonder that, in the UK at least, Impreza sales started suffering and the car's previously untarnished image was suddenly less gleaming.

Subaru realised the error of their ways, and a major revamp of the new Impreza's front end was unveiled as early as 2002's Paris Motor Show, the WRX versions going on sale in the UK by January 2003. Fortunately, this time Subaru got things right. The basic shape of both the four- and five-door Imprezas was as before, but the 2003 model year front end was smoother and less startling. The latest headlamps were altogether more handsome, and the restyled grille was less open-mouthed. The Impreza now looked both grown up and sophisticated, albeit two years later than Subaru had originally intended.

This general upgrade of the Impreza range also saw stiffened suspension put in place for an even flatter handling experience, while further engine and turbo tweaks saw the standard power output now increased to 225bhp – or up to 265bhp if buyers opted for the STi version.

Much to Subaru's relief, both the motoring press and the recently disillusioned band of global Impreza fans seemed impressed with the company's latest efforts, and Britain's *Daily Express World Car Guide 2004* claimed the latest versions were '…almost good enough for the Impreza to reclaim its saloon sports car crown'. In a market where the latest development of the Mitsubishi Evo was grabbing the limelight, that was praiseworthy stuff.

Nowadays, brand-new Subaru Impreza WRXs continue to offer spectacular value when compared like for like with other high-performance saloons, their combination of power, performance, handling, roadholding and affordability continuing to give the range a special appeal. But it's on the used market where the Impreza offers the finest value, with well-maintained examples of the early Turbos now available for shockingly small sums.

It's great news for Japanese performance fans everywhere, because it means that more people than ever can now afford to get behind the wheel of their own Impreza Turbo. The fact that an automotive icon like this can be parked on your own driveway without much financial difficulty is surely worthy of major celebration. It's a car that everybody needs to own at least once; be in no doubt about that. ■

TIMELINE

2000	All-new Impreza line-up announced in Japan
2000	New Imprezas on sale in UK from October; all Turbos now badged WRX
2001	215/242bhp WRX UK300 go on sale in UK in May

2002	WRX STi and STi Prodrive launched in UK in January
2002	New 305PS Performance Pack announced for STi in October
2002	Impreza's new front-end styling announced at Paris Motor Show
2003	Latest Imprezas with new front end on sale in UK from January
2003	Better-equipped WRX SL five-door announced in British-spec
2004	WRX STi 'WR1' on sale in UK from March; just 500 available
2004	New suspension and uprated LSD among changes for 2005 model year

▲ The bug-eyed look of 2000-02 was the Impreza's most controversial moment. Subaru realised the error of their ways and changed things for the better for the '03 model year. (Subaru)

SUZUKI
SC100 GX
pint-pot fun

Back in 1979, most of Europe's Suzuki dealers were busy selling tiny four-wheel-drive machines with about as much on-road performance as a roadkill hedgehog. Then along came this: the new SC100 GX, soon nicknamed the Whizzkid by Suzuki's British importers.

It was the size of a Mini, and yet it was a sporting coupé. Admittedly, the Whizzkid had to rely on just 47bhp from its 970cc four-pot OHC engine, which meant it wasn't fantastically quick even by 1970s standards. In fact, its top speed was just this side of 90mph. But with a low-slung driving position, sharp steering and neat handling, it felt much, much faster. And, thanks to independent coil-sprung suspension all round, it handled well enough to make it enormous fun to drive.

It was almost like a mini-Porsche 911, with its rear-engined layout, coupé looks and raucous-sounding powerplant. A Porsche 911, that is, without the power, the performance, or the

ability to give your sex life an immediate boost. But that didn't stop the SC100 GX becoming a major hit (by Suzuki standards) in the UK and elsewhere.

In fact, by the time imports of the Whizzkid

WHAT WE LIKE...

The world's most affordable sporting car at the start of the 1980s was great fun to drive and dirt cheap to keep. It's still missed by enthusiasts with long memories.

...WHAT WE DON'T

Could have done with more power. Most examples have long since rusted away.

ceased in 1982, after a career of just three years, a total of 4,696 British enthusiasts had taken the plunge. And little wonder: with a bargain UK launch price, the little Suzuki was one of the best-value machines on the market.

We'll admit the SC100 GX wasn't perfect. For a start, it was absurdly cramped inside. For a six-footer to squeeze behind the wheel, the driver's seat had to be in its rearmost position, so that it was touching the seat behind. But that didn't seem to matter. Most owners used the 2+2 Whizzkid as a strict two-seater and made the most of a bit of extra luggage space as a result.

Other motorists didn't know what on earth to make of the little Whizzkid, partly because they'd no idea just how inexpensive this Japanese tiddler really was – and for the street cred of SC100 buyers everywhere, that was great news.

Britain's cost-conscious motorists weren't the only ones to take an interest in the Whizzkid. It also caught the attention of Lotus, the Norfolk-based manufacturer of such sporting legends as the mid-engined Esprit; bizarre but true.

In 1982, when the SC100 GX was about to be discontinued to make way for a front-wheel-drive city car going by the name of Alto, Lotus reckoned there was potential to take over production of the Whizzkid in Britain. Demand for the mini marvel was still high, and Lotus could have done with a low-cost sports car with which to boost its sales. Remember, this was a time when General Motors owned Lotus, as well as having a major financial interest in Suzuki. Transferring production of the seriously popular Whizzkid from Suzuki to Lotus was suddenly seen as a logical step.

Even better was that Margaret Thatcher's government of the time was busy handing out grants and subsidies to companies in areas of high unemployment if they could guarantee the creation of new jobs. The plan was starting to take shape.

Can you image – a Lotus-badged Whizzkid with expertly uprated power, performance and handling? It could have taken the affordable sports car market by storm. It could have turned Lotus into a far more successful specialist manufacturer throughout the 1980s. It could have been exactly what young, cash-strapped fanatics looking for a bit of fun on the side had been crying out for.

But it was not to be. In the end, Norfolk was

▼ Neat two-door coupé styling was quite an achievement for a car no bigger than the original-type Mini. No wonder fans mourned the model's passing in 1982. *(LAT)*

TIMELINE

1976 Suzuki Cervo Coupé announced in Japan with two- or four-cylinder engines

1979 Four-cylinder Cervo renamed SC100GX and launched in UK

1982 Cervo and SC100GX production ceased

deemed an area not worthy of a major government grant, and the SC100 GX quietly faded away in 1982. A sad end for a car with so much more potential than Suzuki ever realised. ▓

SUZUKI SWIFT GTI

supermini on steroids

▲ The Swift GTi's enthusiastic nature and 'chuckable' handling meant plenty of smiles-per-mile when new. These days it makes a cracking good used buy, offering exceptional value for money, too. *(LAT)*

In so many ways, the Suzuki Swift of the mid-1980s onwards was an unexceptional little car. It looked good, was cheap to buy and easy to drive – but then, so were a good many other 'superminis' of the time. When it came to boring second cars, most buyers were happier opting for a Nissan Micra instead.

But then Suzuki did the unthinkable, transforming their three-door shopping trolley into one of the most exhilarating machines the company has ever created: the Swift GTI. Suddenly, Suzuki's Micra-rivalling hatchback had something really worth shouting about, and it didn't take long for young petrolheads on a budget to catch on to the idea.

The Swift GTI was propelled by a twin-cam 16-valve version of Suzuki's otherwise ordinary 1298cc OHC powerplant, specially tuned to pump out an impressive 101bhp at just under 6500rpm. Nothing to write home about? It is when the car it's fitted to weighs in at just 820kg unladen,

endowing the Swift with one of the biggest power-to-weight ratios of any tiny hot hatch.

The result was a Suzuki Swift that would hit 60mph in 8.6 seconds, its top speed being an extra 55mph on top of that. Whilst there were other hatches around that would do the all-important 0–60mph run a tad quicker, few could rival the Swift when it came to adrenalin-pumping, wide-grinned thrills.

The front-wheel-drive GTI would storm away from standstill once its wheelspin was under control, accelerating at what felt like a far more rapid rate than even its figures might suggest. The aural quality of the car was fantastic too, its oh-so-eager 1.3-litre twin-cam engine screaming in delight as the driver made the most of its high-revving nature. Fast gear changes via the standard five-speed 'box added to the fun factor, as did the sharp and precise handling provided by the front-strut, coil-sprung suspension set-up.

Certainly, the Swift GTI was lacking in certain

areas. Its ride was rock hard, its noise levels were high and its lack of weight meant it felt a bit flimsier than a more grown-up hatch. But who cared about all that? The Swift was suddenly attracting hoards of younger buyers who were delighted by its fun factor and sheer affordability.

Make no mistake, the Swift GTI offered fantastic value in its day – and still does now. Halfway through its life, in 1991, this tiny 101bhp funster retailed in the UK at a price that compared favourably with the 90bhp Ford Fiesta 1.6S, the 90bhp Rover Metro GTa and the 72bhp Vauxhall Nova 1.4 SR. None of that dreary threesome could compete with the Suzuki when it came to power, performance, driver enjoyment or value for money.

The Swift range ended up rather sadly in its latter days, with the GTI version disappearing by 1996, leaving just a handful of lowly versions to choose from – by then all built in Hungary. Suzuki did experiment with a 1.6-litre 4x4 version, but this was generally considered a silly idea. That the Swift range continued to be sold until 2004 is impressive; that the GTI disappeared eight years before that is a crying shame. An all-new Swift arrived in 2005, more sophisticated and more grown-up; but a true GTI replacement was nowhere to be seen.

As a used buy now, there's little to touch the Swift GTI. It's cheap, it's just as much fun as it ever was and it's technologically less complicated than its Daihatsu Charade GTti rival – and that can only mean good news for later-life reliability. It's still a tempting prospect. ▩

SPEC

ENGINE: 1298cc twin-cam 16-valve fuel-injected four-cylinder

POWER: 101bhp @ 6450rpm

TORQUE: 83lb ft @ 4950rpm

PERFORMANCE: Top speed 115mph, 0–60mph 8.6 secs

TRANSMISSION: Five-speed manual

CHASSIS: Rack-and-pinion steering; independent coil-spring suspension all round; front and rear disc brakes

▼ An output of 101bhp from a 1.3-litre four-pot was healthy enough. Installed in the lightweight Swift GTi though, it resulted in best-in-class performance. *(LAT)*

TIMELINE

1986	1.3 GTI model joins the latest Swift line-up
1986	UK sales of GTI begin in November
1988	New-look Swift unveiled with more restyled front end
1996	GTI production ceases

WHAT WE LIKE...

It might not be the fastest hot hatch you'll ever drive, but it is a lot of fun. And, crucially, it feels very fast indeed. Even now, a well-preserved Swift GTI is one of the best entries into affordable performance motoring.

...WHAT WE DON'T

Lightweight design means it can feel flimsy and a bit tinny compared with some of the competition. But the Suzuki's value for money and fun appeal more than make up for this.

TOYOTA CELICA
four decades of fun

▲ The seventh-generation Celica range brought dramatic new styling that ensured it stood out in any crowd. By 2005 it was offered in top-of-the-range GT guise, complete with 190bhp, 1.8-litre VVTL-i engine and handling to match. *(Toyota)*

With an ancestry dating right back to 1970, the Toyota Celica has a complex history. So far, no fewer than seven generations of Celica have been launched around the globe, making this one of the most successful coupé lineages the world has ever seen. With the latest versions providing power and performance by the bucket load, the Celica's popularity continues to grow. There's just no stopping this longest-lived of all sporting Toyotas, it seems.

The Celica made its public debut at the 1970 Tokyo Motor Show and marked a major turning point for Toyota. The car's stylists had been unashamedly influenced by America's Ford Mustang of the time, and it was a concept that worked brilliantly. The new Celica's chunky, handsome styling was exactly what American and European coupé buyers were looking for, and the car became an instant hit in almost every market it entered. Toyota had created their first model designed specifically with exports as its main priority.

The Celica first came to Europe in mid-1971, equipped with a 1.6-litre four-cylinder engine. A little while later, the popular Liftback series was announced, with 1.6- and 2.0-litre powerplants, going on sale in Japan from April 1973 and arriving in the UK by 1976.

The most popular version in Britain was the Celica 1600GT Coupé, a machine with real driver appeal thanks to its 1588cc DOHC twin-carburettor engine churning out a very impressive (for the time) 104bhp at 6200rpm. With classic rear-drive handling to match, and all that power fed through an ultra-slick five-speed transmission, the Celica was enough to make homegrown products such as the MGB GT look positively archaic.

Road-going Celicas were real fun machines, and out on the track the newcomer was equally competitive. The climax of this came at the end of 1975 when Win Percy was declared the winner of the 1600 Class of the British Saloon Car

Championship (forerunner of the BTCC), a title he managed to retain the following year. The Celica had arrived in Britain with a bang.

Over a million first-generation Celicas had been sold around the world by the time the Series II models were unveiled in August 1977. These newcomers were larger than their predecessors and, once again, were available in Coupé or Liftback forms, this time with a decent choice of engine, transmission and trim options. The styling seemed softer than that of the original Celica, a point made by many fans of the old-style model. But as Toyota's answer to Europe's Ford Capri and as a worthy and reliable addition to the market, the Series II Celica soon found friends. With 118bhp from its new 1968cc DOHC twin-carb engine, they didn't waste time in discovering just how much fun it could be. ▶

SPEC

CELICA SERIES I 1600 GT COUPÉ

ENGINE: 1588cc DOHC twin-carburettor four-cylinder

POWER: 104bhp @ 6200rpm

TORQUE: 101lb ft @ 4200rpm

PERFORMANCE: Top speed 116mph, 0–60mph 10.2 secs

TRANSMISSION: Five-speed manual

CHASSIS: Recirculating ball steering; independent front coil-spring suspension with MacPherson struts; live rear axle with coil springs; servo-assisted front disc and rear drum brakes

CELICA SERIES IV GT-FOUR

ENGINE: 1998cc DOHC fuel-injected 16-valve turbocharged four-cylinder

POWER: 182bhp @ 6000rpm

TORQUE: 184lb ft @ 3600rpm

PERFORMANCE: Top speed 138mph, 0–60mph 7.8 secs

TRANSMISSION: Five-speed manual

CHASSIS: Rack-and-pinion power-assisted steering; independent coil-spring suspension all round with viscous coupling and permanent four-wheel drive; disc brakes all with ABS

CELICA SERIES VII 1.8 T SPORT

ENGINE: 1796cc DOHC fuel-injected 16-valve VVTL-i four-cylinder

POWER: 180Nm @ 6800rpm

TORQUE: 221.3lb ft @ 4000rpm

PERFORMANCE: Top speed 140mph, 0–60mph 7.4 secs

TRANSMISSION: Six-speed manual

CHASSIS: Rack-and-pinion power-assisted steering; independent coil-spring suspension all round with vehicle stability control and traction control; ventilated disc brakes all round with ABS and brake assist

▲ Toyota's expertise with variable valve timing has meant superb performance for more recent examples of the Celica. *(Toyota)*

▲ The addition of a Liftback model to the original Celica line-up meant useful expansion of the range. The Ford Mustang-influenced styling was obvious but successful. *(Toyota)*

▼ The original Celica, a stunning looking car by the standards of 1970, combined real driver appeal with Toyota's legendary reliability and low running costs. *(Toyota)*

The Series II's styling couldn't have been a greater contrast with what had gone before when the third-generation Celica was announced for 1983, its sharper lines fitting in well with the new ideas for the1980s. This was also the series that saw the first Celica Convertible launched in some export markets, and it was the Series III Celica that chalked up the first of many World Rally Championship victories for Toyota – an amazing seven in all by the end of 1986.

Announced in August 1985, the fourth-generation Celica gained an all-new body and, for the first time ever, front-wheel drive. It came with a 2.0-litre 16-valve engine for the European

WHAT WE LIKE...

Early Celicas now have real classic appeal and are becoming collectable among followers of the1970s. For the rest of us, a Series VI or VII Celica manages to offer great performance, entertaining handling and genuine affordability in a very tempting package.

...WHAT WE DON'T

Most Celicas of the 1970s have long since rotted away, while those from the 1980s have often been thrashed beyond belief, contributing to their low values now. Find a good one, though, and you've got a cracking coupé on your hands – whichever version you opt for.

market, and quickly gained a reputation for fine handling and balance. The new Celica also brought the company an immense amount of publicity through its success in the field of motor sport – and rallying in particular.

This was because of the arrival of the four-wheel-drive GT-Four version in 1986, a 182bhp turbocharged monster with permanent all-wheel drive and some of the finest driving dynamics ever seen in a Celica. So fine was the new GT-Four, it took the flag at no fewer than thirteen World Rally Championship events during its illustrious career, and gave Carlos Sainz the Drivers' Championship in both 1990 and 1992.

Even the road-going GT-Four would hit 138mph flat out, passing the 60mph mark in just 7.7 seconds. This was the most technically sophisticated, best-handling Celica ever to be launched by Toyota, and its success both on the road and on the world's rally circuits was almost guaranteed from the start. It's just a shame it took until 1988 for the awesome GT-Four to become officially available as a UK model.

Yet almost before we knew it, the fifth-generation Celica was upon us, making its public debut at the Frankfurt Show in 1989 and going on sale in Europe during the early part of 1990. The press release of the time boasted: 'The New Celica was developed on the basic concept of creating a car to satisfy the desires of fashion-conscious individuals, providing futuristic features in style and ride.' Well, whatever all that nonsense meant, there was no denying the new Celica was a very fine car – and, as before, a highly competitive one.

Once again, a GT-Four model was developed from the Series V Celica, and with great success. In fact, it was this machine that went on to give Toyota its first ever World Rally Championship title in 1993, an accolade that provided the Celica line-up with invaluable publicity. The Celica name may have been around for a full 24 years by then, but it had never been more prominent in potential buyers' minds. The Celica had become a coupe to be taken very seriously indeed.

The problem with the turbocharged GT-Four version, as always, was its price compared with the lesser models in the range. By 1991, the all-wheel-drive model was retailing at a whopping 30% more than the Celica GT. Yes, you got permanent four-wheel drive in place of the GT's front-drive set-up; and you got a mightily ▶

TIMELINE

1970	First-generation Celica Coupé launched
1971	UK and European sales begin
1973	Mustang-inspired Liftback version launched in Japan
1974	Twin-cam Celica 1600GT joins the range
1975	Celica wins its class in British Saloon Car Championship
1976	Celica Liftback goes on sale in UK
1977	New-look second-generation Celica range announced in August
1978	UK sales of Series II Celica get under way
1981	Facelift sees new front-end styling for Celica
1983	Third-generation Celica appears with sharp, angular styling
1984	Celica Convertible goes on sale
1984	Celica XT replaces ST, but with same 2.0-litre power
1985	Fourth-generation Celica appears, with front-wheel-drive for first time
1986	Celica GT-Four 4x4 goes on sale in most markets.
1987	Awkward-looking new Celica Cabriolet launched
1988	UK sales of GT-Four finally get under way

▶

◀ Most Celicas over the years have been spirited performers, thanks to their excellent engines, capable of competing against Japanese and European opposition with ease. *(Toyota)*

▲ The Celica went through various incarnations during the '80s, though it was the fourth-generation model – complete with front-wheel-drive for the first time – of 1985 that was arguably the most attractive. *(Toyota)*

impressive 201bhp compared with the standard motor's 158bhp. But once the extra weight and the 4x4 powerline drag had been taken into account, the GT-Four's performance was little different from that of the GT, with top speeds of 136mph and 132mph respectively. Meanwhile, standing-start acceleration to 60mph was identical for each model at 7.6 seconds.

Inevitably, it was the standard Celica GT that became the best seller in the fifth-generation line-up. But nowadays, a used GT-Four makes a great buy. While it may not be dramatically quicker than the lowlier GT, it certainly knows how to make the most of all that power in terms of handling and roadholding. When it comes to front-wheel drive versus all-wheel drive, the latter always gives the ultimate grip in all conditions.

When Britain's *What Car?* magazine summed up the latest Celica model back in October 1991, they praised it for its handling, performance and ride quality. And yet the fifth-generation Celica's mere existence had the testers somewhat puzzled when they posed the question: 'But there wasn't

much wrong with the previous Celica, was there?'.

They were absolutely right, of course. Every Celica model seems to have been replaced whilst still in its prime, so nobody was particularly surprised when a new sixth-generation Celica Coupé was unveiled in October 1993. And what a handsome machine it was too, its quad front lamps and curvaceous coupé profile giving it a sexy, sweeping stance that was bang up to date. The almost inevitable GT-Four version followed at the beginning of 1994, the year in which the Celica won the World Rally Championship for the second time, while the latest Celica Convertible arrived soon after.

But it was the seventh-generation Celica line-up unveiled in late 1999 that really brought focus back to the brand. The last few Celicas had tended to be attractive and sporting but not particularly daring. Now, in readiness for the new century and with a concentration very much on cutting-edge design, the 2000 model year Celica was here. And what a stunner it was.

Using an amazing amalgam of sharp edges

◢ The sixth-generation Celica was unveiled in 1993 and, like its predecessor, was made available in all-wheel-drive GT-Four guise. *(Toyota)*

▶ Well-designed interiors and decent ergonomics have tended to be a feature of most Celicas over the decades. *(Toyota)*

and curves, the very latest Celica could never be confused with any rival. It was futuristic and adventurous in the way it looked, and it attracted attention like nothing else in its price range. As *What Car?* magazine pointed out in November 2000, this machine's image was '…not for shrinking violets'.

It was a clever piece of design, a world away from the new MR2 Roadster that appeared in 2000. Where the MR2 was chunky, the Celica was sleek. And where the MR2 was a full-blown convertible, the Celica was an uncompromising coupé.

Under the bonnet, the latest front-drive Celica brought more good news, equipped as it was with a 140bhp version of the latest 1.8-litre VVT-i unit that would find its way into the MR2 Roadster. But whereas the MR2's engine was mid-mounted, the Celica's could be found fitted transversely up front.

Things got really exciting for the all-new Series VII Celica within twelve months of its launch, when a 189bhp version, known as the Celica 190, went on sale. Better still, the following year saw the same engine being used in the most exciting Celica of the 21st century: the awesome Celica T Sport. Equipped with a six-speed manual gearbox, vehicle stability control, traction control, ABS and brake assist, this was the most technologically advanced Celica ever launched. What lay beneath the bonnet was pretty special, too.

It was the very latest VVTL-i version of the existing 1.8-litre lump, making full use of variable valve technology and valve lift expertise. It resulted in dramatically more low-down torque, which created a more dynamic driving style and heightened response at all times. The engine was an absolute joy to experience, and made for one of the most exciting drivers' coupés in a long, long time.

The figures spoke for themselves, with 140mph available flat-out and just 7.4 seconds taken to reach 60mph from rest. But the way this machine behaved out on the open road was far more important than any official performance figures, for this was one of the most communicative 'sensible' coupés in its class. Against some rather bland opposition, the Celica T Sport excelled – just like the original Celica 1600GT had done, way back in 1970. Funny how history has a habit of repeating itself. ■

TIMELINE

1988	Celica Cabriolet dropped after just 18 months
1989	Fifth-generation Celica announced in Japan
1990	Series V Celica on sale in UK this year
1993	Celica GT-Four wins World Rally Championship
1993	Series VI Celica unveiled in October
1994	UK sales of Series VI get under way
1994	GT-Four version of latest model announced
1994	New Celica Convertible unveiled and goes on sale worldwide
1994	Celica GT-Four wins World Rally Championship for second time
1999	Series VII Celica launched with dramatic new styling
2000	189bhp Celica 190 goes on sale in UK in October
2001	Celica T Sport (189bhp) joins UK line-up
2001	500bhp 'Ultimate Celica' concept developed in the USA
2003	Celica GT-Four 4x4 goes on sale in most markets
2004	Limited edition Celica Red and Celica Blue launched

▲ When the Series VII Celica took a bow in 1999, it caused quite a stir. It was one of the bravest styling decisions Toyota had ever taken, but was soon winning acclaim for its cutting edge design. *(Toyota)*

CELICA

TOYOTA
SUPRA 1986–93
power and presence

▲ Big, powerful, effortless and a joy to drive; it's little wonder the new-for-1986 Toyota Supra won so many fans in the battle of the upmarket coupés. (*Toyota*)

The launch of the MR2 and the continued success of each generation of Celica model had proved the competence of Toyota as a manufacturer of fine sporting machines by the mid-1980s. Even so, the launch of the latest model to wear the Supra name was a brave step for the company, and marked a major turning point in its corporate thinking.

The latest Supra arrived in 1986 – although, if we're being pedantic about it, we could claim this was actually the first ever 'proper' Supra, as the previous incarnation of the Supra was officially labelled the Celica Supra and was based on the platform and running gear of … yes, you guessed it, the Celica of the time. Now, Toyota was launching a Supra in its own right, and it just happened to be the most upmarket sporting coupé ever offered by the Japanese giant.

It was a good-looking beast, that's for sure. Long, wide and low, it combined smooth coupé looks with a road presence that seemed to dwarf

the company's cheaper performance offerings. It just looked so 'right' from every angle, the kind of machine that wouldn't have looked out of place on a car park full of Porsche 944s.

Power came from a normally-aspirated version of Toyota's 7M-GE straight-six engine, this time endowed with 24 valves and the obligatory fuel-injection. It was a fairly straightforward, relatively uncomplicated powerplant – but that didn't stop it from developing a highly impressive 201bhp at 6000rpm. This was a serious achievement by mid-1980s standards. Few machines without the aid of a turbocharger managed to pump out more than 200bhp with such consummate ease, and it was a credit to Toyota that they achieved such a high output.

Performance really was effortless, the Supra's subtly growling straight-six engine delivering the power in a way that made other performance machines seem frantic by comparison. And the figures impressed just as much as the behind-the-wheel experience, thanks to a top speed of 135mph. From rest, 60mph was reached in a mere 7.7 seconds, which made standing-starts something of a rewarding experience!

The Supra got off to a good start in every export country it entered, matching its success in Japan. Throughout Europe, in particular, fans of upmarket coupés saw the Supra as a value-for-money alternative to some of the more aspirational marques. Even so, there were some potential buyers for whom even the Supra's 201bhp just wasn't quite enough.

Such critics had to wait until 1989 to have their automotive prayers answered, when the exciting new Supra Turbo hit the streets – and to say it arrived with a bang would be an ▶

SPEC

SUPRA

ENGINE: 2954cc fuel-injected 24-valve normally-aspirated '7M-GE' straight-six

POWER: 201bhp @ 6000rpm

TORQUE: 187lb ft @ 4000rpm

PERFORMANCE: Top speed 135mph, 0–60mph 7.7 secs.

TRANSMISSION: Five-speed manual

CHASSIS: Rack-and-pinion power-assisted steering; independent coil-spring double-wishbone suspension all round with limited-slip rear differential; ventilated disc brakes all round with ABS

SUPRA TURBO

ENGINE: 2954cc fuel-injected 24-valve turbocharged and intercooled '7M-GTE' straight-six

POWER: 232bhp @ 5600rpm

TORQUE: 254lb ft @ 3200rpm

PERFORMANCE: Top speed 155mph, 0–60mph 6.1 secs

TRANSMISSION: Five-speed manual

CHASSIS: Rack-and-pinion power-assisted steering; independent coil-spring double-wishbone suspension all round with limited-slip rear differential; ventilated disc brakes all round with ABS

◀ Normally-aspirated or turbocharged? By 1989 the choice was yours, bringing either 201 or 232bhp to your right foot. *(Toyota)*

▶ The Supra went on to achieve worldwide success, selling more than a million examples during its seven years in production. (Toyota)

understatement. Using a turbocharged and intercooled version of the regular Supra's six-cylinder engine, the new turbo version delivered a huge 232bhp; just as significantly, it developed a massive torque figure of 254lb ft at only 3200rpm, endowing the newcomer with a combination of blistering performance and a minimal need for gear changes in order to make the most of it.

What this equated to was no less than 155mph flat out, and 60mph being reached from rest in a fraction over 6.0 seconds. Even ignoring the size and weight of the Supra, such figures would have been almost incredible; but for a coupé measuring a full 17 inches longer and weighing in at 834lbs heavier than the Porsche 944 of the time, it was simply astonishing. It was the fastest, most powerful and impressive Toyota performance machine ever to go on general sale until then. And it became an instant hit.

In fact, through the Supra and Supra Turbo's seven years on sale, well over a million examples were sold in total, putting this twosome among the best-selling 'niche' models ever offered by Toyota. It was a sad day when, in 1993, the very last Supra Turbo rolled off the production line, even if its successor would prove to be even more exciting.

The appeal of the 1986–93 Supra range continues to this day, particularly given its amazing value for money on the second-hand market. But it's not just the Supra's affordability that sets it apart from some other Japanese coupés; it's also its combination of power, performance, comfort and ease of use.

Get yourself behind the wheel of a Supra Turbo and, despite there being 232 horses eager to be unleashed from under the bonnet, you'll find it a bit of a pussy cat round town. Keep the revs low, enjoy its immense torque and revel in the fact that its five-speed gearbox is a light and

WHAT WE LIKE...

A big coupé with style and performance in equal measures. It may not be the newest performance machine on the block any more, but the Supra still oozes class and desirability.

▶ Long, straight, fast roads were where the Supra felt most at home, capable of swallowing up the miles with consummate ease. (Toyota)

...WHAT WE DON'T

A fairly hard ride was a trait of the Supra throughout its seven years. By 1993, its handling was almost old-fashioned compared with more recent rivals.

slick affair; as easy-to-drive urban transport, a Supra makes a surprisingly pleasant experience. Once the traffic clears and the road opens up ahead of you, though, the Supra Turbo takes on a whole new personality; and how.

Once the boost from the turbocharger makes its presence felt, the Supra Turbo transforms itself into an all-conquering warrior, surging forward at an impressive rate and transforming all stationary objects into a distant blur. Despite such power and performance, the Supra's rear-drive set-up with independent coil-sprung double-wishbone suspension and limited-slip differential handles itself without drama most of the time. This may not be the best-handling Japanese car ever created, as the more enthusiastic driver can easily get the rear end breaking away when pushing the Supra towards its limit, but with confidence and a touch of skill, it's simplicity itself to bring the whole thing back under control and back into line.

It all adds to the fun, even if it does make the car feel just a tad dated by the handling standards of the 21st century. Let's not forget that this machine goes back to the mid-1980s; bear that in mind when driving one for the first time and you're sure to be impressed by what you discover.

You're likely to be equally impressed by the levels of standard equipment installed in the Supra Turbo upon its launch in 1989. Air conditioning, cruise control, central locking, electric windows and mirrors, power seat adjustment and heated door mirrors made up a very comprehensive list for the time. You could even order your super-quick new Supra Turbo with automatic transmission if you wanted, a popular option with the Americans and Japanese but understandably less so with most British buyers.

The Supra may lack the outrageous looks and stunning twin-turbo specification of its successor of the same name, but it is still one of the most impressive all-rounders ever to come out of Japan. It's a handsome beast in an understated sort of a way, and in turbo guise it offers major performance potential even for those on a limited budget.

It may not be as sophisticated or as technologically advanced as a Nissan 300ZX or a Honda NSX, but a Supra Turbo still offers the kind of acceleration and top speed you'd expect from a supercar of the 1980s rather than from a fairly straightforward Japanese coupé. All that torque, all that tyre-shredding performance, all that luxury … it's no wonder the Supra became such a successful alternative to the more prestigious German marques in its day. ■

TIMELINE

1986	Latest Supra launched, bigger than ever and with more power
1986	New Supra goes on sale in the UK in July
1988	New Supra Turbo unveiled at British International Motor Show in October
1989	Supra Turbo hits the streets, offering 232bhp and massive torque
1993	All-new Supra launched; production of existing model ceases

▼ So much torque, so much power, it's little wonder the Supra was such a rewarding driving experience. (Toyota)

TOYOTA
SOARER 1991–2000

smoothly does it

▲ Predecessor of the Lexus SC430, the Toyota Soarer never did make it as an official UK-spec machine, although it has enjoyed success in later years as a popular 'grey' import. *(Author)*

Some of Japan's most interesting models never made it to the UK and other crucial export markets, and the stunningly efficient and seriously desirable Series III Toyota Soarer was one of them, so any examples you spot on British roads now will have been acquired in more recent times as 'grey' imports.

The Soarer name dates back to 1981, when it was applied to a rather angular two-door coupé confined mainly to the Japanese market. The new Series II arrived in 1986, again mainly for domestic consumption. It wasn't until the arrival of the all-singing, all-dancing Series III in 1991 that the Soarer model really got going.

This newcomer featured super-smooth, curvaceous styling and a very contemporary look. It was also the first Soarer designed with export potential in mind, particularly to the USA. That helps to explain why the beauty was styled by the famous Calty Design Studios of California, although a complete change of name would occur before the Soarer was made available in the States in 1992.

The Americans knew the Soarer from the start as the Lexus SC400, enabling Toyota to make the most of a more upmarket brand image. The Soarer

WHAT WE LIKE...

Clean, smooth styling and powerful, evocative engines make this an interesting choice for fans of luxury coupés. That it was known in the States as the Lexus SC400 helped its image no end.

...WHAT WE DON'T

It's another fine Toyota that the British were deprived of when it was brand-new – and for that, the UK importers should have been severely punished!

was so sophisticated, it needed a brand name that aspirational Americans would want to buy into – and Lexus seemed a safer bet than Toyota.

Through various revisions and relatively minor updates, the Soarer remained in production for more than nine years, finally disappearing in December 2000 to make way for the following year's all-new Lexus SC430 (detailed elsewhere). As before, Japan would retain the Toyota Soarer name for home-market sales.

The Series III Soarer was an impressive machine, both inside and out. Initial engine choices comprised a 250bhp 4.0-litre quad-cam V8 or a 2.5-litre twin-turbo, although the latter wasn't sold in the USA. By 1995, a 3.0-litre version had joined the range, sold in some markets as the Lexus SC300.

The 4.0 GT line-up must rank as the most desirable Soarer, the effortless V8 powerplant offering a brilliant combination of refinement and performance. With a 150mph top speed and 0–60mph in a mere 6.9 seconds, this was a seriously quick machine. Yet the whole experience felt far from rushed, no doubt a tribute to the four-speed 'intelligent' automatic transmission's efficiency and smoothness, as well as the superlative ride quality.

These weren't the tautest of machines when it came to fast cornering, as Toyota had to keep comfort levels high – particularly in the USA. However, the coil-sprung double-wishbone-suspension set-up and optional traction control system combined to offer a more than adequate handling and roadholding package, without diluting the Soarer's opulent, upmarket, Lexus-inspired image at all. And if you wanted, you could even pay extra for air suspension.

The Series III Soarer deserves recognition for so many things, not least for being the first ever coupé to wear a Lexus badge and for being the first member of the Soarer family created for sales outside Japan. So why was it never given a chance in Britain, of all places? It's a mystery. ∎

SPEC

ENGINE: 4.0-litre 32-valve quad-cam fuel-injected V8

POWER: 250bhp @ 5600rpm

TORQUE: 260lb ft @ 4400rpm

PERFORMANCE: Top speed 150mph, 0–60mph 6.9 secs

TRANSMISSION: Four-speed automatic electronically controlled transmission (ECT) with power/normal shift modes

CHASSIS: Speed-sensitive power-assisted rack-and-pinion steering; independent coil-spring double-wishbone suspension all round; optional traction control system; ventilated disc brakes all round with ABS

TIMELINE

1991	Third generation of successful Soarer line launched in May
1992	Special-edition, better-equipped Twin Turbo Limited launched in July
1992	Rebadged version (Lexus SC400) goes on sale in USA
1994	3.0 GT joins the range in January
1996	2.5-litre models now fitted with VVT-i engine
1997	2.5-litre VVT-i receives minor power increase (225PS)
2000	Production of Series III Soarer ceases in December
2001	New (Series IV) Toyota Soarer/ Lexus SC430 goes on sale

◀ Lift the bonnet and marvel at the 4.0-litre 32-valve V8, a smooth and effortless powerplant that has no trouble easing 250bhp from within. *(Author)*

TOYOTA
STARLET GT TURBO
from dull to dynamic

▲ While most standard Starlets were boring little machines that tended to be bought by retired gentlefolk, the GT Turbo was a different kind of animal altogether. This pocket rocket was fun, frisky and a very fine driver's car. (Author)

It's surprising, for a company with a history of producing some exceptional performance cars over the years, that Toyota never made more of the Starlet in the UK. Maybe it was because of the prohibitive import restrictions placed on Japanese cars for so long; whatever the reason, there's no denying that most Brits considered the Starlet a reliable but terminally boring machine.

Britain's motoring press generally loathed the Starlet, and *What Car?* magazine struggled to find a good word to say about the smallest Toyota in October 1991. 'Dull little engine matches dull performance and even duller ride', they complained. And who could blame them? With just the Starlet 1.0 GL on sale by then, it was hardly a machine to set an enthusiastic driver's adrenalin racing.

That is because the UK never officially received the awesome Starlet GT Turbo, a miniature hot hatch that managed to transform

WHAT WE LIKE...

Never an official UK import, so any Starlet GT Turbo is going to be rarer than the average hot hatch. Despite that, there's no problem sourcing spares or finding fellow enthusiasts willing to offer help and advice. It's an unsung hero in a world of characterless small cars.

...WHAT WE DON'T

Standard Starlets were as dull as a whole bag of very dull things, so you'll have to expect the odd snigger from the uneducated. Once they see for themselves the potential of the GT Turbo, they'll soon come round.

an inherently dull design into an exhilarating and really rather rapid machine. From the late 1980s through to the mid-1990s, the Starlet GT Turbo provided young Japanese enthusiasts with yet another high-performing, sharp-handling excuse to hit the streets and have some fun.

At the heart of the GT Turbo was a 1331cc DOHC 16-valve fuel-injected four-pot motor, aided by the boost from Toyota's very own CT-9A turbocharger. By the time the GT Turbo finally disappeared in 1996, it was pumping out a glorious-sounding 133bhp at 6400prm, with the excitement of a red line stretching all the way to 7000rpm-plus. It was enough to propel the fairly lightweight Starlet to 60mph from rest in a mere 6.9 seconds, with a top speed just this side of 120mph within easy reach. And it was enough to guarantee an immensely rewarding driving experience.

The Starlet Turbo was a real fun machine, from its throaty engine note to its super-sharp handling. Thanks to some serious work by Toyota engineers, the standard front-wheel-drive Starlet's all-coil suspension set-up was tautened, lowered and transformed to provide flat, kart-like handling. Throw into the equation extremely precise rack-and-pinion steering and a highly effective anti-lock braking system and you had all the right ingredients for fast safe fun.

The Starlet GT Turbo wasn't just great on paper but was a genuinely rewarding and entertaining machine when driven enthusiastically. And when you think how characterless, almost tedious its lowlier versions were, such a transformation was little short of miraculous. Here was a tiny hot hatch with real charisma, created from one of the world's least interesting 'superminis' of the time. Toyota had done some fine work in the past, but this was an achievement of near biblical proportions.

The really cruel aspect of all this, of course, is that British buyers never got the chance to buy brand new Starlet GT Turbos for themselves. Such a machine could have provided a welcome relief from various go-faster Fiestas of the time, but it was not to be.

Happily, Britain's 21st century Japanese car enthusiasts are a more determined and resourceful lot, which is why healthy numbers of second-hand performance Starlets have since found their way to the UK; and about time, too. ■

SPEC

ENGINE: 1331cc DOHC 16-valve fuel-injected turbocharged four-cylinder

POWER: 133bhp @ 6400rpm

TORQUE: 157Nm @ 4800rpm

PERFORMANCE: Top speed 119mph, 0–60mph 6.9 secs

TRANSMISSION: Five-speed manual

CHASSIS: Rack-and-pinion steering; independent coil-spring suspension all round; disc brakes all round with ABS

TIMELINE

1987 Starlet Turbo S launched with 1.3-litre 12-valve engine

1989 Special GT-Limited brings four-wheel ABS and extra equipment

1990 Softer-styled new Starlet range sees debut of latest Starlet GT

1992 More powerful version of DOHC engine now fitted

1992 New GT-Limited version launched with alloys, air con and more

1994 Starlet GT facelift sees round headlamps on many versions

1994 GT-Advance special launched with LSD, anti-roll bars and other features

1996 All-new Starlet sees launch of Glanza V performance version

TOYOTA
MR2 SERIES I
mid-engined masterpiece

▲ Sports car fans everywhere sat up and took notice when the first-generation MR2 hit the streets. This wedge-shaped mid-engined funster got off to a flying start. *(LAT)*

The idea of a mid-engined two-seater sports car wasn't exactly untried prior to the launch of the exciting new Toyota MR2 in 1984. The highly successful Fiat X1/9 had been around since the early 1970s, after all, and was still selling in fair numbers. And the near-supercar Lotus Esprit had used the concept to great effect for almost as long. In typical Japanese fashion, Toyota managed to take the idea of a mid-engined sportster and very nearly perfect it.

Coincidentally, the MR2 wasn't the only mid-engined two-seater being launched by a major manufacturer in 1984. In the States, the Pontiac division of General Motors was busy unveiling the new Fiero range the same year, with styling not completely dissimilar to that of the MR2. But where the Toyota product looked sharp and exciting, the Pontiac was a little bulbous and awkward from most angles. Where the Toyota enjoyed the power of a high-revving 16-valve twin-cam engine, the Pontiac made do with an

ancient pushrod effort known as the Iron Duke. It's little wonder the Fiero soon faded from favour even in its home market, while the exciting new MR2 went from strength to strength throughout its five-year career.

Had Fiat decided to further develop the X1/9 throughout the 1980s, the MR2 might have had a tougher fight on its hands. Happily for Toyota, the X1/9 was badly neglected during its final few years of life, enabling the new MR2 to be seen as a vastly more modern, better-performing alternative.

One advantage the X1/9 had over the MR2 was its excellent value for money. By the time the innovative new Toyota went on sale in the UK in 1985, it cost considerably more than its Italian rival. But enthusiasts throughout Britain were soon won over by the newcomer's superb design, top class engineering and great fun factor. Despite being a more highly developed product than the Fiat, the MR2 was still a raw, exhilarating and thrilling drive.

Home-market MR2s came with a choice of single overhead-cam 1.5-litre (83bhp) or twin-cam 1.6-litre 16-valve (122bhp) engines, each mounted transversely just behind the driver. For the UK and other key export markets, just the twin-cam version was made available. Toyota figured there would be only a small market for the lower-powered model in the UK, and didn't want to run the risk of its significantly poorer performance affecting the image of the range as a whole. British buyers – then just as much as now – expected strong performance, and that's exactly what the 1.6-litre motor was there to provide.

The engine itself had been seen before in the Corolla GT Coupé, but this was the first time it had been mid-mounted in any Toyota. The configuration provided the MR2 with impressively even weight distribution, which was obviously a major aid to handling, but it was the engine itself that provided the initial thrills.

The maximum power of 122bhp was developed at 6600rpm, so it was an engine that thrived on hard work, and the more it was worked, the better it sounded. It was a fairly gruff engine note, but none the worse for that, and with the revs being fully exploited most of the time, it seemed to be simply in its element.

In the usual Toyota tradition, the MR2's five-speed gear change was slick and precise by the standards of the 1980s, enabling any keen driver to make the most of the power potential on offer. And that was great news, because with a top speed of 121mph and the 0–60mph sprint in only 7.6 seconds, any 16-valve MR2 was capable of providing countless thrills per journey.

Thrills that really kicked in when the car was subjected to a high-speed jaunt along any winding A-road, where the extraordinarily good levels of handling and roadholding really shone through. In mechanical make-up, the MR2 was fairly straightforward, thanks to its all-coil MacPherson strut suspension, rack-and-pinion steering and disc brakes all round. But with its mid-engined layout and taut suspension set-up, the MR2 managed to go round corners at the kind of speeds – and provided the kind of thrills – that drivers of front-engined rivals could only dream of.

I remember buying a 1988 MR2 that, by then, was twelve years old, had covered a hefty mileage and was hardly the most cherished example around. Yet, compared with other second-hand sports cars I'd owned in the past, that ageing Toyota was still enormously rewarding to drive at speed. Acceleration was still more than sprightly, the handling and levels of grip were still astoundingly good, and the level ▶

SPEC

ENGINE: 1587cc DOHC fuel-injected 16-valve four-cylinder

POWER: 122bhp @ 6600rpm

TORQUE: 105lb ft @ 5000rpm

PERFORMANCE: Top speed 121mph, 0–60mph 7.6 secs

TRANSMISSION: Five-speed manual

CHASSIS: Rack-and-pinion steering; independent coil-spring suspension all round with MacPherson struts and front and rear anti-roll bars; disc brakes all round (ventilated fronts)

◀ In 1.6-litre form, the MR2 enjoyed an output of 122bhp - enough to ensure perfectly adequate performance for most owners. The engine itself came straight from the Corolla GT Coupe of the time. *(Toyota)*

▲ The MR2's mid-
engined layout
and striking styling
gave it instant
appeal among
driving enthusiasts
and poseurs alike.
No wonder
waiting lists were
soon building in
just about every
export market.
(Toyota)

of enjoyment gained from every single journey
was incredible for a car that had cost me so little.
It may not have been the most pristine MR2 on
the street, but it was great fun to own – and
impressively reliable, too.

That, of course, was another advantage that
the new-for-1984 Toyota MR2 would have over
its Fiat X1/9 arch rival, the latter being renowned
for its fragility, quality control problems and dire
reputation for premature rusting. Suddenly, here
was an alternative from Toyota that was not only
faster and more fun to drive, but was almost
guaranteed to be phenomenally reliable. It was a
Toyota, after all. For anybody reared on the
unreliability and unpredictability of Italian and
British sports cars of old, it was like a breath
of fresh air.

Ah yes, fresh air. Surely a 'proper' sports car
needed to offer some kind of removable roof for
wind-in-the-hair motoring if it was to be taken
seriously by all potential buyers. Well, perhaps so,
because as early as 1986 Toyota revealed the new
MR2 T-Bar – a targa-topped addition to the

range, with two removable roof panels
divided by a central strengthening brace.
The panels themselves were easy and
quick to remove, and the effect was
quite dramatic. Just like the now seriously ancient
Fiat X1/9, the MR2 was a summer fun car with
the roof in the boot, and a snug machine in the
winter months with the panels back in place.
Compared with a more traditional canvas-topped
convertible, it offered the best of all worlds.

It didn't take long for Toyota's MR2 to gain
itself an enthusiastic following throughout the
world, not least in the UK. British sales got under
way in the spring of 1985, and by the end of that
year there was an official waiting list still growing
in length. The motoring press were just as
impressed as the buyers, with every magazine
and newspaper road test praising Toyota's latest
sportster for its performance, handling and all-
round fun appeal.

Britain's *Autocar* magazine had closely
followed the development progress of the MR2,
witnessing as early as 1983 a prototype being

Like every other magazine in the UK and further afield, *Autocar* would be bowled over by just how good the MR2 was. In its first road test of the newcomer in March 1985, *Autocar* enthused particularly about the MR2's get-up-and-go: 'Grip when accelerating from rest is really outstanding and partly responsible for the impressive set of performance figures. The best getaway is achieved right on the maximum ▶

WHAT WE LIKE...

Sharp styling, great handling and eager performance made this the most desirable affordable two-seater of the 1980s. Its mid-engined layout also marked an important turning point for Toyota.

◀ Neat handling and sharp steering helped guarantee a rewarding drive for the MR2 motorist. *(Toyota)*

...WHAT WE DON'T

What is there possibly to dislike about the utterly brilliant MR2? Oh all right, here's something: abused examples are now looking tatty and can suffer from rust, but really that's about it; these things are still amazing machines.

tested at speed on the Zolder circuit in Holland. With the car were teams of engineers from both Toyota and Lotus, and many motoring pundits assumed the new mid-engined test car would be some forthcoming new model from Lotus. *Autocar*, though, knew otherwise, recognising the machine as the following year's new Toyota two-seater – and, understandably, they couldn't wait to get behind the wheel.

▼ Was this the car the Fiat X1/9 should always have been? The X1/9's lack of investment through the '80s helped the MR2 get established remarkably quickly. *(LAT)*

revs (7600rpm) and is just enough to allow the rear tyres to break traction and provide the optimum launch…'

Interestingly, the MR2 was a heavier machine than many experts had predicted, tipping the scales at 975 kilograms unladen. For a small two-seater sports car, it was no lightweight, partly accounted for by the penalty of the double-bulkhead bodyshell design. So just how was it that Toyota managed to achieve such excellent performance figures?

Happily, the MR2's 4A-GE (as Toyota referred to it) twin-cam engine was a cracker, one of its neatest bits of engineering being what might best be described as a two-stage throttle.

Upstream of the conventional butterfly throttle design were four additional throttle flaps, worked by actuators which were controlled in turn by a vacuum switching valve (VSV) and ECU. When the engine was turning over at under 4650rpm, those additional throttles remained closed, but at higher revs, the ECU no longer sent signals to the VSV, thus causing it to stop operating, allowing atmospheric pressure to be led from the VSV to the actuators, which then opened the supplementary throttles completely. High gas speeds, efficient fuel mixing and cylinder filling were achieved at low revs, while the full advantages of increased breathing from four valves per cylinder were enjoyed at the top end.

That may not sound particularly exciting or groundbreaking by current standards, but in the mid-1980s it was quite an innovation – and one that worked highly effectively. Keeping the revs

high in all kinds of driving situations gave a surge in performance that the enthusiastic driver simply revelled in, particularly when it allowed him to beat the competition in a standing-start test.

But the MR2 wasn't just about outright performance; it was also about being the best-handling Toyota then available, a fact underlined by America's *Car & Driver* magazine when trying an MR2 for the first time in Japan: 'On the hellaciously fast 2.5-mile Yamaha motorcycle test course near Hamamatsu, the MR2 was surprisingly poised. The handling stayed calm and collected right up to tire-sliding speeds, just as advertised. The Celicas and the Supras also on hand for comparison were falling all over themselves.'

That was warm praise for a car that had originally been envisaged as a commuter runabout. In fact, that was even the inspiration for its name, MR2 being an abbreviation of the rather clumsy 'Mid-engined Runabout 2-seater'. So how come it ended up as a seriously desirable sports car instead?

During its five years of development, the design was changed quite drastically, with more of an emphasis on performance and sports car image as time went by. Yet, the end product managed to remain true to its original concept, for it was indeed one of the most practical, manoeuvrable, convenient sporting offerings ever to hit the market. It's true that it lacked the usefulness of the Honda CRX's 2+2 layout, but that was hardly the point. The MR2 was one of the easiest-to-live-with sports cars ever created, as well as one of the most rewarding.

By the time the final Series I MR2 rolled off the production line in 1989, no fewer than 166,104 examples had been built, a healthy figure for what was a fairly specialised sports car. Hard-tops, T-Bars and even a 150bhp supercharged version (aimed mainly at Japan and the USA, not for UK consumption) had been built, all of them snapped up by ever-eager buyers who appreciated the Toyota's unique mix of qualities.

The original MR2 still has a loyal and enthusiastic following today, with the best examples starting to creep back up in value and become highly sought after among fans of modern classics. Owning a Series I MR2 has always been a rewarding experience, and never more so than in the 21st century. It's an icon, a modern-day legend, an inspiration; an all-time classic whose influence spread far wider than Toyota probably ever intended. And it's a car every enthusiast must own at least one of before they die. ■

TIMELINE

1984	MR2 unveiled in Japan to rapturous reception
1984	British launch at Birmingham's Motor Show in October
1985	UK sales get under way in the spring
1986	MR2 T-Bar goes on UK sale in the autumn
1986	Supercharged MR2 announced (not for UK)
1989	Series II MR2 launched, replacing the original

▼ The MR2 T-Bar provided the best of both worlds, it's snug-in-winter and fun-in-summer layout being an obvious advantage over more conventional convertibles of the time. *(Toyota)*

TOYOTA
MR2 SERIES II
growing up fast

▲ New, softer styling was a world away from the sharp, angular looks of the original MR2. Not everyone approved, but that didn't stop the Series II model from enjoying major success and a decade-long production run. (LAT)

The arrival of the Series II MR2 in 1989 marked another change of direction for Toyota in terms of its styling. Where the original MR2 had been small, angular and very sharp looking, the latest model to wear the badge was bigger, more curvaceous and appeared a lot more grown up. It was still a highly sporting machine, an uncompromising two-seater with its engine still mid-mounted. But it was also more sophisticated and refined in just about every sense.

Fans of the old-style MR2 weren't all convinced by the Series II's new look, criticising it for having less attitude than their beloved favourite. Somehow, the latest MR2 didn't shock onlookers in quite the same way as did the original. But that didn't stop it from being a huge success, with UK sales being particularly buoyant throughout its ten-year career.

The timing of the MR2's new look couldn't have been better, for the 1990s would see greater use of curves where straight lines had

previously ruled in the styling stakes. The latest MR2 looked like a product ahead of its time – a fortunate situation, given that its eventual replacement wouldn't arrive until the start of the new millennium.

Beneath the MR2's softer new look sat a familiar layout, with an independent coil-sprung suspension set-up, impressively sharp rack-and-pinion steering and disc brakes all round. ABS wasn't available initially, but would become standard equipment later.

Where the original MR2 used 1.6-litre power, the newest version had been upgraded to 2.0 litres – in fact, the latest version of Toyota's 1998cc twin-cam 16-valve lump, an engine with plenty of grunt and all the right sound effects to match. For the first time too, the MR2 was now offered in the UK with a choice of two different outputs.

Buyers who didn't demand the fastest sports car on the street were attracted by the entry-level MR2, using a 119bhp version of that fabulous engine. Mind you, it was no slouch, propelling this cheapest version in the range to a top speed of 129mph, passing the all-important 60mph mark in a very respectable 8.3 seconds. That might not sound particularly exciting, but it felt commendably quick from the driver's seat. Being a little bit cheaper than the more powerful MR2 GT, it was also great value for money.

Yet for many MR2 buyers, the need for speed made that extra expense worthwhile, which meant that most opted for the 158bhp GT. With a top speed of 137mph and the 0–60mph dash in just 7.6 seconds, this was the MR2 that enthusiasts soon started lusting after, particularly as it was such an entertaining drive into the bargain.

Some early examples of the Series II MR2 did suffer from an unexpected handling difficulty, where sudden oversteer could catch out even the most experienced of drivers. But Toyota ▶

SPEC

MR2 2.0 – 119bhp

ENGINE: 1998cc DOHC fuel-injected 16-valve four-cylinder

POWER: 119bhp @ 5600rpm

TORQUE: 130lb ft @ 4400rpm

PERFORMANCE: Top speed 129mph, 0–60mph 8.3 secs

TRANSMISSION: Five-speed manual (automatic optional)

CHASSIS: Rack-and-pinion steering; independent coil-spring suspension all round with MacPherson struts and front and rear anti-roll bars; disc brakes all round (ventilated fronts)

▲ A choice of power in the Series II MR2 meant up to 173bhp by 1994, the year when the latest GT version was launched. *(Toyota)*

MR2 2.0 GT – 158bhp

ENGINE: 1998cc DOHC fuel-injected 16-valve four-cylinder

POWER: 158bhp @ 6600rpm

TORQUE: 140lb ft @ 4800rpm

PERFORMANCE: Top speed 137mph, 0–60mph 7.6 secs

TRANSMISSION: Five-speed manual

CHASSIS: Rack-and-pinion steering; independent coil-spring suspension all round with MacPherson struts and front and rear anti-roll bars; disc brakes all round (ventilated fronts)

MR2 2.0 GT – 173bhp

ENGINE: 1998cc DOHC fuel-injected 16-valve four-cylinder

POWER: 173bhp @ 7000rpm

TORQUE: 137lb ft @ 4800rpm

PERFORMANCE: Top speed 136mph, 0–60mph 7.4 secs

TRANSMISSION: Five-speed manual

CHASSIS: Rack-and-pinion steering; independent coil-spring suspension all round with MacPherson struts and front and rear anti-roll bars; disc brakes all round (ventilated fronts)

WHAT WE LIKE...

Bigger and roomier than the original MR2, the latest model also offered a choice of power outputs for the UK market. The MR2 had grown up in every way.

...WHAT WE DON'T

Fanatics of the Series I didn't immediately take to the smooth new look, but plenty of other buyers loved it. Early handling difficulties were soon overcome – which was just as well.

The outright 'sportiness' of the latest-generation MR2 came as a pleasant surprise to anybody concerned that the model had matured too much. Happily, despite its extra size and greater refinement, the newcomer was still a hugely entertaining experience, praised by the motoring press for its character and charisma. Even as late as 1999, Britain's *The Express World Car Guide* was enthusing '...the MR2 still manages to make your spine tingle with superb feedback through the steering and a stubby gear lever that's easy to flick through the gears.' That was high praise for a ten-year-old sports car that by then was up against some far newer competition.

But typically, Toyota never neglected the MR2 or allowed it to stagnate. It's true that the Series II's styling was altered hardly at all during its ten years or so in production, but its equipment levels were improved significantly in later years, while 1994 also saw the GT being replaced by a new 173bhp version going by the same name.

Curiously, this most powerful derivative of the Series II ever offered in the UK boasted almost identical performance to its 158bhp predecessor, with just 0.2 of a second shaved off the 0–60mph time. Where this latest engine scored was in its flexibility and its even more free-revving nature, with maximum power developed at an adrenalin-pumping 7000rpm. It may not have been much faster than the previous GT, but the driver had even more fun finding that out.

Japan and a handful of export markets (but not the UK) were also offered 2.2-litre normally-

wasted little time in addressing this problem and, with the suspension retuned and the foibles sorted, the latest MR2 was soon reinforcing the perception that mid-engined cars really did offer the finest grip and handling.

aspirated and 2.0-litre turbo alternative powerplants, the latter in particular being a bit of a beast. It's just a shame such a more powerful version was never made more widely available, given that the MR2's mid-engined layout and well-designed chassis could easily cope with the extra horses. Sadly, it simply wasn't to be.

As with the first of the MR2s, the Series II was available in a choice of Coupé or T-Bar guises, the latter proving a popular choice with open-air fanatics and sun worshippers. Whichever was chosen, you'd find exactly the same impressive performance, fine handling and massive fun factor as part of the package.

You also got a surprisingly practical car for your money. Compared with its predecessor, the new-look MR2 offered more room inside for even fairly big adults, as well as a useful amount of extra luggage space. The latter point impressed *What Car?* magazine in 1991, when they pointed out that '...at least you can get more than a toothbrush in the boot.'

Toyota made a wise decision by making the MR2 such a practical car, as this was a model aimed at a wider audience than before. Sales of the Series I MR2 hadn't just been to out-and-out enthusiasts who cared far more about performance and handling than

they did about user-friendliness or practicality. It had, Toyota discovered, also appealed to middle-aged couples as an entertaining second car, providing a useful extra boost to sales. By making the Series II an even easier vehicle to live with, Toyota knew it was expanding its appeal still further.

Don't let this put you off owning a Series II MR2. Practical it may be, but this machine is no hairdresser's special. It's a fabulous mid-engined device with great performance, entertaining handling and a wonderful low-slung driving position. And even now, it still turns heads and looks so, so good.

Many motoring writers coined the phrase 'mini Ferrari' when describing the curvaceous MR2, and they were partly right. This, though, was a Ferrari with reliability and great build quality thrown in. Suddenly, its likeness to a classic Italian stallion had diminished... ◼

TIMELINE

1989	New-generation MR2 replaces old-style model
1990	T-Bar version launched for open-top fun
1994	158bhp version replaced by new 173bhp GT
1999	Production ceases by the end of the year
2000	Series III MR2 roadster announced in spring

▼ Get behind the wheel of a well-tuned MR2 GT and revel in its spirited performance. This is still a very rewarding machine to take for a spin. *(Toyota)*

TOYOTA
MR2 SERIES III
the roadster arrives

The worldwide success of the previous two generations of MR2 sports cars really put the pressure on Toyota to come up with an outstanding replacement for the new millennium. So when the wraps were about to come off the Series III MR2 for the 2000 model year, there was an understandable buzz of excitement.

Three things were widely assumed about the newcomer. Firstly, it would be available in both coupé and targa-top guises, following the previous success of both versions. Secondly, it would still be mid-engined for the finest handling experience in its class. And thirdly, it would be even more powerful than the outgoing MR2 GT.

Oh well, one out of three was something, I suppose. The MR2 for the 21st century was indeed mid-engined, as before. But it was also a full convertible model – though Toyota preferred the name Roadster – for the first time ever, as well as being significantly less powerful than the GT it replaced.

Yes, less power. Fewer horses. Not so much oomph. However you wanted to put it, there was no disguising the fact that, at 138bhp, the new MR2's maximum power was well down on the old-style MR2 GT's 173bhp. Its engine was smaller too, coming in as a 1.8-litre twin-cam 16-valve unit in place of the previous 2.0-litre. What exactly was going on?

Fortunately for enthusiasts everywhere, one drive of the latest-generation MR2 was enough to convince most of them that this was indeed a car good enough to carry that illustrious badge forward. Engine size and ultimate power may have been down, but the spirited performance and fantastic driver feedback were still there in droves.

The top speed was more than adequate for most owners' needs at 131mph, taking 7.8 seconds to reach 60mph. Compare such figures with those for the MR2 GT in the previous chapter and you'll find there's not a huge amount of difference, showing that Toyota had achieved the

SPEC

ENGINE: 1794cc DOHC fuel-injected 16-valve VVT-i four-cylinder

POWER: 138bhp @ 6400rpm

TORQUE: 125lb ft @ 4400rpm

PERFORMANCE: Top speed 131mph, 0-60mph 7.8 secs

TRANSMISSION: Six-speed manual (from 2002)

CHASSIS: Power-assisted rack-and-pinion steering; independent coil-spring suspension all round with MacPherson struts front and rear; ventilated disc brakes all round

seemingly impossible. Here was a sporting machine with a smaller, less powerful engine than the model it replaced, yet it still managed to offer very nearly the same kind of performance.

This was partly thanks to a reduction in weight compared with the old-style MR2. More crucially, however, the latest model to bear the name also made full use of Toyota's extensive variable valve technology expertise, hence the VVT-i tag for the new powerplant. It gave extra flexibility throughout the rev range, making up with real enthusiasm what the engine lacked in on-paper power.

MR2s have always been about the all-round driving experience rather than the best set of official performance figures in the industry – and the new-for-2000 model continued this tradition. By the standards of the new century, the acceleration figures were pretty impressive for a 1.8-litre convertible, but it was the way the car felt that was far more important, and here the MR2 didn't let the side down; not one bit.

The mid-engine layout, taut all-coil suspension and impressively sharp rack-and-pinion steering all worked together to create a modern-day sports car with real driver appeal. Handling and grip were first class; in fact, the way any enthusiastic driver could power an MR2 into a tight bend and come out the other side smiling and unscathed was guaranteed to put smiles on faces.

The MR2's low-slung driving position gave it an immediate head-start over uninspiring rivals such as the MGF when it came to feeling fast at any speed. And, of course, its slick and quick manual transmission was a joy to use and helped to make the car such fun to drive.

Britain's motoring press was as impressed with the long-awaited newcomer as the public seemed to be. Back in November 2000, *What Car?* magazine praised the MR2 for being '…superb to drive' and for boasting '…game performance.' In fact, just about the only thing the magazine's testers could find to criticise was the MR2's lack of storage space – which for a mid-engined two-seater sports car was hardly the end of the world.

In typical fashion, Toyota didn't leave the MR2 alone for very long, and by 2001 they ▶

▲ Superbly designed cockpit and terrific driving position helped ensure the latest MR2 felt like a 'proper' sports car. *(Toyota)*

▼ The MR2 Roadster isn't the fastest convertible on the planet, but its sharp steering and impressive handling guarantee a rewarding drive with plenty of feedback. *(Toyota)*

WHAT WE LIKE...

Gorgeous, chunky styling with real attitude helps to keep the MR2 name alive and well. A more entertaining choice than its front-engined rivals, with performance to match its great handling and superb chassis.

...WHAT WE DON'T

Power was down on the previous MR2 GT, although the driving experience was just as strong; sequential transmission option isn't to everyone's taste.

▶ Despite being radically different from the two previous generations of MR2, the Roadster had no trouble establishing a loyal and enthusiastic following. *(Toyota)*

▼ Mid-engined fun – part of every MR2's DNA. *(Toyota)*

were embarking upon improvements; or rather, changes. The launch of a new sequential-style semi-automatic transmission wasn't met with universal acclaim, Britain's *Car* magazine including the new MR2 SMT (sequential manual transmission) in its Top Ten list of most disappointing cars of the year. The magazine explained that '...humans change gear better' than the new set-up, and suggested SMT was a '...complication too far.'

With most MR2 buyers opting for standard manual transmission, this wasn't too serious an issue, and things improved dramatically in 2002 when a whole raft of updates saw all MR2s fitted as standard with six-speed gearboxes, limited-slip differential (LSD), vehicle stability control (VSC), traction control and brake assist. It all helped to make the MR2 even more of a foolproof performance car, keeping everything under control even when it was pushed to the limit with a total novice at the wheel.

The best news of all was that such extra features didn't dilute the MR2's enthusiast appeal. LSD in particular meant great news for enthusiastic drivers, providing extra traction in all conditions by continually transferring torque to the wheel with more grip – and all without losing engine speed. These latest updates didn't improve the MR2's official performance figures, but they made a big difference to its at-the-limit behaviour and meant more use could be made of what power was available.

The latest MR2 was all about useable power and performance, which in real-life motoring counts for a lot. That it was also as much fun to drive as its forebears said a lot about the ingenuity of the boffins at Toyota.

By 2003, with interest in modified cars increasing all the time, Toyota GB launched a new body kit for the MR2 range, a three-part set-up comprising front spats, side skirts and rear bumper extensions. By the following year, a limited edition

MR2 – simply known as the Red – was on sale, featuring a red leather interior, red hood and special badging.

But in real terms, the 2000-onwards MR2 changed remarkably little over the years, no doubt because its loyal customer base liked it just the way it was. There were faster, more powerful sportsters around when the MR2 Roadster first hit the streets, but Toyota's highly communicative little gem was instantly hailed as one of the most fun experiences in its class.

It also boasted impressive value for money, the UK-spec version costing less than an MGF 1.8i VVC, a Mazda MX-5 1.8i S, or a BMW Z3 1.8 entry-level model. Toyota had got its pricing policy spot-on yet again, making the MR2 a realistic proposition for large numbers of sports car buyers. It's little surprise then, that the MR2 Roadster soon established itself as another strong seller in the two-seater class.

Toyota took something of a risk with the new Roadster by dropping the idea of a hardtop, coupé-style MR2 altogether, as well as endowing the newcomer with significantly less power than its top-of-the-range predecessor. But buyers didn't seem to care; and with good reason.

Even now, the MR2 Roadster still boasts cutting-edge styling, fantastic dynamics, superb handling and roadholding, as much performance as most convertible buyers demand, and an ease of ownership that's particularly important in this sector of the market. This was a machine exactly right for the new millennium, and Toyota's brave decisions about the future direction of the MR2 brand were soon paying off handsomely. ▪

TIMELINE

2000 Series III MR2 roadster launched in UK in the spring

2001 Sequential manual transmission version announced

2002 Six-speed transmission and LSD among updates for 2003 model year

2003 New MR2 body kit announced by Toyota GB

2004 Limited edition MR2 Roadster Red goes on sale in the UK

▲ By 2002, the MR2 Roadster was being fitted with six-speed transmission, limited-slip differential and traction control as standard, making for an even greater driving experience. *(Toyota)*

▼ The Roadster may have been less powerful than some of the MR2 derivatives that had gone before, but weight-saving design and clever engineering always ensured decent enough performance figures. *(Toyota)*

TOYOTA
SUPRA MkIV
supercar sensation

▲ With twin turbochargers working overtime, it's little wonder the hi-tech new Supra pumped out a whopping 326bhp in its fastest form. It was quite simply the most powerful car from any mass-market manufacturer in its day. *(Toyota)*

Even by the time the old-style MkIII Toyota Supra was about to cease production in 1993, it was still a good-looking machine and, in turbo guise particularly, was seriously quick. But nothing stands still forever, and with the latest Nissan 300ZX grabbing so much of the Japanese supercar limelight, Toyota knew something had to be done. Perhaps nobody, though, was quite prepared for exactly what was to come,.

The all-new MkIV Supra caused a shockwave in the automotive world when it first hit the streets in 1993, not just because of its sensational, sexy, swoopy new styling but also because of what lay under the bonnet. By the time British imports got under way in autumn of the same year, anticipation was high and the excitement among Toyota fans was frenzied.

The entry-level new Supra was a normally-aspirated version following in its predecessor's footsteps of using straight-six power, this time a 2997cc 24-valve DOHC masterpiece. And,

remarkably, this non-turbocharged powerplant managed to pump out a hugely impressive 220bhp at 5800rpm, not far off the figure achieved by the previous Supra Turbo.

That, of course, was exciting enough. Or rather, it wasn't. Because Toyota had another trick up its corporate sleeve in the shape of the utterly outrageous Supra Twin Turbo, a brand new flagship that used the same 3.0-litre engine as its lower-powered cousin but, thanks to a pair of seriously effective turbochargers working sequentially, had no problem generating an incredible 326bhp at 5600rpm. Quite simply, you couldn't buy a more powerful machine from any mass-market manufacturer anywhere in the world, so that despite tough opposition from the likes of Nissan and Honda, Toyota was once again top of the performance tree.

With an unrivalled power-to-weight ratio of 210bhp per tonne (compared with 'just' 149bhp per tonne from the previous Supra Turbo), ▶

SPEC

SUPRA

ENGINE: 2997cc 24-valve DOHC fuel-injected straight-six

POWER: 220bhp @ 5800rpm.

TORQUE: 210lb ft @ 4800rpm

PERFORMANCE: Top speed 139mph, 0–60mph 6.7 secs

TRANSMISSION: Six-speed manual or four-speed automatic

CHASSIS: Rack-and-pinion power-assisted steering; independent coil-spring double-wishbone suspension all round with limited-slip rear differential and traction control; ventilated disc brakes all round with ABS

SUPRA TWIN TURBO

ENGINE: 2997cc 24-valve DOHC fuel-injected straight-six with twin turbochargers and intercoolers

POWER: 326bhp @ 5600rpm

TORQUE: 325lb ft @ 4800rpm

PERFORMANCE: Top speed 156mph, 0–60mph 5.1 secs

TRANSMISSION: Six-speed manual or four-speed automatic

CHASSIS: Rack-and-pinion power-assisted steering; independent coil-spring double-wishbone suspension all round with limited-slip rear differential and traction control; ventilated disc brakes all round with ABS

◄ Swoopy, curvaceous styling was bang up to date by the standards of 1993. The latest model to carry the Supra name certainly knew how to turn heads. *(Toyota)*

▲ Monstrous rear spoiler helped provide plenty of downforce at speed – an essential feature of any machine with a 156mph top speed. *(Toyota)*

this amazing new supercar promised so much; and it delivered it in style. Top speed was a terrific 156mph; and taking just a fraction over 5.0 seconds to shatter the 60mph target, this twin-turbocharged hedonist was scorchingly quick. It would even hit the magical 100mph figure from standstill in only 12.3 seconds, according to *Autocar* magazine's first test of the newcomer in September 1993.

To say the motoring press were completely bowled over by what they experienced at the wheel of the Supra Twin Turbo would be a gross understatement. *Autocar* enthused: 'Toyota has produced what is, in our view, the quickest front-engined, rear-drive car yet point-to-point – and that includes the new BMW M3.' Quite an accolade.

But there was far more to both of the new Supra models than pure power. These were performance machines through and through, with superb handling, grip and driver appeal. The new Supra's suspension was a hugely effective double-wishbone set-up with traction control and limited-slip differential helping to keep the Twin Turbo's acceleration and speed under control. Having massive ventilated disc brakes all round provided the kind of stopping power rarely experienced before; the Supra was, thus, a commendably safe machine.

With traditional rear-wheel drive and all that power on tap, it was possible for inexperienced drivers to get into trouble in a Supra. (Well, what else would you expect?) But road testers of the time were universal in their praise for the Supra Twin Turbo's handling and roadholding, often caught using the kind of hyperbole normally reserved for vastly more expensive machines from Modena.

Autocar's testers simply did not want to leave the Supra's driving seat, so taken were they with the all-round driving experience and high levels of excitement: 'With double wishbones at each corner and state-of-the-art Michelin Pilot tyres, the Supra has heroic levels of grip and a level of body control that we have not seen in this class or any other below that of the very fastest and most expensive supercars', they declared.

They went even further in their summary, claiming the Supra offered '…a new class standard for performance and new world standards of grip for a front-engined, two-wheel-drive car.' For any machine to receive such praise from hard-to-please road testers was a notable event. The fact that it was said about a coupé from Japan was simply unprecedented.

So back in 1993, what were Toyota GB charging for a machine that could rival the very best from any manufacturer anywhere in the world? Presumably something this good and this exciting would be out of reach of anybody other than the odd multi-millionaire? Well, not quite. In

fact, the Supra Twin Turbo (the only version of the new-look Supra line-up ever officially offered in Britain) while certainly not being given away, was still much less expensive than a Honda NSX, an entry-level Porsche 911 Carrera, or a Jaguar XJS V12, and was over 40% less than a Ferrari 348tb.

Fair comparisons? Absolutely. And they even stack up when you study in detail the power on offer from each of those manufacturers, because despite having the joint-smallest engine of that particular group, the Toyota managed to churn out an effortless 326bhp – a figure that outstripped the Honda's 274bhp, the Porsche's 250bhp, the Jaguar's 308bhp and the Ferrari's 300bhp. When it came to the most performance for your pounds, it seemed there was nothing out there to touch the oh-so-desirable Supra Twin Turbo.

It's no surprise that the awesome new Supra attracted so much attention throughout 1993, although its role within the Toyota family line-up would always remain 'niche'. In fact, no matter how fast, powerful and relatively affordable the newcomer was, it seemed there would always be a majority of buyers who would choose an arguably more prestigious badge than Toyota's on which to spend their money. Perhaps that explains why, over a five-year period, a mere 623 Supra Twin Turbos were officially imported to the UK, a pitifully low figure. ▶

WHAT WE LIKE...

The Supra Twin Turbo was the most powerful car from any major manufacturer in its day, and you can't get much better than that. The fact that it's also outrageous to look at and guarantees an adrenalin rush every time you take to the wheel ... well, who wouldn't find room for a MkIV Supra in their collection?

...WHAT WE DON'T

With tarmac-ripping performance and a rear spoiler bigger than a wardrobe, any Twin Turbo is going to attract unwanted attention from the police. If you're determined to lose your driving licence in a hurry, this could be the ultimate car in which to do it.

◀ Road testers of the time reckoned the Supra Twin Turbo brought new levels of grip for a front-engined, rear-drive car. And they were right. *(Toyota)*

▼ Like many of the most hi-tech Japanese coupés, the Supra was criticised by some folk for being almost too clinical and too efficient. Some people are just never satisfied, are they? *(Toyota)*

The good news is that a rather larger number of used MkIV Supras have since found their way to Britain as 'grey' imports, which has helped to swell substantially the numbers available now on the used market. But whether you choose to buy a UK-spec car or a Japanese import, you'll need to decide which model suits your needs best.

All 623 'official' Supras sold in Britain were Twin Turbos, but a fair proportion of 'grey' imports have been of the normally-aspirated model. With seriously strong performance even from this entry-level version, it makes a tempting proposition for anybody who doesn't crave the ultimate in power. But if you're basing your choice of a non-turbo Supra on the assumption you'll save on insurance costs, you'll almost certainly be disappointed. In fact, the extra premiums charged by most insurance companies for 'grey' imports mean it's unlikely to be any less expensive to insure than an 'official' Twin Turbo. Worth bearing in mind, isn't it?

Remember too, that the Japanese market was offered both hard-top and targa-top versions of the MkIV Supra, so a reasonable selection of each tends to be available to anybody looking for a second-hand 'grey' import.

You also need to have a think about how you like to change gear, because a large proportion of all Japanese-spec Supras come with the four-speed automatic transmission that proved so popular in the car's homeland. By comparison, British buyers tended to prefer the six-speed manual gearbox (built in Germany by Getrag), a close-ratio device that was as slick and precise as you'd expect from such a highly developed supercar. The choice is yours. If a manual gearbox is a must for you, just be prepared to shop around and hold out for what you really want. Sooner or later, the Supra of your dreams will show up.

And a dream machine it is, too – even if, like anything else on the road, it's not completely perfect. In its day, the MkIV Supra was criticised for its lack of rear seat accommodation (yet, it was only ever meant to be a 2+2…) and its poor stowage space (the boot is tiny for what is a fairly large car). But if such concerns are important to you, perhaps you should be looking at a nice sensible estate car instead?

A more important criticism in its day centred around the Supra's lack of any real character, a claim that *Autocar* lost no time in agreeing with when the Supra first arrived in the UK, suggesting the car's slightly clinical feel might deter real enthusiasts. 'For the depth and integrity of its engineering, it deserves to be praised long and loud', said the magazine's testers about the Supra Twin Turbo, before going on: 'Yet the anticipation of a long drive at dawn won't keep you awake the night before. This car earns your respect in the first five seconds, yet is one the true enthusiast could drive for five years without ever actually loving.'

It was a bizarre situation in which Toyota found themselves. Here was a machine that, in terms of power, performance and sheer outrageousness, was more than a match for any supercar from any other manufacturer. And it was also a car with none of the annoying quirkiness, foibles or difficulty of driving traditionally associated with such marques as Ferrari. And yet, by making the all-new Supra Twin Turbo so outrageously good and so highly accomplished, Toyota was being criticised for creating a product that lacked character, charisma, or heart.

Fortunately for the Supra, many enthusiasts across the world chose to ignore such criticism, discovering instead the unique mix of attributes offered by the Supra; power, performance, acceleration and the ability to rearrange your

◢ Sit down, get comfortable, fire up the twin-turbo powerplant and get ready for a truly exhilarating drive. The MkIV Supra means business. *(Toyota)*

▶ 220bhp in non-turbo guise, or another 106 on top of that as a twin turbo? The choice is yours. Either way, you're in for a great time. *(Toyota)*

internal organs
during any standing-start sprint were
an essential part of the Supra's appeal. So was
the fact that it was an easy machine to drive, and
a reliable proposition in everyday use. Here was
one of the world's few supercars (along with the
Honda NSX) that combined all you ever wanted
in terms of adrenalin rush with the kind of
ownership experience that made the whole thing
relatively painless.

As with any extreme performance car, a Supra
Twin Turbo isn't cheap to insure and, at around
15–18mpg overall, can seriously dent your bank
balance if you pay your own petrol bills. But it's
also an incredibly efficient, impressively reliable
and perfectly practical choice for anybody looking
for one of the ultimate second-hand coupés.

My main criticism of any 1993-onwards Supra
would be its fairly drab and unexciting interior,
but I'd balance this by pointing out the
ergonomic excellence of the dashboard, the
surprising comfort of the front seats and the
near-perfect driving position. I'd also put it all
into perspective by taking a look at how little a
well-preserved second-hand Supra Twin Turbo
can cost to get on your driveway right now.

There has never been another Japanese
performance car quite like the Toyota Supra, and
maybe there never will be again. But the fact
that there are good supplies of used examples
available in the UK nowadays at highly affordable
prices is surely something worth celebrating.

If a big, powerful Japanese coupé is the stuff
you dream of, you need a very good reason not
to be swayed by a Supra; and if it's the Twin
Turbo version you opt for, you'll soon be finding
yourself at the wheel of one of the greatest
supercars ever created in the 1990s. ∎

TIMELINE

1993 All-new Supra unveiled in
normally-aspirated and Twin
Turbo models

1993 UK-spec imports of Twin
Turbo on sale by autumn

1995 Entry level limited-edition
Supra SE launched in some
export markets

1997 Final UK imports on sale by
year end

1998 VVT-i technology for
non-turbo means extra
power (225bhp)

1998 Minor interior revisions for
both models

2002 Supra MkIV production
finally wound down

▲ While British
buyers tended to
prefer the Supra's
six-speed manual
transmission, many
Japanese owners
preferred the four-
speed automatic
alternative. Bear
this in mind when
buying a
secondhand 'grey'
import. *(Toyota)*

▼ Although
official UK imports
of the Supra
ceased as early as
1997, this
awesome machine
remained in
limited production
right through to
2002. Even then, it
was still seen as
massively
desirable. *(Toyota)*

GREY IMPORTS

Thanks to 'grey' imports, you'll now find a great selection of desirable Japanese cars on sale in the UK that were never offered through official channels. And as the numbers of 'grey' imports have increased, so has their acceptability; insurance hassles and uncertainty over spares availability are now a thing of the past.

By far the easiest way to buy a 'grey' car is to visit a specialist dealer who actually imports the vehicles from Japan. Such companies bring used cars to the UK in small quantities at a time, deal with all the paperwork, sort out the necessary testing and pay any tax that is due before selling them on. From a consumer's point of view, it's as easy as buying any other vehicle; all the hard work is done for you.

Do be careful, though. Like any car, a Japanese 'grey' import is susceptible to having its mileage altered, particularly when 'km/h' speedometers are swapped for 'mph' replacements. One importer I spoke to claimed cars even have their mileages altered before they've left their ship at the British dockside.

The best advice is to make sure the dealer you're buying from is a member of the British Independent Motor Trade Association (BIMTA), who can get involved and offer a conciliatory service if a dispute arises – but only if the trader concerned is a BIMTA member.

When buying from any member, make sure you ask them to provide an official BIMTA Certificate of Authenticity for the car you're interested in, as this offers you invaluable peace of mind. Every year, BIMTA claims, around 2000 vehicles stolen in Japan end up being imported to the UK and sold on to unsuspecting buyers. But a BIMTA Certificate of Authenticity will confirm whether or not a vehicle was ever registered as stolen in Japan, and will also prove there's no outstanding finance on it.

BIMTA can also provide odometer checks, a must if you're in any doubt about the vehicle you're buying. The vast majority of imports are sold in Japan via one of the country's 140 auction houses, and BIMTA has access to the records of almost all of these.

DOING IT YOURSELF

Up to 40,000 second-hand Japanese vehicles are imported to the UK each year, but not all by traders. So what happens if you want to bypass UK dealers completely in an effort to save money? Well, you can arrange your own import, although many Brits end up losing money when it all goes wrong, so it's essential you have a reliable and dependable agent in Japan, as most car auctions there are 'trade only'.

Then there's the issue of what to do with the vehicle once the hammer falls and it's yours. An agent in Japan should be able to arrange almost everything for you, from attending the auction and bidding on your behalf to such complicated issues as arranging transport to the docks, completing all the necessary paperwork, organising the shipping process and what happens once your vehicle arrives either in Southampton or Bristol. A good agent is worth every yen of his commission.

The arrival of your 'grey' import in the UK marks the start of another complex process, as you must pay the import duty and VAT that is now due. HM Customs & Excise will insist the purchase price of the vehicle in Japan is liable for VAT, as is the cost of the import duties that must also be added. You will be unable to bring your car away from the UK docks without first paying the duty and tax that are due; and even then you won't be able to drive your car home, as it still won't be registered for use on British roads.

Registration itself is relatively straightforward if the vehicle is at least ten years of age. However, any Japanese import less than a decade old must now undergo an ESVA test (replacement for the original SVA test), introduced in 2004. Whereas the old SVA was simply a check to ensure any vehicle non-type approved for UK use was up to British and European standards, the ESVA is more stringent.

Extra criteria are covered within ESVA, including emissions, noise testing, the fitment of suitable alarms and the suitability of a vehicle's instrumentation for British usage. And within ESVA is the requirement for an official model report, applicable to most Japanese imports manufactured from January 1st 1997 onwards.

And just because your car passes an ESVA test, don't assume it's automatically legal to use on the road once it's registered. ESVA is not a test of roadworthiness, so assuming your import is at least three years old it will still need to pass a standard MoT test, too.

The cost of getting a Japanese import through an ESVA test varies hugely from model to model. However, most UK importers I spoke to reckoned on spending anywhere between £700 and £1500 (in 2005) per vehicle simply to meet ESVA criteria, before they could even think about trying to register the vehicles in the UK.

BRITISH AUCTIONS

The complication of finding yourself a reliable agent in Japan able to source an import for you can be averted if you choose to attend a British auction house that specialises in freshly imported vehicles.

It's pretty much the same as an ordinary car auction, except that all the vehicles being sold are freshly arrived in the UK and have yet to undergo ESVA testing or the registration process. It's a way of locating a vehicle that you can actually see before you buy, without having to pay any kind of a dealer's premium. However, as with importing a car yourself, you then have to go through the ESVA (if applicable), MoT and registration processes before you can use the vehicle in the UK.

AND FINALLY...

A quick word about damage: if a recent 'grey' import is showing any signs of wear and tear (scratched or grazed paintwork, for example), it will most probably have occurred since it was sold at auction in Japan. Once the hammer falls, any bound-for-Britain import then has a difficult journey ahead of it, being shunted from auction house to car park to ship to docks to car park over a period of several weeks. It's not unusual for parking damage to occur, and you need to be on the lookout for this when inspecting any future purchase.

Don't forget, too, that most Japanese-spec cars tend to be less well protected against corrosive road salt than their British-spec counterparts, and it may well be worth investing a little in a thorough professional treatment of the underside with Waxoyl or similar. You will probably be able to negotiate this into the price if you're buying from a dealer, but always ensure the job has been done well and to your satisfaction. ∎

MODIFYING

▲ Created as a Pace Car for the American Champ Car racing series, this special Lexus SC430 was re-tuned to provide a healthy 312bhp, as well as being treated to race-spec suspension, Eibach racing coil springs, Bilstein shock absorbers and 18-inch front and 19-inch rear SSR wheels. Sadly, this version never made it to production reality. *(Lexus)*

Enthusiasts of Japanese performance cars have a thriving scene open to them throughout the world, but particularly in the UK where some of the most popular makes and models have a real fanatical following. Whether it's a modified Civic VTi or a 'chipped' Impreza Turbo that takes your fancy, you'll find no shortage of fellow fanatics, specialist companies and even magazines willing to advise and entertain.

On the magazine front, the UK has no less than three specialist titles dedicated to the Japanese car scene. The logically named *Japanese Performance*, produced by CH Publications; the equally appealing *Banzai*, published by Unity Media; and the most recent launch, *J Tuner*, from Future Publishing. All three feature fantastic modified cars, readers' rides, all the latest accessories, vital information on specialists, news from the club world and a whole lot more.

These magazines are available from newsagents nationwide, and each has its own loyal band of readers. Their respective success is well deserved, too; with so many magazines in the 'modified'

sector focusing on uprated European models, it was only a matter of time before at least one title appeared catering purely for fans of Japanese cars. That there are now three such magazines available is fantastic news.

EXTRA OOMPH

You have only to glance through one of these magazines or do an internet search under your favourite make and model of Japanese car to realise there's no shortage of specialists around willing to help improve your motor. Whether that means an engine chip for a few extra brake-horsepower, a full-on body kit for head-turning looks or a suspension upgrade guaranteed to ensure roll-free cornering, you'll find plenty of companies anxious to attract your custom.

Among the simplest and most affordable upgrades available for most models are performance air filters and aftermarket exhaust systems, the combination of which could add a handful of extra brake-horsepower to your car's output, as well as aiding its responsiveness. But what if you want to go further?

You could always have your engine re-chipped; plenty of owners do. But what exactly does this entail? In simple terms, it's all to do with fuel injection and engine management systems. The new, upgraded chip fits into your car's ECU and basically 'ups' the fuelling and the ignition timing. This generates extra power, a quicker throttle response and better acceleration, particularly effective in the case of a turbocharged car.

No problems there then. Except it's not quite as simple as that. Any reputable specialist who's chipping your car will reset the CO level and raise the fuel pressure to cope with it all, as well as ensuring an excellent state of tune for the engine. The car will then be put on a rolling road and run carefully up to the desired power level; less sympathetic treatment could cause serious damage to your engine. Bear all this in mind when shopping round for a chipping specialist, and at all costs avoid anyone down at the pub who says they can '…do it for fifty quid'.

BRAKES AND SUSPENSION

Any major increase in power brings the predicament of whether your standard braking and suspension systems can cope – and there's no all-encompassing answer to this. If in any doubt, seek advice from a specialist.

If an improved braking system is what's needed, you might consider drilled, vented or grooved new discs. The idea behind these is to aid brake cooling, repel water and moisture and keep the pads themselves as clean as possible. The difference with vented discs is that, to look at, they resemble two discs stuck together but with a gap between that fills with cold air. Many of today's performance cars already have vented discs fitted as standard, though rarely of the drilled type.

All these disc designs work extremely well. After all, water being constantly forced against discs and pads must have somewhere to go. Grooved and drilled discs allow for this, thus preventing the water from ruining the compound of the brake pads and leading to brake fade or outright failure. It's all very clever stuff.

For the ultimate in braking upgrades, you'll need to be adding top quality four-pot callipers (for extreme cooling under very hard braking) to your list of requirements. Or you could always opt for something like an AP racing performance brake kit, available for a growing list of models and consisting of a pair of vented front discs, lightweight alloy anodised mounting bells, four-pot alloy callipers, purpose-designed calliper mounting brackets and Mintex high-performance brake pads. That's quite a package – and it also comes with a commensurate price tag.

Braking upgrades are a fine idea. But go too far and you'll find the new braking force passing extra stress onto your car's anti-roll bar bushes, steering joints and bushes, suspension bushes and so on. All these areas will also need uprating if you go too far with your brakes. Then you need to ask yourself whether your dampers are stiff enough and your car low enough to cope with the extra braking. It's a similar story with the spec of your tyres.

The moral of the story? Upgrade your brakes and suspension sensibly, don't go over the top and end up ruining your car.

THE WHEEL THING

The same advice applies equally to wheels and tyres, as any major changes here can have knock-on effects elsewhere. So once you've set your heart on a set of shiny new alloys, what's the magic formula when it comes to deciding which size to go for? Should you stick with standard width or go all the way and have absolute monsters fighting to escape from under your arches?

There's no hard and fast rule when it comes to sizing. For the ultimate in one-upmanship, plenty of people go for the biggest they can squeeze in without fouling the arches, which could mean 17-inch rims on certain Honda Civics, while other people might be happy with 16s. A lot of it's down to personal preference.

The starting point is inevitably a good aftermarket wheel retailer who can tell you instantly what the biggest wheel is that can be sensibly used on your machine. They know their stuff, they've been into modded cars for years and they're worth listening to. But is it always best to go for the biggest sizing? Well, not necessarily. The bigger and fatter the wheels and tyres, the more likely they are to follow track lines in an ▶

uneven road surface, which could mean you're fighting with your steering wheel a lot more than before.

While fitting fatter rims will, in most cases, improve your car's roadholding, there is a point beyond which any such benefits cease. If 16s result in the ultimate grip and handling, is there any point going for 17s just to be one-up on the 'competition'? Well, that's your call. Just don't expect an automatic improvement in roadholding following from each bigger size.

If you're intent on fitting a monstrous set of rims, it's also worth investigating the effects on your particular car's brakes and steering before actually taking the plunge. That's why any modifications you're likely to carry out on your car in the future need to be planned carefully.

Think about what you're trying to achieve, study the various ways of getting there, look at the costs involved and talk to as many fellow owners and specialists as you can. Every modification you carry out will almost certainly affect something else on your car, so the order in which you carry out such mods is vital.

But get it right, and you'll have a car to be truly proud of, and a machine even more rewarding to drive than its maker intended.

INSURANCE ISSUES

Whether your Japanese sports or performance car is completely standard or highly modified, you need to make sure you've got adequate insurance cover arranged. That isn't necessarily as straightforward as you might think, although the situation has improved over the last few years. It's not so long ago that most mainstream insurers wouldn't consider offering cover on a 'grey' import, for example. Happily, they've now been forced to adapt to market changes and, anxious not to lose any business, most will insure the kind of Japanese models that were previously considered taboo.

If it's a 'grey' import you're trying to insure, you'll find most insurance companies will consider offering cover, depending on your own circumstances and the extent of any modifications carried out. Do be aware that even a fairly modest 'grey' import will be required to have a Thatcham-approved immobiliser fitted (and your insurer would need proof of this via a fitter's certificate) before most mainstream insurance companies will offer cover.

As for the actual

◄ One of the simplest (and least expensive) ways of gaining a slight increase in power is to invest in a performance air filter or induction kit, courtesy of companies like K&N and Pipercross. If that's not enough for you, then you're probably thinking along the lines of an engine re-chip... *(K&N)*

premium, you'll find most 'grey' imports will cost anywhere between 25 and 50 per cent extra to insure, even if the car in question is almost identical in specification to its officially-imported counterpart. In most cases too, insurers will insist on a higher compulsory excess for your policy, often averaging twice the amount of excess implemented for a UK-spec model. Bear this in mind when comparing policies offered by different companies.

So why does all this extra expense exist with insurance for 'grey' imports? For a variety of reasons. 'Greys', it seems, are statistically more likely to be stolen or involved in accidents than official UK-spec models. (There's no obvious, logical reason for this – but since when did statistics take logic into account?) 'Grey' imports also tend to be better equipped and higher-spec than UK cars, which means even a minor shunt can involve the replacement of more trim, trickier paint schemes, unique bodywork sections and so on. Whatever the reasons for the difference, however, there's very little you can do about it.

Except, of course, the crazy course of action that some owners of 'grey' imports have tried over the years – by not telling their insurers that the Impreza, EVO, MX-5 or whatever parked on their driveway is in fact a 'grey' import. Don't be tempted by this, because if ever you are forced to make a claim, your insurance company's assessors are well trained enough to spot a 'grey' from an official import at twenty paces.

It's a similar situation when trying to insure a UK-spec car that's been modified. At first, it may seem tempting not to admit to your car having

been 'chipped' or to your suspension and braking systems having being uprated. But, again, if you're unfortunate enough to have an accident and any such modifications are discovered by an assessor, it could make your entire insurance policy null and void – and you won't receive any payment.

Even fairly basic modifications, such as an aftermarket set of alloys, should be declared to your insurer when arranging cover. You may pay a little extra for your policy, but at least you'll know your car – and its expensive new wheels – are adequately covered should the worst ever happen.

If you're spending a serious amount of cash on improving, upgrading or modifying your much-loved Japanese machine, the last thing you should be cutting back on is your car insurance. It just doesn't make sense.

GO FOR IT!

Whatever the make, model or specification of Japanese performance car you find yourself owning, you can rest assured it's one of the best-engineered vehicles in its class and, almost certainly, one of the finest to drive. So whether it's an ageing 200SX, a classic 240Z, a twin-turbo Supra or a standard MR2 that finds its way into your life, just make sure you enjoy every moment you spend behind the wheel.

The Japanese car scene has rarely looked more interesting, and whatever your budget, there are now some great used – and new – choices out there. It's time to go shopping. It's time to go Japanese. ■

▼ Transforming the looks of your beast can be as straightforward as fitting a new set of alloys – and there's certainly no shortage of different styles, sizes and specifications available these days. Your insurance company should be made aware of any changes to your car's original specification. *(Wolfrace Wheels)*